BOOKS BY TRUMBULL HIGGINS

Winston Churchill and the Second Front
Korea and the Fall of MacArthur
Winston Churchill and the Dardanelles
Hitler and Russia
Soft Underbelly

TRUMBULL HIGGINS

THE
Perfect Failure

Kennedy, Eisenhower, and the CIA
at the Bay of Pigs

W · W · NORTON & COMPANY

NEW YORK · LONDON

The text of this book is composed in Primer, with display type set in Centaur. Composition by the Maple-Vail Manufacturing Group. Book design by Marjorie J. Flock.

First published as a Norton paperback 1989

Library of Congress Cataloging-in-Publication Data
Higgins, Trumbull.
    The perfect failure.

    Bibliography: p.
    Includes index.
    1. United States—Foreign relations—1961–1963.
2. Cuba—History—Invasion, 1961.   3. Kennedy, John F.
(John Fitzgerald), 1917–1963.   4. Eisenhower, Dwight D.
(Dwight David), 1890–1969.   5. United States. Central
Intelligence Agency.   6. United States—Foreign relations
—1953–1961.   I. Title.
E841.H54   1987   327.73   87–5720

ISBN 0-393-30563-5

W. W. Norton & Company, Inc., 500 Fifth Avenue, New York, N.Y. 10110
W. W. Norton & Company Ltd., 37 Great Russell Street, London WC1B 3NU
2 3 4 5 6 7 8 9 0

To MY WIFE

Contents

Many Americans could ask themselves, why a war in Vietnam, thousands of miles away, why millions of tons of bombs dropped on Vietnam and not in Cuba? It was much more logical for the United States to do this to Cuba than to do it ten thousand kilometers away.[1] —*Fidel Castro, 1974*

I guess the way you learn to do things is to do them imperfectly.[2] —*McGeorge Bundy, 1979*

Who would have thought that it would some day be judged a crime to carry out the orders of the President of the United States.[3] —*Richard Helms, 1973*

We must face the fact that the United States is neither omnipotent nor omniscient . . . and that therefore there cannot be an American solution to every world problem.[4] —*John F. Kennedy, November 1961, after the Bay of Pigs*

Preface

As a specialist in military fiasco, the author cannot but be attracted to what Theodore Draper, Irving Janis, and Harry Rositzke all have deemed the perfect failure of the Central Intelligence Agency at the Bay of Pigs. Not merely is the public and semipublic literature already enormous, but the fear expressed by many over recent years that we again may face various unpleasant aspects of the Bay of Pigs in Nicaragua and elsewhere has been growing apace. It should be emphasized that this is not a history of the CIA nor one of Cuba; rather it is concerned with the failure of the United States government under two administrations to cope with the problem of Fidel Castro between 1959 and 1961. Reference will necessarily also be made to the successful practice run for the Bay of Pigs in the Guatemala operation of 1954.

Of distress to many liberals will be John F. Kennedy's own well-justified anxiety regarding those "bastard" historians who "are always there with their pencils out."[5] Of pain to conservatives may be the conclusion that the opposition to the Bay of Pigs was largely confined to moderates and liberals among American policy makers. It is often underestimated just how many men at and near the top actually do oppose absurdity in advance and not just after the event from the secure advantage of hindsight. Therefore, history should honor those who had the courage and opportunity to express such wisdom at the time.

Apart from the rapidly growing memoirs and transcripts at the Columbia, Eisenhower, Hoover, Kennedy, Princeton, and the U.S. Naval Institute libraries, including those papers released under the Freedom of Information Act, the author has interviewed many of the principals involved—regrettably, on occasion, off the record. Obviously, the author's association with some of these men carries with it the danger of bias as well as the advantage of richer authenticity. As for documents alone, Theodore Draper's words should be remembered: "Not only do . . . officials make policy; they do much to control the history of their policy-making."[6] Yet another danger recently cited is that of Robert Bowie: "The policy-maker, unlike an academic analyst, can rarely wait until all the facts are in. . . . He thinks in terms of odds and probabilities, rarely in terms of carefully reasoned analytical judgments or certainties. He is very often under strong pressure to do something, to take some action, even if all the facts are not yet available to him."[7]

Past restrictions on sources for this period of growing frustration for American policy, interestingly, have made the principal protagonists and their aides appear even more inadequate than they actually were. Careful scrutiny of the pressures on the Eisenhower and Kennedy administrations in Washington, as well as of their prejudices and self-interest, often affords a more convincing explanation for their actions and their errors than their self-interested and implausible arguments at the time and afterward. Explanations of error should not be used as justifications for mistakes. Instead, such explanations should become the basis for avoiding the full impact of the still more carefully planned fiascos of the future.

The author wishes to express his appreciation for assistance rendered by Mary Carr, Theodore Draper, Kermit Lansner, Herbert Parmet, Thomas Powers, Arthur Schlesinger, John Taylor, and Peter Wyden.

New York, December 1986

I
Guatemala's "Fortune" and "Success"

Well, if we don't look out, we will wake up some morning and read in the newspapers that there happened in South America the same kind of thing that happened in China in 1949.[1] —*John Foster Dulles, 1953*

How is it that you do not fear Yugoslavia, and, in fact, help her? She is a Communist country.[2] —*Ché Guevara, 1960*

Now what can we do? We can do what we did with Guatemala. There was a Communist dictator there that we inherited from the previous Administration. We quarantined Mr. Arbenz. The result was that the Guatemalan people themselves eventually rose up and they threw him out.[3] —*Richard Nixon, 1960*

*T*HE TRADITION of American filibustering in the Caribbean in general and in Cuba in particular long preceded John F. Kennedy's intervention at the Bay of Pigs in 1961. Even after relinquishing its direct rule over Cuba in 1901–1903 following that island's recent liberation from Spain, in the famous Platt Amendment to the treaty establishing nominal Cuban independence the United States government carefully established the right of military intervention in Cuba in order to protect its interests at any time. During an era of open American imperialism in Latin America, this right of intervention in Cuba was no dead letter, as may be seen in the landing of U.S. Marines to guard American properties and business interests from 1906 to 1909, in 1912, and from 1917 to 1922, this last intervention under the cover of a supposed German threat.

By 1933, however, President Franklin D. Roosevelt, by resisting strong pressure to intervene against radical Cuban attacks on American business, had inauguarated a new policy toward Latin America. Within another year, Roosevelt's Good Neighbor policy had culminated in the abrogation of the bitterly resented Platt Amendment, except for the retention of the U.S. naval base at Guantánamo Bay in southeastern Cuba. Ostensibly guarding one of the maritime passages to the Caribbean, in practice the Guantánamo base gave the United States a continuing potential for easy intervention in the island, although the USA's legal right to do so had now been waived.[4]

Following Roosevelt's death, the gradual American return to imperialism in Central America, provoked largely by the sporadic growth of communism in this touchy region, resulted in pressure on the Truman administration to intervene in Guatemala. There the increasingly leftist government of President Jacobo Arbenz Guzmán had begun to threaten the traditional dominance of the local economy by big American companies, particularly the United Fruit Company. Although asked for arms in 1952 by General Anastasio Somoza, the long-time dictator and good friend of the United Fruit Company in Nicaragua, with which to clean up the Arbenz regime, the Truman administration would eventually abandon a momentary effort by the CIA (Operation Fortune) to take advantage of this offer. Somoza himself had deemed the undertaking too risky and had evidently overestimated the support he would obtain from

President Truman and from Walter Bedell Smith, then Director of Central Intelligence. Indeed, in National Security Council Directive 16, dating back to 1948, the Truman administration already laid down its basic Latin American policy—namely, that, with a few possible exceptions, communism in the region was not yet taken seriously at this time. Presumably, this was the reason that the United States signed Article 15 of the charter of the Organization of American States pledging against military intervention, even indirectly, in Latin America for any reason whatsoever.

Adolf Berle, a prominent Democrat formerly in the State Department who, like Allen and John Foster Dulles in the past, had been a legal representative for the American companies involved in Guatemala, had encouraged Somoza's request in 1952 on the avowed grounds that Guatemala was already in the hands of a Russian-controlled dictatorship. Resistance by the normally anti-Communist Assistant Secretary of State for Inter-American Affairs, Edward Miller, Jr., who had been initially bypassed in the CIA's discussion of arms for Somoza as well as by Undersecretary of State David Bruce, finally resulted in Secretary of State Dean Acheson turning down Operation Fortune as premature. Acheson detested Berle, in any event.

Liberal Latin American leaders such as José Figuéres Ferrer, the pro-American President of Costa Rica, likewise, had repeatedly opposed U.S.-sponsored intervention in Guatemala under any cover whatsoever. The Central Intelligence Agency, however, continued to report that the Arbenz regime was arming its supporters in the labor unions against both its own conservative army and possible external invasion from El Salvador. The agency denied having taken any covert action to assist such an invasion.

A month after Eisenhower entered the White House, his avowedly more anti-Communist administration was confronted with the prospective seizure of extensive United Fruit Company properties in Guatemala on the part of the Arbenz government. Largely as bureaucratic cover, in revised basic policy statement NSC. 144 on March 18, 1953, the National Security Council agreed to refrain from overt U.S. unilateral intervention in the internal affairs of other American countries in accordance with existing treaty obligations. But in two more highly classified annexes to the staff study preceding the statement, it was noted that since Latin American countries would probably not yet favor even limited multilateral intervention, except in the case of a clearly identifiable Communist regime, the United States would have to consider unilateral intervention, regardless of the treaty violations involved and the resulting anti-Yankee reaction in Latin America. Adolf Berle now privately believed that the United States could not possibly tolerate a Communist state in Central America, although this former liberal somewhat regretfully admitted that the era when the United States could just send in the Marines had long since passed.

Consequently, in March 1953, the still weak Operations Coordinating Board of the National Security Council confined itself to contemplating various propaganda operations against Arbenz officials. But Senator Henry Jackson's Senate subcommittee as well as Ambassador Spruille Braden, Berle, and Allen Dulles, the new Director of Central Intelligence, all continued to push for organizing and arming Guatemala's conservative but squabbling neighbors against Arbenz. Eisenhower had appointed Allen Dulles to the Central Intelligence Agency despite Dulles's constant refusal to coordinate the various intelligence agencies of the U.S. government. The President accepted this weakness in his new appointee, saying that he would "rather have Allen as my chief intelligence officer with his limitations than anyone else" he knew.[5]

Given the administration's reluctance to engage in open unilateral action in Latin America, the only way Eisenhower had left to oppose communism by force was through the secret operations of the Central Intelligence Agency. Thus, on March 29, 1953, Colonel J. C. King, Chief of the Western Hemisphere Division of the CIA, along with United Fruit Company, sponsored another premature, small, and unsuccessful uprising at the town of Salamá in Guatemala in an effort to subvert the indifferent Indian population in the region. The result of this poorly planned attempt was to drive the already nervous Arbenz government into a previously unnecessary dependence upon the Soviet bloc for arms supplies, since the United States government refused to provide arms for a regime "strongly influenced by the Communists."[6]

Not surprisingly, a most important National Intelligence Estimate of May 19, 1953, noted that the situation in Guatemala remained adverse to U.S. interests and that Communist influence would probably continue to grow as long as President Arbenz remained in power. Redistribution of United Fruit Company and other properties would be used to mobilize the hitherto inert peasantry in support of the administration. The NIE next stated that the army was the only organized element capable of changing this situation, but that its command and most of its forces would remain loyal to Arbenz unless they were personally threatened by the Communists or by serious disorders. The NIE concluded that a united Guatemalan army could defeat any of its hostile Central American neighbors, which, however, were unlikely to go beyond clandestine subversion into an open military intervention in Guatemala. If actually attacked, Guatemala would seek to invoke the Rio Treaty of 1947 and the UN Charter against such an external action. Arbenz himself, probably not a Communist, had now become emotionally committed to agrarian reform and found

Communist leaders among his most ardent and useful supporters, although he could still break with them. Two days
later, a State Department memorandum to the new Assistant
Secretary of Inter-American Affairs, John Moors Cabot, mentioned its covert policy of boycotting aid to Guatemala while
working for military assistance pacts against Arbenz with El
Salvador, Honduras, and Nicaragua.

Three months later, on August 19, hostile American policy
toward Guatemala was further spelled out in a draft paper prepared in the State Department, which was now taking a more
anti-Communist tone under John Foster Dulles and was eager
for another success by the CIA, such as that against Mossad-
egh in Iran at the same time. Nevertheless, the traditional
bureaucracy of the State Department continued to oppose such
policy on the grounds that the loss of Latin American good will
would be a disaster far outweighing the advantage of any success gained in Guatemala. Covert action was too risky for the
same reason, since the danger of exposure of the United States
trying a Russian seizure of Czechoslovakia in reverse was too
great. In accordance with NSC.11, the draft paper finally came
down in favor of making use of the Organization of American
States, employing direct unilateral U.S. action only as a last
resort. A tendency by the top-level 10/2 Committee of the NSC
earlier in August toward covert operations against the Arbenz
government in Guatemala had anticipated the State Department draft, but all the dilemmas faced by the Kennedy administration in Cuba in 1961 were already befogging the necessarily
more cautious State Department in Guatemala during Eisenhower's first year in office.

Continual drum beating for United Fruit Company by the
exceedingly well-connected lobbyist Thomas Corcoran, the
support of the powerful Democratic Senator Lyndon Johnson,
and John Foster Dulles finally won over Eisenhower's sharp-

minded new Undersecretary of State Walter Bedell Smith, and another effort against Arbenz was considered in the autumn of 1953. The Republican Assistant Secretary for Inter-American Affairs John Cabot had now become partially converted to activism, apart from having close relations with United Fruit Company through his brother, its former president. And Eisenhower himself may have been convinced by the former Director of Central Intelligence, Undersecretary of State Walter Bedell Smith, as well as by Eisenhower's brother Milton, that Guatemala was going Communist. And, indeed, on September 20, a rebellious Guatemalan general, Carlos Castillo Armas, wrote President Somoza of Nicaragua of these promising indications.[7]

Consequently, in November, Colonel Albert Haney of the Central Intelligence Agency was ordered to set up a new agency organization at Opa-Locka Marine Air Base in Florida, an organization carefully separated from the conservative and indignant Colonel King and his Western Hemisphere Division, which had previously been in charge of covert operations in Guatemala. Success in some low-profile endeavor against the then only Communist-influenced state in the New World seemed valuable to the agency in building up credit with the new administration. Haney soon decided that, if possible, a nonmilitary and non-United Fruit Company approach to the problem of overthrowing Arbenz was desirable because of King's previous failures. Given the lack of rebellious sentiments among the still-cowed Indian population of the country, the officer corps of the Guatemalan army appeared to be the most powerful, if also the most vulnerable, element of Guatemalan society.

Apart from Raymond Leddy of the State Department, Haney's superiors in the CIA were to be Deputy Director for Plans Frank Wisner, Special Assistant for Paramilitary Psychological Operations Tracy Barnes, and Richard Bissell. The latter two would again be in charge at the Bay of Pigs. Allen Dulles also feared that Eisenhower might never approve of an open American military role in Guatemala, another parallel with the Bay of Pigs. And, like Colonel King, Wisner feared the premature exposure of Haney's bluff in the use of limited invading force and propaganda. Nevertheless, Allen Dulles pushed through a compromise plan for some secret U.S. military support—he had no other real choice in this matter.

At the same time, aggressive new American diplomats were appointed to Central America, such as Ambassador Whiting Willauer of the CIA's old CAT airline in China, who was sent to the vital post in neighboring Honduras, where he borrowed CAT pilots for the future rebel air force against Arbenz. Most spectacular of these appointments, however, was that of John Peurifoy in October 1953. A flamboyant, pistol-packing Dixie Democrat, Peurifoy was appointed Ambassador to Guatemala, in his own words to crack the big stick. Peurifoy had already made his reputation as an anti-Communist Ambassador to Greece before becoming *de facto* diplomatic theater commander for all Central America. As a highly expendable Democrat in the event of failure, with some success he might also bring that still powerful party along on a bipartisan policy for Guatemala. The advantages for the Eisenhower administration in having the two brothers, John Foster Dulles and Allen Dulles, heading the State Department and Central Intelligence Agency, respectively, is readily apparent here.

In December 1953, Peurifoy spent a lengthy evening with President Arbenz and left convinced that the stubborn Guatemalan executive could not be bullied into an anti-Communist stance. In fact, in a famous phrase similar to Vice-President Nixon's subsequent appraisal of Fidel Castro, Peurifoy cabled

Washington, saying that if Arbenz was not a Communist, the Guatemalan would "certainly do until one comes along," and that "normal approaches will not work in Guatemala." Peurifoy's new position embodied a large element of bluff, but President Eisenhower's "good man" in Guatemala did not shrink from the possibility of "considerable bloodshed." That Peurifoy was not acting on his own had already been made clear to the somewhat naïve Ambassador of Guatemala, Guillermo Toriello, in Washington on January 16, 1954, when, in Eisenhower's own language, the President gave Toriello "unshirted hell" for "playing along with the Communists."[8] On that occasion, the President had talked at length about the dangers of communism, while, until abruptly dismissed, the Ambassador dwelt upon the issue of United Fruit Company as the real threat to the sovereignty of Guatemala. Unfortunately, both men were right.

Eisenhower's avowed anger with the insistent Toriello may have been, in part, politic at a moment when the French defeat in Indochina was looming, but it also may have stemmed still more from a warning by Eisenhower's stern, old wartime buddy, Undersecretary Smith. According to Smith, Arbenz may have claimed to Peurifoy that Guatemalan Communists were honest men who visited Moscow only to study Marxism rather than to receive orders. Nevertheless, at the CIA level, Colonel King was again overruled by Wisner and by Allen Dulles himself, when the Colonel warned them that Haney's plans would start a civil war in Central America. The determined CIA Director simply consulted his ever-available brother, John Foster Dulles, and was given the go-ahead for the confident Colonel Haney.[9]

Haney lost no time in expediting his arrangements in February and March 1954. A tough and insubordinate guerrilla operator from the Korean War, William "Rip" Robertson, was assigned as liaison officer to President Somoza of Nicaragua. Training camps, secret radio stations, and airstrips were built in Nicaragua and Honduras, as well as a powerful additional radio station on Swan Island in the Caribbean and another radio station in Guatemala itself, the last being programmed to operate on the same wave lengths as the regular Guatemalan stations. Old P-47 and P-51 fighter planes and C-47 transports were sent to Panama for future use, and, last, but not least, Colonel Carlos Castillo Armas was chosen by the agency to head the proposed invading force from Honduras. Unlike his more independent successor in Guatemala, Miguel Ydígoras Fuentes, the weak Castillo Armas had received the full support of such doubters as Colonel King, to say nothing of ardent hawks such as Colonel Luis Somoza of Nicaragua. But like the anti-Arbenz Guatemalans, Eisenhower's careful assistant for National Security Affairs, Robert Cutler, expressed doubts regarding the choice of Castillo Armas and even about allowing indigenous forces to select their own leaders with American support. And, as was to happen again with his future choices, E. Howard Hunt, CIA political-action chief for the operation, found his preferred presidential candidate, Dr. Juan Córdova Cerna, not even in the running.

In March, President Eisenhower sent his more-than-eager Secretary of State to a meeting of the Organization of American States in Caracas to garner some ostensible legal cover for the forthcoming CIA plans in Guatemala. In the Venezuelan capital, the feared, but unpopular John Foster Dulles was able to push through only a weak resolution against communism in the New World, without any multilateral action by the OAS against Guatemala. In his effort to convince the Latin Americans that communism in Guatemala constituted a "serious threat," Dulles probably lost more by antagonizing the reluctant Latin governments with his bull-in-a-china-shop tactics than he gained in nominal support against Arbenz. After all, powerful memories of earlier and repeated U.S. intervention in Central America remained a lot fresher in Caracas than awareness of any more recent and far less visible machinations, actually or allegedly directed by Moscow.

Upon returning home, Dulles fired John Moors Cabot as Assistant Secretary of Inter-American Affairs. In spite of Cabot's United Fruit connections, Dulles considered him too liberal. Sadly for the aggressive Secretary, Cabot's supposedly more conservative replacement, Henry Holland, immediately objected to the too public and too military nature of Operation PB Success, as the CIA plan was code-named. The bad-tempered Bedell Smith promptly told Holland to forget his (Holland's) "stupid ideas" and get on with the job of overthrowing Arbenz.[10]

By April, the angry Undersecretary observed with concern the "sustained frantic efforts" by Guatemalan emissaries to procure light arms, planes and artillery from Western Europe. Smith expressed anxiety that Guatemala would "evade [the] strict U.S. embargo" in order to build up the military strength of Communist groups in the country. Such groups, the State Department now estimated, had grown to 2,000–3,000 men, or almost half the strength of the regular Guatemalan army, which persisted in its loyalty to Arbenz. On April 23, President Eisenhower warned Congress that Guatemala was spreading its Marxist tentacles into El Salvador. And in Honduras, Ambassador Willauer was working night and day arranging air crews for the rebels' twelve-plane force, not to mention holding the Honduran government in line as the main CIA base against Guatemala. With matters so propitious for action, on May 11 Secretary Dulles could only lament that so far it had been "impossible to produce evidence clearly tying the Guatemala government to Moscow."[11] Clearly, the scene was set for the prompt materialization of such evidence.

At last, on May 15, a Swedish freighter, the *Alfhem,* which had been tracked for a month, since sailing from Stettin in Poland with an estimated 2,000 tons of unsuitable Czech and German arms, docked at Puerto Barrios in Guatemala to be received by Arbenz's minister of defense himself. The next day, Allen Dulles chaired a meeting of the Intelligence Advisory Committee, the top American intelligence chiefs from the U.S. military and the State Department. Professing chagrin that the *Alfhem* had slipped by its American trackers, the committee decided without delay that this was the long-sought pretext for intervention in Guatemala on behalf of Castillo Armas and his small group of exiles impatiently marking time in neighboring Honduras.

The President now warned congressional leaders that he would not just sit around any longer, but would stop all future shipments of arms to Guatemala. The State Department went into a frenzy of activity to find some legal pretext, such as an alleged violation of the Caracas Resolution, to take forcible steps against Guatemala. At a staff meeting of the State Department and the U.S. Joint Chiefs of Staff on May 21, General Matthew Ridgway, Army Chief of Staff, asked if Nicaraguan troops might be sent to Guatemala "as an alternative to the use of U.S. troops," a typical Ridgway question at a time when the administration was secretly debating the possibility of American intervention in Indochina in order to save the French after the spectacular fall of Dien Bien Phu. Unhappily, the Somoza forces in Nicaragua were deemed, even by their aggressive dictator, as "incompetent" for action in Guatemala, so Admiral Arthur Radford, Chairman of the Joint Chiefs of Staff, was left with only contingency plans to be prepared against any future orders. Admiral Robert Carney, Chief of Naval Operations, reported that the navy was already carrying out air surveillance at sea against further arms shipments for Guatemala.[12] Enough was enough.

The next day Secretary Dulles asked the President for authority to halt suspicious foreign vessels on the high seas off the coast of Guatemala—by force, if necessary—and to examine their cargoes. On May 24, Eisenhower informed congressional leaders of this new order, not fully effective until May 27, while Dulles next told the British about it and expressed hope for their cooperation. But on May 25, the highly experienced Deputy Undersecretary of State, Robert Murphy, warned Dulles that Dulles's new policy was "wrong" and might be "very expensive over the longer term." Murphy concluded that this new American action confessed "the bankruptcy of our political policy." "Instead," argued Murphy, "of political action inside Guatemala, we are obliged to resort to heavy-handed military action on the periphery of the cause of trouble. While I do not question the usefulness of a display of naval force in Central America under present circumstances, forcible detention of foreign shipping on the high seas is another matter. Our present action should give stir to the bones of Admiral von Tirpitz," the First World War German Admiral whose policies helped bring both Great Britain and the United States into war with Germany in 1914 and in 1917. Finally, the State Department's legal adviser reported that such U.S. naval action would violate several American treaties and could be considered an act of war.

Speaking of the Tirpitz era, on the same day, in conversation with the British Ambassador Sir Roger Makins, John Foster Dulles remarked that "the British would forgive us if we learned some lessons from British blockade practice in the First World War."[13] Despite Dulles's suggestion that communism in Guatemala might spread to British Honduras, Makins rejoined that his government's reaction might not be all that the Americans would desire. And, indeed, the reaction of British Foreign Secretary Anthony Eden was not to accept any *de facto* American blockade of British shipping on its way to Guatemala.

Meanwhile, the busy Secretary had told Eisenhower that a dangerously well-informed *New York Times* reporter in Guatemala, Sidney Gruson, was following the Communist party line. As a result of pressure on this powerful newspaper by Allen Dulles, Gruson was kept out of Guatemala during the unfolding of the CIA's counterrevolution there—another parallel with President Kennedy's problem with *The New York Times* during the Bay of Pigs, except that Kennedy would not descend to false charges of communism in order to get his way with the *Times*.[14]

The Dulles brothers were really up against it in Latin America as well by now. For example, on May 23, Louis Halle of the State Department Policy Planning Staff penned a memorandum to his superiors emphasizing that the major problem currently was Indochina, rather than playing, as Halle put it, the unconvincing role of an "elephant shaking with alarm" before a Guatemalan mouse as a spectacle for an audience of dubious Latin Americans. Halle notwithstanding, on May 28, Eisenhower approved NSC.5419/1 on U.S. policy in the event of what was quaintly called Guatemalan aggression in Latin America. The National Security Council accepted a Joint Chiefs of Staff suggestion that the United States would intervene unilaterally only as a last resort, since multilateral intervention with Latin American states obviously was preferable to the extent it was feasible.[15]

During the first week of June, repeated conversations between Ambassador Peurifoy in Guatemala and the State Department revealed that the purpose of blockading Guatemala was more to disrupt its maritime trade than just to prevent a further influx of arms from the Soviet bloc. But while confusion festered between the State Department and the U.S. Navy over what was to be stopped or inspected at sea, on June 8 President Arbenz responded to the American pressure with a *de facto* state of siege involving the suspension of civil liberties in Guatemala. On June 11, the CIA heard that Arbenz was resisting warnings from his army officers to oust Communists from his government on pain of being thrown out of office himself by June 15. The unyielding President replied that he would fight to the last man among his worker and peasant supporters. Finally, on June 14, American authorities in Hamburg halted the loading of antiaircraft shells from the Soviet Union destined for Guatemala from that German port.

By June 14, Allen Dulles had warned Press Secretary James Hagerty to prepare for evasive action before the press, since officially the United States government knew nothing of what was about to transpire in Guatemala. The next day at a final White House meeting of the National Security Council on Operation PB Success, Eisenhower told the two Dulles brothers and the Joint Chiefs of Staff that they now had to win because, in effect, the United States was already committed. Careful preparations were made, however, to discourage adverse congressional reactions in case the operation did not succeed.

Consequently, when on June 18, as the lower echelons of the State Department had feared, Foreign Secretary Eden rejected American requests to search British shipping, the President would not agree with his still-innocent Press Secretary. In his diary, Hagerty has written that "the State Department made a very bad mistake, particularly with the British, in attempting to search ships going to Guatemala. ... As a matter of fact, we were at war with the British in 1812 over the same principle. I don't see how with our traditional oppo-

sition to such search and seizure we could possibly have proposed it, and I don't blame the British for one minute for getting
pretty rough in their answers."[16] But Eisenhower made it very
clear that, in view of the American commitment, the time for
second thoughts was over, an essential point that he stated to
both Senator Thruston Morton of Kentucky and to his own
aide, General Andrew Goodpaster.

The power of the Dulles coalition, backed by the President,
finally became manifest on June 18 when less than two hundred
poorly trained followers of Colonel Castillo Armas at last strag-
gled across the Honduran frontier and cautiously advanced a
few miles into Guatemala. Protecting rapid and facile retreats
was becoming a necessary component of the CIA's raggle-tag-
gle military operations. More importantly, Castillo Armas's weak
forces were covered by three P-47 fighter planes and a couple
of Cessnas, with CAT pilots from General Chennault's and
Ambassador Willauer's old China organization, against absolutely no Guatemalan air opposition. Defections from Guatemala's tiny air force had totally paralyzed it. But in their
spectacular, if minuscule, operations over Guatemala, the
P-47s did meet some of the antiaircraft fire so characteristic of
Soviet-supplied countries.

This conspicuously *opéra bouffe* invasion was sustained by
a deafening radio barrage from nearby CIA stations, especially
that on Swan Island in the Caribbean, directed by David Phillips of the agency. A CIA memorandum of Allen Dulles noted
on June 20 that the Castillo Armas forces were relying exclusively "upon the possibility that his entry into action will touch
off a general uprising against the Guatemalan regime. . . . The
entire effort is thus dependent upon psychological impact rather
than actual military strength. . . . The use of a small number
of airplanes and the massive use of radio broadcasting are
designed to build up and give main support to the impression

of Castillo Armas' strength as well as to spread the impression of the regime's weakness."[17]

As so often happens with the employment of psychological techniques as a substitute for real war, matters did not go well. In the field, Castillo Armas's widely scattered forces, too weak for any deep or effective penetration of their homeland, waited in vain under CIA orders for a revolt, or even local desertions, by the Guatemalan army. In another parallel to the Bay of Pigs, the Arbenz government instead appealed to the United Nations, catching the U.S. delegate, Henry Cabot Lodge, in barefaced lies denying covert American intervention and quite unprepared to beat a Soviet veto by transferring the Guatemala appeal to the U.S.-dominated Organization of American States. The United Nations Security Council then passed a French resolution urging members to abstain from any action likely to cause bloodshed in Guatemala. Well might Eisenhower seethe over the behavior of his NATO allies, Britain and France, in not supporting him on this vital issue.

Worst of all, late on June 20, Colonel Haney informed Allen Dulles that his tiny air force had lost three planes to small-arms fire in Guatemala, thereby seriously weakening Castillo Armas's chief military asset. As in the marginal operation in Cuba in 1961, the State Department and CIA had kept U.S. support for Operation Success minimal to conceal American participation, but a backup of U.S. naval and air forces was already standing by, ready for emergencies. Instead of employing such forces to aid Castillo Armas in the field, as suggested by Lieutenant General Charles Cabell, his Air Force deputy in the CIA, Dulles cleared with Bedell Smith the sending of two more old Honduran P-51s offered by President Anastasio Smorza to support the invaders. Unhappily for such a neat solution, Assistant Secretary of State Holland, always anxious about the visibility of CIA activities in Central America, demanded a direct appeal to the White House to authorize sending the two planes. In a famous meeting on June 22, the President settled the dispute between Secretary of State Dulles and Henry Holland. According to Eisenhower's ironic account, he decided in Allen Dulles's favor when told by Dulles that the prospects of Castillo Armas were nonexistent without two P-51 fighters to replace his losses. With such replacements, there was supposedly a 20-percent chance of success. Whatever Dulles's actual estimates—and less amusing figures range from 50 to 80 percent—Eisenhower reasoned once again that, although the CIA incursion was openly violating U.S. treaty obligations, he had better be the winner in an operation throughout which he had been opposed to sending in the Marines.[18]

The Eisenhower administration took care of its small war on the diplomatic side with equal dispatch. On June 23 and 24, Secretary Dulles warned both his Paris embassy and Ambassador Lodge at the United Nations that if the French and British continued backing Guatemala in the United Nations, President Eisenhower "would feel entirely free" to cease supporting them in Indochina, North Africa, Cyprus, and Egypt. Lodge replied from New York that a split among the NATO allies would please the Russians very much, but Dulles insisted that the whole value of regional organizations like the OAS, which the United States could still dominate, was "at stake." On June 24, Lodge, therefore, exercised a veto in the UN against the Anglo-French resolution on Guatemala. He reported to Washington that his warning was received with great solemnity by the British and French delegates in New York.[19]

Actually, Eisenhower was even angrier than his diplomatic representatives had made out. On June 24, he told Hagerty that if the British expected "a free ride" on Cyprus, he would teach "them a lesson"; they had "no right to stick their nose in matters which concerned this hemisphere entirely." The next morning Sir Winston Churchill and Anthony Eden, arriving in Washington to discuss the far more important crisis in Indochina, learned that the Monroe Doctrine was far from dead in the Eisenhower White House. But after all, the British Prime Minister, as an old buccaneer against the shipping rights of neutrals, cannot have been as shocked by Eisenhower as was Eden by his own bête noire, John Foster Dulles. If Eisenhower pleased his old British friends by no longer contemplating sending marines into Indochina to bail out the collapsing French, on Central America he and Dulles "talked cold turkey" to Churchill and Eden, much as he was accustomed to doing during the bitter crises of the Second World War. As Churchill had already observed, Anthony Eden was sometimes foolish in quarreling with the Americans over petty Central American issues of little concern to Great Britain.[20]

That afternoon of June 25, the British and French delegates abruptly abstained from voting against the United States on the Guatemala issue in the United Nations. The United States thereby won in the Security Council by the slight but decisive majority of 5 to 4 votes. The new government of Pierre Mendès-France in Paris, frantic to obtain Anglo-American support against the Sino-Soviet bloc in Indochina, was in no position to resist what Charles de Gaulle has justly termed the Anglo-Saxons. In a sense, success in Guatemala was a small compensation for the loss of Tonkin China for the Eisenhower administration in 1954. John Kennedy would face a similar, painful choice between Laos and Cuba in the spring of 1961 and, like Eisenhower, would give precedence to the problem closer to home. Only Lyndon Johnson would make the far less practical choice in favor of much too distant and demanding South Vietnam.

Likewise, from June 25, renewed and intimidating light

bombing of selected points in Guatemala, coupled with the
jamming of local radio stations amid misleading instructions
broadcast from outside the country, finally provoked a revolt
by the Guatemalan army leaders against the Arbenz government within another two days. The officer corps had particularly feared a vain attempt by Arbenz to arm the leftist popular
militia as a direct threat to its own power. Foreign Minister
Toriello now appealed directly to John Foster Dulles in vain,
but by June 27 was informed by Ambassador Peurifoy that the
United States demanded "a clean sweep" of the whole Arbenz
government, although futile efforts were still being made by
the Guatemalan army to avoid swallowing the unpopular Castillo Armas as its new junta leader. To top matters, without
permission from his CIA superiors in Florida, under the pressure of the eager President Smorza, a rebel plane piloted by
soldier of fortune "Rip" Robertson of subsequent Bay of Pigs
fame bombed and beached an offshore British freighter incor-
rectly suspected of carrying arms or ammunition to Arbenz.
Even Richard Bissell of the CIA has admitted that this went
beyond the established limits of policy. Meanwhile, in Washington, lower-echelon State Department and British protests
on moral grounds were brushed aside as ruthlessly, as had
been Arbenz, Toriello, and Eden.[21] As Eisenhower had said, in
his administration the United States did not quit halfway, at
least not in almost defenseless Guatemala. Thus, by July 1954,
Castillo Armas was at last fully installed in power in Guatemala City, thanks entirely to his powerful and persistent friends
in Washington, and President Eisenhower made no effort in
private to conceal his keen satisfaction with this achievement.

The Central Intelligence Agency basked in congratulations
on its dangerously facile victory in Guatemala, and, among
others, Tracy Barnes, Richard Bissell, and E. Howard Hunt
received commendations from their gratified Director, Allen

Dulles, who, according to Bissell, had been on the top of running Operation PB Success. Indeed, so glowing was Allen Dulles that he described Arbenz's fall as a new and glorious chapter in U.S.–Latin American history. Ché Guevara, who was also in Guatemala at this juncture,[22] would derive different lessons from the instructive episode of Operation Success—lessons such as the need for mobilizing a whole people against external attack as well as for the early purge of an inherited conservative office corps while there was still time. In the future, Fidel Castro would prove to be his apt pupil.

In any case, Operation Success, as fundamentally a psychological tour de force, greatly influenced agency planners in the future for the Bay of Pigs, as has been conceded by Richard Bissell himself. The CIA was now authorized by NSC.5432 / 1 on September 3 to take "increased action against Communist penetration" in Latin America, with unilateral U.S. action, as before, to be undertaken ostensibly "only as a last resort." The fact remained that neither in Guatemala nor earlier in Albania nor later in Indonesia or Cuba would the CIA actually ever have enough available and competent dissidents to mount a successful military operation, apart from the perennial problem of the deniability of the U.S. role. But for the time, the facile victory of Operation Success evoked a sense of obligation to the Central Intelligence Agency on the part of Castillo Armas and his successor, the agency's original choice for President of Guatemala, Miguel Ydígoras Fuentes. On the other hand, because of widespread and often violent criticism in Latin America of the CIA concerning this operation, in January 1955 Democratic Senator Mike Mansfield of Montana proposed the creation of a Joint Congressional Oversight Committee to supervise more seriously such CIA activities.[23]

Although he did manage to establish a congressional subcommittee on the CIA, Mansfield failed to achieve full and

joint congressional committees because of the threat to the
minority system implicit in existing congressional committees. Furthermore, an alarmed Eisenhower said that any such
committees would have to be created over his dead body, in
part because he feared that one might be directed by Senator
Joseph McCarthy or some other congressional blabbermouth.
In fact, in September 1954, the President had already tried to
head off any publicity-seeking congressional committee by
authorizing his own investigation of the Clandestine Services
with the so-called Doolittle committee. That this committee
was safely under the control of the same intelligence agencies
it was meant to appraise may be seen in its famous conclusion
that to compete with world communism, "hitherto accepted
norms of human conduct do not apply. If the United States is
to survive, long-standing American concepts of 'fair play' must
be reconsidered." Among the limitations on the Central Intelligence Agency that should be removed, according to the Doolittle committee, were any restraints upon the Director or his
DD / P—that is, Deputy Director for Plans (i.e., Operations).[24]

In February 1956, in order further to preempt the creation
of Mansfield's original congressional committees, at the recommendation of the Hoover commission Eisenhower set up
what eventually would be called the President's Foreign Intelligence Advisory Board to deal with both press leaks on the
CIA and the growing use of science and technology in intelligence matters thereafter. Former Ambassador Joseph P. Kennedy, who served briefly on this last board, soon resigned after
deciding that it was no more than window dressing to appease
a Congress then thoroughly uninterested in embarrassing the
CIA in any way. In 1976, the House and Senate Select Committees on Intelligence would reach essentially the same conclusion regarding the Foreign Intelligence Advisory Board under
both Eisenhower and Kennedy. Only by 1980, did Congress

finally make the intelligence agencies responsible to its oversight committees, although how little this would improve
matters in the ensuing Reagan administration remained to be
seen.

Neither this board nor a more ephemeral Eisenhower
watchdog committee over the CIA—the Operations Coordinating Board of the National Security Council, established in 1953
in part as a circuit breaker to protect the President from direct
knowledge of covert operations—succeeded in exercising any
serious control over the Central Intelligence Agency, according to two prominent and indignant members of the Foreign
Intelligence Advisory Board, Robert Lovett and David Bruce.
Both men had had a great deal of experience in government
service—Bruce had been an old rival of Allen Dulles in Office
of Strategic Services days—and each decided that "final approval
. . . of the O.C.B. inner group can, at best, be described as *pro
forma*" and that "no one, other than those in the C.I.A. immediately concerned . . . has any detailed knowledge of what is
going on." As a consequence, CIA operations of the sort that
Ambassador Charles Yost has termed ham-handed experi-
ments in subversion were often conducted in direct conflict
with official State Department policy and were sometimes
unknown to the lower echelons of the department.[25]

For example, in February to May 1958, in a less successful
but far more accurate foreshadowing of the Bay of Pigs operation than Guatemala, the CIA failed to subvert or overthrow
the purportedly Left-leaning government of Sukarno in Indonesia. Unknown to the U.S. Ambassador there and publicly
disavowed if privately approved by both Eisenhower and John
Foster Dulles, this operation never got off the ground when its
Sumatra-based rebels refused to fight effectively against
Sukarno's regular military forces. Finally, in May 1958, a CIA
American pilot supporting the rebels was shot down and cap-

tured in a B-26 bomber. Allen Dulles then dropped the whole
operation as quietly as possible, leaving the local Communists
stronger than ever.

As a consequence, Frank Wisner, Deputy Director for Plans—
that is, of the clandestine operations of the CIA—lost his job,
and the Foreign Intelligence Advisory Board told an angry
Eisenhower that there had been no proper planning for the
operation by anyone in the fissiparous agency. Indeed, said
the board with unaccustomed spunk, the affair had been over-
controlled by a nervous John Foster Dulles in distant Washington, a judgment remarkably similar to many on Dean Rusk's
activities during the Bay of Pigs. Later on, despite the secret
review mechanisms of Gordon Gray's more potent Special
(5412) Group of the National Security Council, which actually
had been supervising the CIA since 1955, approximately three-
fourths of all covert-action projects would never be reviewed
or approved by any committee outside the agency itself before
action was undertaken. As Eisenhower's prudent aide General
Goodpaster concluded, the CIA remained a weakly controlled
enterprise throughout the Eisenhower years, despite stren-
uous efforts by the President to supervise it effectively, but from
a discreet distance.[26]

Weak control of the CIA or not, on September 25, 1956,
under the impetus of the Operations Coordinating Board of
the National Security Council as well as that of the Joint Chiefs
of Staff, in NSC.5613 / 1 the President approved of a statement
that read: "If a Latin American State should establish with the
Soviet bloc, close ties of such a nature as seriously to prejudice
our vital interests . . . [the United States must] be prepared to
diminish Governmental economic and financial cooperation
with that country and to take any other policy, economic or
military actions deemed appropriate."[27]

I I
Fidel's Cuba

Castro will have to gravitate to us like an iron filing to a magnet.[1] —*Nikita Khrushchev, September 1960*

It is only to posterity that revolutionary movements appear unambiguous.[2] —*Henry Kissinger, 1961*

If we start assassinating Chiefs of State, God knows where it all will end?[3] —*Franklin Roosevelt to OSS chief William Donovan, 1944*

*I*N MARCH 1958, the accelerating growth of Fidel Castro's guerrilla movement in the Sierra Maestra mountains of southeastern Cuba precipitated a State Department freeze on the delivery of American arms to the Cuban government. This early attempt to disassociate Washington publicly from its long-time man in Havana, President Fulgencio Batista, was resisted vigorously by the new United States Ambassador in Cuba, Earl T. Smith. Claiming that both his professional embassy staff and the CIA Station Chief in Havana were undercutting him in their advocacy of a deal with Castro, and supported by Spruille Braden and Arthur Gardner, his predecessor in Cuba, the increasingly anxious and angry Smith vigorously argued for the continuation of the customary U.S. policy of supporting Batista for the business and anti-Communist reasons prevalent most of the time since the nominal abrogation of the Platt Amendment in 1934. Actually, by November 1958, John Foster Dulles and William Wieland, who headed the State Department's Caribbean desk, were seeking a third force to replace Batista in Cuba, although the experienced and more liberal Wieland was rapidly losing hope for even that unlikely solution.[4]

Since the issue of when Fidel Castro really became an active Communist, as opposed to a theoretical Marxist, and thus whether or not an American deal with him was ever really possible in the early stages of his rise to power, rapidly became so intensely partisan a political question in the United States, few conclusions will satisfy everyone on this score. Nevertheless, the effort on the part of the more professional elements of the State Department and the CIA to disengage the United States from Batista's rapidly sinking popularity in Cuba seemed wise, however hopeless the possibilities of establishing an effective alternative to Fidel Castro may appear to have been in retrospect. After all, it was only in December 1958, at the last minute before Castro's accession to power, that Allen Dulles belatedly passed on to an indignant President and the National Security Council a firm warning from Ambassador Smith that if Castro took over, Communists and other extreme radicals would probably participate in any government Castro formed. At the same time, on December 23, the State Department, in actual practice already headed by Christian Herter, informed the confused President that the Cubans no longer supported Batista, that Fidel Castro was the least anti-American member of his own faction, and that evidence of Communist dominance in Castro's movement remained insufficient. At any rate, the State Department concluded, Batista must quit the presidency of Cuba and should probably leave the country as well.

Just how serious were the steps taken that same month by the new, more cautious CIA Station Chief in Cuba, James Noel, and by American business interests in Cuba led by William Pawley to try to create a non-Batista junta as an alternative to

Castro remains somewhat uncertain. Pawley, incidentally, was close to Richard Nixon and, according to Eisenhower, harbored a pathological hatred for Castro. Eisenhower's characteristic approval of a search for a middle way between Batista and Castro reflected that perennial dream of American foreign policy makers—a compromise between corruption and communism. Allen Dulles, however, did discuss with Admiral Arleigh Burke, the strongly anti-Communist Chief of Naval Operations, the forcible prevention of Castro's coming to power. Within the State Department, which half-heartedly had sponsored Pawley's earlier attempts and those of the CIA to block Castro's ascent to power, Admiral Burke found full support for forcible opposition to Castro only from Robert Murphy. Subsequently, to avoid open violation of the U.S. Neutrality Act, Pawley would recommend to Eisenhower illegal activities against Castro only under the aegis of the CIA.

Influenced by Colonel J. C. King, the agency's Chief of the Western Hemisphere Division, Allen Dulles now feared possible widespread bloodshed as a result of a change of regime in Cuba. Dulles may also have rewritten a CIA report on Castro to President Eisenhower in a more hostile vein, although he was warned by Colonel King and by his Inspector General, Lyman Kirkpatrick, Jr., that even the Cuban middle class had already deserted Batista. For that matter, six months later Dulles himself would testify secretly that both Batista's army and people had deserted him. In fact, said Dulles, "everybody deserted him." Kirkpatrick, who had set up BRAC, Batista's police section to repress Communist activities within Cuba, was mortified when word of BRAC's frequent use of torture finally leaked out to an angry Cuban public.[5] Not surprisingly in these circumstances, Secretary of State John Foster Dulles, now mortally sick, greeted Castro's arrival to power at the beginning of January 1959 with the gravest doubts as to whether this was good or bad for the United States.

With Batista's abrupt and somewhat unexpected flight from Cuba at the end of the year and Castro's delirious popular reception in Havana, the State Department on January 8 hastened to assure the new Cuban government of the sincere good will of the United States. Allen Dulles then testified, in a closed briefing of the Senate Foreign Relations Committee on January 26, 1959, that Fidel Castro himself did not have "any Communist leanings," nor was he "working for the Communists." More accurately, Dulles told the suspicious Senators that Castro "apparently has very wide popular backing throughout the island." The CIA Director added that "American intervention there at this time or even before, would have had disastrous effects throughout the whole hemisphere and I see no alternative—this is a matter of policy. But from the intelligence point of view, American intervention would seem now to be a move which would be counterproductive."[6]

The next month, however, reporting secretly to Eisenhower, Dulles warned that Castro was moving rapidly toward a complete, if not yet Communist, dictatorship in which Communists were already infiltrating all organs of Cuban government and society. In Annex B to NSC.5902/1 on February 16, while the continued U.S. policy of nonintervention still remained official, it was stated that Latin Americans "tend to believe that the United States overemphasized Communism as a threat to the Western Hemisphere and consequently, they tend to take insufficient precautions against internal Communist subversion. . . . This played into the hands of the Communists, who since the Guatemala experience, were camouflaging their revolutionary aims and identifying Communism with . . . national aspirations."[7]

Once firmly in power, Ché Guevara, not at all desirous of U.S. good will, had already busied himself with seizing the files of Batista's anti-Communist police section, BRAC, and promptly had its Director shot. Meanwhile, profiting from Guevara's experience in Guatemala, Castro promptly purged the old Batista army of its conservative officer corps. With the customary disapproval of Colonel King, Allen Dulles now declared that the agency had to start recruiting men of the Left for potential anti-Castro Cuban projects. To start matters rolling in this new direction, King's superior, Richard Bissell, Deputy Director for Plans, was allowed to bring in several German refugees from the Eastern European Division of the agency to liberalize King's conservative and rather independent Western Hemisphere Division.

The no-longer-acceptable and certainly unqualified American Ambassador Earl T. Smith had already been recalled after last-minute attempts to induce Batista to quit on his own accord. Smith was replaced in February 1959 by Philip Bonsal, an optimistic diplomat of great experience in Indochina, who admired Castro personally, as he had previously admired the unfortunate General Henri Navarre. By Indochina standards, Bonsal did not yet consider the new Cuban leader a real Communist. Unhappily for the success of Bonsal's mission, as a result of a reporter's provocative question in mid-January at the Havana Hilton, Castro had already remarked that, henceforth any American effort to intervene in Cuba would result in 200,000 dead gringos in his country. For the moment, however, Castro had to content himself with imprisoning or shooting only his domestic opponents.

On a visit to Venezuela in January, Castro proposed to his rapidly cooling host, President Rómulo Betancourt, the liberation of Puerto Rico from the United States. In March, Castro attacked both the Venezuelan and Costa Rican governments for not opposing the United States, although elements among these two governments had been his previous closest supporters. Shortly afterward, Castro may have been responsible for supervising several unsuccessful small raids on the Dominican Republic, Haiti, Panama, and Nicaragua by groups from Cuba. At the same time, he also charged reactionary Americans with planning an invasion of Cuba with the many Batistiano refugees and former wealthy sugar planters who had already fled Castro's confiscations, frequently to an embittered and a restless refuge in Florida.[8]

In mid-April 1959, Castro visited Washington to the great irritation of Eisenhower, who hurriedly left town to avoid the embarrassment of seeing him. In the course of this much-publicized visit to obtain arms, if not aid, the Cuban leader had a lengthy discussion with Vice-President Richard Nixon, who concluded that Castro was either under Communist discipline or at least incredibly naïve about communism. Thereafter, in his own words, the Vice-President became the strongest and most persistent advocate of forcibly overthrowing Castro by arming Cuban exiles against him. In fact, according to Castro, Nixon favored using the U.S. armed forces to assist the invading exiles.

At this juncture and for sometime afterward, Nixon's views failed to convince either the White House, the supposedly dangerous liberals of the State Department, or even Richard Bissell and Frank Bender of the CIA. However, under the influence of his increasingly alarmed Station Chief in Havana, James Noel (code-named "Nelson"), Allen Dulles again warned the President of the growing Communist infiltration of the Castro regime. It is also possible that Castro, as Philip Bonsal has suggested, may have been misled regarding the state of American opinion because of the generally cordial reception that he had received outside of Washington on his April visit to the United States. In this connection, Undersecretary of State Christian Herter informed Eisenhower on April 22 that

Castro was "a most interesting individual, very much like a child in many ways, quite immature regarding the problem of government, and puzzled and confused by some of the practical difficulties now facing him. In English he spoke with restraint and considerable personal appeal. In Spanish, however, he became voluble, excited and somewhat 'wild.' "[9] At the same time, though, the CIA told the President that Castro, while an enigma, was also a born leader of great personal courage of conviction and that it would be a serious mistake to underestimate him. Whether born leader or confused child, Castro himself subsequently asserted that he had been a Communist long before he had seized power, although even this was almost certainly exaggerated after the event to meet his future political requirements.

With the forced resignation in July 1959 of the anti-Communist Manuel Urrutia Lléo and Castro's initial selection as provisional president of Cuba, many of Castro's more moderate supporters, the CIA and the State Department concluded that Castro had betrayed the original promises under which he had gained power. The arrest in October of Major Húber Matos, military chief of Camagüey Province, the systematic replacement of other non-Communists with Communists, and a purge of Castro's cabinet in November 1959 made Communist dominance of Cuba unmistakable to the now-horrified Ambassador Bonsal. In fact, Bonsal had come around to considering Castro's current orations reminiscent of Hitler's at his most hysterical, while the State Department was now considering building up a coherent resistance inside Cuba to reject Castro.

Admiral Arleigh Burke, the agressive Chief of Naval Operations, was confirmed in his long-held view that Castro was a Communist who had Russian support because of Soviet interest in controlling the world's narrower sea lanes. On Novem-

ber 5, Acting Secretary of State Christian Herter recommended
to Eisenhower the encouragement of opposition to Castro, both
inside and outside Cuba, in the most discreet possible fashion
in view of Latin American sensitivity to overt American intervention. Four days later, the President approved of the State
Department's recommendation, and the United States was at
last launched upon a still officially secret war against Cuba.[10]

In December 1959, Colonel King submitted a memorandum
to Allen Dulles, observing that the "far left" dictatorship in
Cuba, if permitted to stand, would encourage the seizure of
American property in other Latin American countries. King
recommended four actions against Castro, which met with the
approval of both Dulles and of Richard Bissell, his Deputy
Director for Plans. Among these was one that Dulles accepted
on December 11—namely, that "thorough consideration be
given to the elimination of Fidel Castro," because neither his
brother Raúl nor Ché Guevara had "the same mesmeric appeal
to the masses." Less evasively, the recommendation concluded: "Many informed people believed that the disappear-
ance of Fidel would greatly accelerate the fall of the present
Government."

In order to head off Bissell's rival clandestine organization,
Colonel King recalled his Station Chief Jake Engler from Venezuela. On January 18, 1960, Engler (code-named "Enders")
set up a new task force of the Western Hemisphere Division
as a planning team against Castro in a still only nominally
priority operation. In late 1960, a cadre of Cuban instructors
was to be sent to the Panama Canal Zone to be trained in provoking their anti-Castro compatriots to make small uprisings
along the Cuban coasts. Unfortunately for King's hopes, this
half-hearted new operation, then called WH / 4 or the Cuba
Task Force, would come under Bissell and Tracy Barnes's
direction rather than his own.

Notwithstanding his approval of Colonel King's explicit memorandum of the previous month regarding Castro's assassination, on January 18, 1960, Allen Dulles informed the Special Group of the National Security Council, supervising agency activities in Cuba, that "we do not have in mind the quick elimination of Castro, but rather actions designed to enable responsible opposition leaders to get a foothold."[1] The rationale for anti-Castro leaders' obtaining a possible foothold obviously arose from a National Security Council discussion of the previous week about seizing Cuba. Eisenhower had objected to any such action, saying that no Russian bases had yet appeared on the island. The President had then also agreed with Secretary of the Treasury C. Douglas Dillon that, in deference to the priorities of Latin American opinion, right-wing dictator Rafael Trujillo, President of the Dominican Republic, should be thrown out before Castro. At a National Security Council meeting on January 14, it was stated that Castro was moving toward introducing communism so skillfully as to give the United States no excuse for intervention. Clearly, the administration was on the horns of a dilemma regarding what to do about Cuba and how to justify any course of action.

Bonsal's temporary recall to Washington in January 1960, following "indignities" to himself on the part of Castro, signaled a public hardening of the American line toward Cuba, although the Ambassador still favored some *modus vivendi* in order not to push Castro toward even further extremes. In fact, he still hoped that Castro would remain a neutral in the cold war. In writing up a public presidential warning embodying his relatively moderate views, Bonsal stated that, while the United States intended to continue its policy of nonintervention according to its treaty commitments, Cuba was not doing likewise. After some hesitation at a meeting with his State Department advisers on January 25, Eisenhower proposed using

the unenthusiastic Organization of American States to push
the U.S. case. Two days earlier, Eisenhower had suggested
strengthening the American garrison at Guantánamo in Cuba.
Finally, losing his famous temper, he concluded that "Castro
begins to look like a madman" and added that the United States
should impose a unilateral blockade on Cuba. The angry President now roundly declared that if the Cuban people got "hun-
gry" enough from such a blockade, "they will throw Castro
out." Bonsal replied that the United States "should not punish
the whole Cuba people for the acts of an abnormal man."[12]

In February, calming down under State Department pressure, Eisenhower embargoed all arms shipments from the
United States to Cuba. The Soviet agreement at the same time
to purchase 5 million tons of Cuban sugar over the next five
years, as well as a series of mysterious incidents culminating
in a successful attempt—possibly by the CIA—to blow up the
French ammunition ship *La Coubre* in Havana harbor in early
March, drove the Cuban government to step up the seizure of
American property of all kinds, the total value of which would
eventually amount to almost $1 billion. Indeed, Castro com-
pared the sinking of *La Coubre* with that of the USS *Maine* in
Havana harbor in 1898. This provocative analogy would be
followed by Castro's Pearl Harbor within another thirteen
months.

On March 9, the pessimistic but realistic Colonel King
informed his subordinates of his fear of a Cuban attack upon
the U.S. naval base at Guantánamo Bay and added that, but
for the "highly unlikely" elimination of both Castro brothers
and Ché Guevara "in one package," the CIA operation could
be "a long drawn-out affair" since "the present government
will be only overthrown by the use of force." The next day, at
a meeting of the National Security Council, Admiral Burke,
declared that the United States needed a real leader for the

anti-Castro forces since "many of the leaders around Castro were even worse than Castro." Allen Dulles replied that the major anti-Castro leaders, such as they were, were no longer in Cuba. Somewhat irrelevantly, President Eisenhower expressed his fear of another Black Hole of Calcutta, evidently for the Americans remaining in Cuba. In short, in both the administration and the agency the search for some provocation to intervene against Castro continued apace.

On March 14, the more restricted Special Group supervising the CIA met with the agency in the White House to consider the proposed organization of the Cuba Task Force. There ensued a general discussion of the consequences if the Castro brothers and Guevara "should disappear simultaneously." Admiral Burke again argued that "the only organized group within Cuba today were [sic] the Communists and there was, therefore, the danger that they might move into control." Interestingly, Allen Dulles felt that such an eventuality "might not be disadvantageous because it would facilitate a multilateral action by the O.A.S. [Organization of American States]."[13] Colonel King admitted that so far there were few Cuban leaders capable of taking over from Castro in case of his overthrow. Assassination was not openly discussed since the President was apparently present at this meeting. In any case, Eisenhower had already urged Allen Dulles to take stronger action against Castro and not just attack sugar refineries. Outside of the National Security Council, Eisenhower was a lot less discreet in his private discussions with selected officials.

Thus, on March 17, the President would approve of Richard Bissell's four-part program of covert action (appropriately codenamed Operation Pluto) against Castro's regime so as to obtain a policy more acceptable to the OAS, but in such a manner as to avoid any appearance of U.S. intervention. As a result of this program, Eisenhower initially authorized Bissell to organize the innumerable and disparate Cuban refugee factions into a public political organization that would eventually be called the Frente Revolucionario Democrático. It was believed that this would require about four or five months to achieve—months, as it turned out, of increasing frustration, confusion, and difficulty. Bissell's fourth and most important point—the organization of a paramilitary force outside of Cuba of about 800 men for a landing from bases in Guatemala and Nicaragua—met with less immediate presidential approval and, indeed, eventually resulted in Eisenhower's rewriting his private papers to make it appear that he had never approved of any military planning for any Cuban landing, let alone one at the Bay of Pigs.

Of this March 1960 plan, Thomas Mann of the State Department reported that "ultimate success" of a landing was based upon "a sizable popular uprising or substantial follow on forces." Since an effective popular uprising was "unlikely," the United States would be faced with abandoning the landing force accompanied by a consequent loss of prestige, or transforming the invaders into guerrillas, or openly intervening with American forces. Such flagrant violations of U.S. treaties would result in virtually no support for the United States in either the OAS or United Nations, as well as enhancing Castro's popularity in Cuba. Should the guerrilla option be taken, the CIA assumed that Cuban volunteers would rally about small company-sized military catalysts scattered through the mountains of Cuba. It was estimated that it would take about six to eight months to raise and train outside of Cuba such a force of some 300 or more men. Thomas Mann, however, preferred open American intervention since it was more in accord with U.S. traditions.

The third point of the March 17 program stipulated that action against Cuba would be supported by a powerful propaganda offensive, including radio broadcasts transmitted by the radio station built for the Guatemala operation in 1954 by the then-Colonel Edward Lansdale on Swan Island, a dependency of Honduras in the Caribbean southwest of Cuba. A covert intelligence and action organization inside Cuba completed the CIA's plans at this stage.[14] Of course, subsequently both Eisenhower and his aides have denied that Operation Pluto constituted a decision to invade Cuba at all.

As a consequence, the ambitious and gratified Bissell was now ordered to switch his attention from preparing Tibetans in Colorado for subversion in Communist China to training approximately 20 to 30 guerrilla cadre leaders in the Canal Zone instead. His assistant would be the impetuous and unpopular Tracy Barnes, who had also participated in the Guatemala operation in 1954. Like the Guatemala operation, the chain of command through which the Clandestine Services normally operated was once again bypassed by a separate staff organization reporting exclusively to Bissell and Barnes. This enabled Bissell's doubting and perhaps jealous Deputy Richard Helms, formerly responsible for clandestine operations in Cuba, including attempts to assassinate Castro, carefully to remove himself from as much responsibility as possible. Of more immediate importance, Colonel King's conservative Western Hemisphere Division was also excluded from the Cuban project for fear that, among other things, it would bring back the old Bastista crowd if it were successful in Cuba. Sherman Kent, who headed the CIA Board of National Estimates, was simultaneously cut out of knowledge of any Cuban plans. Finally, Vice-President Richard M. Nixon considered himself the action officer within the White House for the project as a whole. According to his military aide Brigadier General Robert Cushman of the U.S. Marine Corps, Nixon wanted nothing to go wrong. To ensure this, Cushman was appointed coordinator among the various government agencies.

Less eager for action was Acting Secretary of State Christian Herter, who, having replaced the dying John Foster Dulles,
complained that since the latest CIA National Intelligence
Estimate on Cuba had failed to find Communist influence on
Castro dominant, it would be impossible to gain a two-thirds
vote in the skeptical Organization of American States for legal
action against Castro. The State Department also harbored a
well-justified fear that Latin American votes against Cuba would
depend upon more substantial and dramatic U.S. economic
aid programs for their own development progress. Ambassador
Bonsal's return to Cuba on March 20, the day after a declara-
tion of economic war on the United States by Ché Guevara,
now Castro's revolutionary economics minister, was similarly
inauspicious. Nevertheless, Bonsal continued to advise restraint
in American actions against Castro on the depressing grounds
that the Cuban leader derived much of his popular support
from his anti-Americanism. On April 22, Castro, better informed
on American policy than the U.S. Ambassador, publicly and
accurately declared that Washington was organizing a well-
prepared and premeditated plan of action against the Cuban
government, a plan that, he informed an audience of half a
million in Havana a week later, had already materialized in
Guatemala with CIA and State Department support.

Earlier in the month, Castro had with some difficulty wiped
out a guerrilla group operating in the hills against him, and he
suspected with good reason that another such group had been
launched from the U.S. naval base at Guantánamo. At least at
this time Castro did not seem to know about Admiral Burke's
earlier advocacy of employing a full American division to rescue some 30 touring U.S. Marines kidnaped in June 1958 in
a raid by Raúl Castro's mountain guerrillas, a raid not authorized by Fidel Castro. To Burke's disgust, Robert Murphy and

Roy Richard Rubottom, the usual liberal Assistant Secretary of State for Latin American Affairs, had then been able to thwart this particular excuse for open American intervention. Three weeks later, after a State Department threat to resume U.S. arms shipment to Batista, the Marines had been returned to the Americans by Raúl Castro unharmed. In any event, by 1960 the Cuban leader could hardly have been unaware of the open recruiting of volunteers against him among the loquacious Cuban refugees in Miami and New York, where the CIA had at last been able to patch up an agreement of sorts between several of the more prominent refugee faction.[15]

A significant final economic break took place in June 1960, when, in a major miscalculation of the availability of oil tankers on the world market, American oil companies in Cuba, with the support of Washington, refused to refine the newly delivered Russian oil. As Philip Bonsal had feared, this refusal resulted first in the seizure of the remaining U.S. refineries by the Cubans and, thereafter, in Cuba's enforced dependence upon the Soviet Union for increased economic support. In July, as another step in his new program of economic action against Castro, President Eisenhower cut down the generous Cuban sugar quota for 1960, a preliminary to eliminating it entirely the next year. For Bonsal, with the dumping of economically dependent Cuba on Russia's doorstep, the United States turned its back on thirty years of statesmanship in Latin America. For Ché Guevara, this was a long-overdue American step, and one that he desired anyway, since, as an orthodox Marxist at this stage, he deemed such capitalist benefits symbols of an obsolete colonial yoke. But most important, Eisenhower, by now completely fed up, felt that this imposition of what he called economic sanctions against Cuba would naturally lead to "other moves" against Castro, moves of an "economic, diplomatic [and] strategic" nature.[16] American relations with Cuba had deteriorated to the level of those with Japan in July 1941.

Some of these "other" American moves appeared in the form of a powerful radio station that the CIA began to operate on May 17 from Swan Island. The purpose of the new station was first to attack Rafael Trujillo, the gradually weakening dictator of the Dominican Republic, and subsequently to attack Fidel Castro, its real target. Secretary Herter had felt that the OAS would never support the United States against Castro unless the unpopular right-wing dictator was also attached. He also feared that the alternative to an unpopular U.S. takeover was a pro-Castro coup in the Dominican Republic. Later on, the CIA would buy time for similar purposes on commercial radio stations within the continental United States. In June 1960, the agency was finally able to set up Eisenhower's long-desired Frente Revolucionario Democrático (FRD) in an attempt to unite the leading anti-Castro groups among the many struggling Cuban factions in the United States.

In early July, Nikita Khrushchev, apparently alarmed, announced to Castro's keen humiliation that "figuratively speaking, if need be, Soviet artillerymen can support the Cuban people with their rocket fire if aggressive forces in the Pentagon chose to start intervention against Cuba." Soon afterward, the Soviet leader also proclaimed that the Monroe Doctrine, having outlived its time, should now be buried as a corpse. Khrushchev further offered to help Castro in disposing of that stern guardian of the Monroe Doctrine, the U.S. naval base at Guantánamo.[17] In the upshot, Castro, to the accompaniment of hysterical enthusiasm, announced the confiscation of key American properties in Cuba. The island would no longer be a *de facto* American colony, however domineering his more ambiguous but more distant suppliers in Eastern Europe might become.

As a consequence of this contretemps, Allen Dulles and the

Central Intelligence Agency warned President Eisenhower that
the Soviets might already be installing short-range missles in
Cuba, notwithstanding their avowed reliance only upon long-
range missiles in the Soviet Union to defend their potential
outpost in the Antilles. In March, a National Intelligence Estimate had concluded, however, that the Russians would not
risk war with the United States to protect Cuba; and in June,
Eisenhower himself had decided that Khrushchev would not
enter into a mutual security pact with Cuba because of the
Russian's awareness that the United States would not tolerate
it. In any case, as the Cuban leader unwisely boasted in July,
22,000 tons of Czech small arms were already arriving for
Cuba's rapidly expanding popular militia. This gave Cuba the
largest Latin American army by the autumn of 1960, a force
at this time variously estimated to be composed of some 240,000
regulars and militia, according to the U.S. Department of State.
Ambassador Bonsal reported to Washington that Castro had
begun to import arms only in May 1959 and, frightened by
growing U.S. hostility, to obtain them from the Soviet bloc only
by the summer of 1960.[18]

At the same time, the first of what the Senate Select Committee has said involved at least eight attempts to assassinate
Castro was inaugurated. Such techniques had long been contemplated within the agency, and both Arbenz and Chou En-
lai had already been discarded as potential targets for sundry
sane reasons. Castro himself estimated in 1975 that there had
been no less than twenty-four such CIA attempts on his life,
but the Maximum Leader had never been known for the mod-
eration of his claims or charges. On July 21, responding to a
Cuban volunteer's offer to arrange an accident to Raúl Castro
within Cuba, Tracy Barnes, Bissell's Deputy in Clandestine
Operations, and Colonel King, still included in the assassination plans, offered a picayune $10,000 for the "successful

completion" of this task. Whether under orders from Allen
Dulles or not, this offer was withdrawn almost as soon as it
was made, but the CIA was launched upon a variety of absurd
schemes, ranging from the mere discrediting of Fidel Castro
by causing his beard to fall out to the outright murder of the
Cuban leader by means of hired Mafia chieftains.

The responsibility for these particular fantasies, which
brought about the exploitation of the agency by the Mafia
without any results at all and eventually the utter discrediting
of the CIA beyond the wildest hopes of Communist propaganda, remains a point of contention. Bissell, King, and Colonel Sheffield Edwards, Director of the agency's Office of
Security, would subsequently blame one another for thinking
up the idea in the first place, while E. Howard Hunt has char-
acteristically claimed credit for himself. In any case, Robert
Maheu, who hired these Mafia figures, was to offer approximately $150,000 to John Rosselli, Santos Trafficante, and Sam
Giancana. To Attorney General Robert Kennedy's particular
embarrassment, when he was told some of the story in 1962,
Giancana was currently on the FBI's list of the ten most wanted
criminals in the United States. Among the more practical of
these absurdities was one in which the Mafia was to poison
Castro with pills to be given to him by his alleged mistress,
Marie Lorenz, if possible coinciding the murder with an invasion of Cuba by anti-Castro refugees. This last idea of sched-
uling Castro's assassination with the invasion of Cuba was also
one of Hunt's several proposals and would, in fact, eventually
be incorporated into Bissell's plans for Cuba.[19]

Meanwhile, Eisenhower had been resisting Republican
pressure for action against Castro before the election by warning Republican members of Congress that the use of United
States forces against Cuba would turn all of Latin America
away from the United States toward communism, although he

hastened to add that he would not tolerate a Communist government in Cuba. But on August 18, long despairing of any OAS stand against Cuba, Eisenhower, upon receipt of the CIA plan for a guerrilla war against Castro, privately approved a budget expanded to some $13 million for such a project. The President further authorized the use of Defense Department personnel and equipment for the training of anti-Castro Cubans in Guatemala, since Miami and Panama had involved too much publicity. In an order whose echo would be heard in the future under Kennedy, Eisenhower forbade the employment of the American military in combat, to the great disappointment of Richard Nixon and his supporters, desperate for some such spectacular action before the election.

Eisenhower was disappointed by Bissell's continued inability to set up a provisional Cuban government-in-exile, saying that without such a government with real popular support, he would never approve of any kind of invasion of Cuba. As with Indochina in 1954, the President was a master at providing caveats enabling him not to intervene in the many places throughout the world where people expected him to intervene.[20] Like Charles de Gaulle, Eisenhower was a popular military hero; thus, much less than his more liberal successors, Eisenhower would not have to play the patriot in order to win elections.

III
The Hot Potato

Cipriano Castro once again reoccupied the center of the stage as the Latin dictator most distrusted by the Roosevelt Administration. By the summer of 1904 the President reached the conclusion that Castro was "riding for a fall" and that, in such circumstances "if he has a fall," we had better give it to him![1] —*Richard Challener on Theodore Roosevelt*

The liberals are waiting to see Nixon let Cambodia go down the drain just the way Eisenhower let Cuba go down the drain.[2] —*President Nixon to Henry Kissinger, 1970*

I believe the American people will never approve direct military intervention by their own forces [in Cuba], except under provocations against us so clear and so serious that everybody will understand the need for the move.[3] —*Eisenhower to John F. Kennedy after the Bay of Pigs*

O N SEPTEMBER 2, 1960, Senator John F. Kennedy opened his campaign for the presidency with remarks in Maine at increasing variance with some of his earlier opinions on the subject of Fidel Castro and Cuba. For example, in October 1959, in his book *The Strategy of Peace,* in a statement much criticized subsequently by Republicans, Senator Kennedy had suggested that if the Eisenhower administration had given "the fiery young rebel a warmer welcome in his hour of triumph, especially on his trip to this country," Castro might not have gone over to the Communists.[4] Eleven months later, however, the Senator, now Democratic presidential nominee, had discovered that Castro was already "a source of maximum danger" and that "the big task of the next Administration" would be "to contain this revolution in Cuba itself, and not have it secretly spread through Latin America." Indeed, in July 1960, Kennedy had been introduced by the CIA to several leaders of the anti-Castro resistance soon to be headed by José Miró Cardona.[5] How much Kennedy learned of the agency's plans for Cuba remains speculative, although it seems to have been a good deal.

On September 21, 1960, as Fidel Castro, while staying at the Hotel Theresa in Harlem, met Nikita Khrushchev in a carefully publicized encounter in New York, Senator Kennedy proclaimed to an audience in Tennessee that he was "not satisfied to see a Communist satellite 90 miles off the coast of Florida, eight minutes by jet. Those who say they will stand up to Khrushchev have not demonstrated any ability to stand up to Mr. Castro (applause)." And on September 23, Kennedy added that Cubans fighting Castro both at home and in exile should be sustained until they are free of communism.[6] Provoked by these and subsequent Kennedy assertions that he intended to enforce the Monroe Doctrine and not permit a Soviet base in Cuba, on October 18 the Republican presidential nominee, Richard Nixon, hinted to the American Legion in Miami Beach that a number of steps had already been taken and would continue to be taken toward a political and an economic guarantee against what he now publicly termed the intolerable cancer of the Communist Castro regime. Equally provoked, Castro made savage personal attacks upon Kennedy, whom he called an ignorant millionaire in a speech before the United Nations on September 26.

Ten days following Nixon's remarks, apparently fearing an anti-Castro invasion of Cuba before the election, Kennedy replied to Nixon, suggesting that some anti-Castro forces both inside and outside Cuba deserved American aid. This speech infuriated Nixon, since, notwithstanding Allen Dulles's private denial to the Vice-President that he had told Kennedy anything of significance, Nixon feared that his rival had been unofficially informed by Dulles during an authorized briefing in July of the Eisenhower administration's covert plans for Cuba. Still more inclined to jump to alarming conclusions, the Cuban delegation at the United Nations notified the General Assembly that Havana expected a large-scale invasion of the island in the near future, an invasion to be mounted with the support of the American military services. Equally concerned, Adlai Stevenson, campaigning for Kennedy, was reassured by the latter that he really intended to let the Organization of American States handle Cuba rather than have the United States alone take care of Castro by arming Cuban exiles. And former Secretary of State Dean Acheson warned Kennedy that the latter's campaign rhetoric was locking him into untenable positions for the future.[7]

Nixon's further complaint on October 22 that Kennedy's implied advocacy of arming the anti-Castro Cubans represented "probably the most dangerously irresponsible recommendation that he'd made during the course of the campaign" was true, at least in retrospect. But, as Arthur Schlesinger has pointed out, while Nixon was enraged at what he considered Kennedy's supposed hypocrisy in openly advocating a necessarily secret policy of the administration, his criticism of Kennedy actually applied to his own policy still more, since he had long privately favored arming the Cuban rebels against Castro. In fact, one wonders what Nixon had in mind when he said that Kennedy's policy (and his own in secret) would violate five American treaties, "would lose all our friends in Latin America . . . [and] would be an open invitation to Mr. Khrushchev to come . . . into Latin America." To complicate further his policy of inconsistent competition with the inconsistent

Kennedy, Nixon was also pushing secretly for an invasion of Cuba from Guatemala before the election for the sake of helping his own candidacy. Apparently, in the final heat of the political campaign, both candidates lost track of just who was being more hypocritical, and, if at this juncture the arguments of either happened to be logical, such arguments were hardly being uttered for the sake of their logic.[8]

During those competitive political debates between the presidential candidates over Cuba, CIA plans for aid to the anti-Castro Cubans had likewise undergone serious amplification. In this period, Richard Bissell and Colonel Edwards of the CIA also decided to brief Allen Dulles and General Cabell more openly regarding their plans to assassinate the Cuban leaders. Whether, in his turn, Dulles directly—or, more likely, obliquely—obtained Eisenhower's authorization for these assassination attempts remains doubtful, since it was designed to be under the doctrine of plausible presidential deniability. Nevertheless, meeting with the National Security Council on August 18, the President in effect may have authorized the assassination of Patrice Lumumba of the Congo, although, as with Trujillo later on, Lumumba's murder was eventually handled, at least on the surface, by the local opposition at the last moment before Kennedy's inauguration.[9]

The initial CIA plan for the invasion of Cuba had envisaged the infiltration of a few hundred anti-Castro guerrillas into the Cuban mountains, particularly of the Escambray chain, where there already were an indeterminate number of men allegedly operating against Castro. Because of the State Department's refusal to countenance the training of such guerrilla forces within any American-controlled territory, including the U.S. Jungle Warfare School in Panama, the training was to take place from July on in the still presumably favorable political atmosphere of the secret camps in President Miguel Ydígoras

Fuentes's Guatemala. According to Ydígoras, who had been the CIA's original choice for its operation against Arbenz, he had granted the CIA its base at Trax in the Guatemalan mountains in return for American concessions on the sugar quota and for U.S. support against the British in British Honduras. At the same time, in view of the growing uneasiness of the Mexican government, the anti-Castro FRD sponsored by the CIA, had to be moved from Mexico City to Miami, notwithstanding the presence of at least two hundred of Castro's intelligence agents in that increasingly Hispanic city.

By the autumn of 1960, however, the arrival of large quantities of Czech arms for Castro's rapidly expanding militia, the increasing reluctance of the terrified peasantry to feed the anti-Castro guerrillas, the penetration of the disorganized guerrilla bands by Castro's experienced agents, and the growing difficulty and ineffectiveness of aerial supply to the weakening resistance in the Escambrays gradually induced the CIA to drop its relatively modest plan for guerrilla infiltration of Cuba. Indeed, Allen Dulles himself, like several more prudent members of the agency, was already dissociating himself from the fiasco of the anti-Castro guerrillas in Cuba. Moreover, even as early as January or February 1960, the Cuba Task Force planners had contemplated a small amphibious strike force to supplement guerrilla action and by June had begun to form a small Cuban anti-Castro tactical air force.

In September 1960, Admiral Robert Dennison, Commander of the Atlantic Fleet in Norfolk, Virginia, was informed by a subordinate of a CIA request for a large landing ship (LSD), the USS *San Marcos* in Puerto Rico, as well as smaller landing craft for purposes unknown. The angry Dennison promptly called General Lyman L. Lemnitzer, Chairman of the Joint Chiefs of Staff, and was told he would receive a CIA briefing in due course. Lemnitzer, of course, was an old colleague of

Dulles from the days when they helped prevent northern Italy from becoming Communist during the German surrender in 1945. Meanwhile, Dennison's immediate superior, Admiral Burke, was checking on the CIA's mysterious and proliferating activities in Guatemala.

By November 4, four days before the presidential election in the United States, the Central Intelligence Agency ordered a most reluctant four-hundred-man Cuban guerrilla unit, already in training in Guatemala, converted into a larger, fully conventional amphibious invasion force, except for some sixty men, who were to be retained in their original status as a diversionary guerrilla force. Under these new circumstances two Marine Colonels—Jack Hawkins for amphibious war and Stanley Beerli for the air support—were now given control of the amateur guerrilla trainees in Guatemala, since, as usual, guerrilla techniques undertaken in the Escambrays against former professional guerrillas had failed. Unfortunately, Colonel Hawkins knew little of CIA procedure and, in a critic's words, acted as if he were commanding an orthodox military unit, notwithstanding his extensive experience of guerrilla war in the Philippines. Another Marine, Nixon's aide Brigadier General Cushman, already deemed the operation "pretty hairy" and thought that if it failed, standby U.S. forces, preferably Marines, "should jump in." Realistically, Cushman thought the operation already so large that "everybody in the world would know the U.S. is behind this."[10]

Likewise, in the Defense Department, neither Secretary Thomas Gates nor Undersecretary James Douglas of the Special Committee reviewing the Cuban project nor the Joint Chiefs of Staff themselves showed much faith in guerrilla warfare and still less in the new concept of a small-sized invasion by Cubans alone. Gates called the Cuban landing forces wholly inadequate, an opinion evidently derived from Colonel Edward

Lansdale of Vietnam fame, while Douglas wanted to disassociate the Defense Department from any assumption that its
loan of training personnel to the CIA implied Defense Department approval of the Cuban project. Lansdale also warned about
lack of popular Cuban support for such a small invasion force.
In any case, the Joint Chiefs of Staff continued to conceive of
intervening in Cuba as a process of aiding the guerrillas and
not as a military invasion at all.

Undoubtedly, Eisenhower's anxieties over a Castro attack
on Guantánamo during October and November 1960, an anxiety that resulted both in Marine reinforcements and in mine
fields being hastily laid around the naval base, gave the U.S.
Navy additional cause for the belief that any invasion of Cuba
could hardly be unrelated to an overt and acceptable American
intervention. In any case, the careful Eisenhower kept saying
to Dulles and Bissell that he would go along with them, but he
wanted to be sure that the damned thing worked.

Whether the Central Intelligence Agency had similarly
assumed that the United States would openly intervene in Cuba
as a result of the aggressive speeches of the now probable
presidential victor John F. Kennedy is not certain. Nevertheless, Tracy Barnes's earlier appointment of a liberal European,
Gerry Droller (code-named Frank Bender), to take charge of
guerrilla recruiting for the Cuba project in the last analysis
would appear to have relied on the general assumption of ultimate American intervention. In an assignment inherently so
difficult, Bender's ignorance of both Latin America and the
Spanish language—and, indeed, of elementary tact—would
aggravate all the problems of coordinating a highly variegated
anti-Castro force for any kind of military operation. It would
also serve to make Bender an ideal scapegoat for Robert Kennedy when all went wrong. Fortunately, thanks to his reactionary rival and subordinate political action officer E. Howard

Hunt (code-named Eduardo), Bender would necessarily be bypassed more and more on refugee affairs in Miami, although Hunt proved to be an equally disastrous selection for such an undeniably thankless job.[11]

Another possible cause for the drastic change of CIA planning away from guerrilla war may be seen on November 3 and again on November 16. On the first occasion, Undersecretary of State for Political Affairs Livingston Merchant openly inquired at the Special Group reviewing the Cuban project, whether planning for "direct positive action" simultaneously against Fidel Castro, Raúl Castro, and Ché Guevara had yet been undertaken by the CIA. General Cabell replied for the agency that "action of this kind is uncertain in results and highly dangerous in conception and execution" as an operation against all the Cuban leaders at once. Therefore, Cabell claimed, the possibilities of Merchant's question were "beyond our capabilities."[12] In short, with assassination plans either dormant or held very closely within the agency and guerrilla activities a failure, an outright invasion, albeit by Cubans alone, seemed a more desirable supplement to the other programs.

But when, on November 2, Richard Bissell had outlined to an appalled and indignant Admiral Dennison the naval aspects of the new CIA plans for an amphibious invasion (appropriately to be code-named Bumpy Road), Dennison asked who was to defend his undermanned outpost at Guantánamo in case of such immediate action. Fortunately, Eisenhower soon put off the mid-November date of the proposed Cuban amphibious operation on the all-too-obvious grounds that nothing else was ready yet either. Dennison would be given almost no intelligence on Cuba during the next three months in spite of his repeated complaints to Bissell that he knew nothing of the capabilities of Castro's armed forces. In fact, Dennison's warships would almost sink a CIA ship near the eventual invasion site, since the embattled Admiral knew almost nothing of the CIA plans either.[13]

Given the intense interest aroused by the purportedly different policies of the two presidential candidates toward Cuba, it is not surprising that leaks about the purpose of the CIA camps in Guatemala now began to appear. Starting with the Guatemalan paper *La Hora* on October 30, 1960, which described preparations for the invasion of Cuba as well under way in Guatemala, the story was picked up by the *Hispanic American Report* of Stanford University in early November. Tipped off about this, the November 19 issue of *The Nation*, a national American publication, went to press with an editorial urging U.S. news media with correspondents in Guatemala to check on the *La Hora* and Stanford reports concerning what *The Nation* termed a "dangerous and hare-brained" project.[14] Informed by *The Nation* of its forthcoming editorial, *The New York Times* began printing stories abut the training camps in Guatemala and finally, on November 1, published a page-1 statement by Foreign Minister Raúl Roa of Cuba at the Untied Nations, warning that the Untied States was planning an invasion of Cuba from Guatemala within the next few days.

On November 13, under congressional pressure from the Democrats triumphant in the recent election, President Eisenhower ordered the U.S. Navy, including an aircraft carrier, to protect the east coast of Guatemala to prevent possible support from Cuba for a rovolt by one-third of the Guatamalan army at Puerto Barrios against President Ydígoras. In an airborne landing employing B-26 bombers manned by anti-Castro refugees in Guatemala, anti-Castro Cuban soldiers from the Trax base, and experienced U.S. Air Force pilots, the CIA managed to put down the revolt against Ydígoras in short order. On November 18, acting at the recommendation of Allen Dulles, the Eisenhower administration allowed the CIA director and

Bissell to inform the new President-Elect for the first time of its plan to help the anti-Castro guerrillas. This was wise, since well after the election on November 20 *The New York Times* finally printed an interview with President Ydígoras, who branded reports of anti-Castro Cuban plans for an offensive from Guatemala against Cuba as "just a lot of lies."[15]

Notwithstanding such blunt denials, the cat was finally out of the bag. As President Kennedy would put it later in the disillusioned spring of 1961, what occurred in Guatemala was not news until it appeared in *The Times*. Within another fortnight, denials in *The New York Times* had elicited confirmation regarding Cuban bases in Guatemala from the *Saint Louis Post-Dispatch*. Thereafter, a steady trickle of reports concerning hanky-panky in Guatemala appeared in the still generally unconcerned American press.[16]

When, on November 18, 1960, in Palm Beach, President-Elect Kennedy received from two men he most admired, Allen Dulles and Richard Bissell, his second and now fairly specific briefing on the agency's plans for Cuba, in all probability Dulles and Bissell made no mention of any plans to assassinate Castro. While Theodore Sorensen has written that from this moment Kennedy harbored grave doubts regarding the size, daring, and concealability of the CIA invasion plan, Kennedy still gave the impression that he generally agreed with it, pending his final official approval. After all, he had just been elected on an anti-Castro platform, to the joy of the Cuban refugees and to the equal pleasure of CIA Director Allen Dulles.

Dulles, who has been described as the last of the great romantics of intelligence, was also among Kennedy's first notably conservative reappointments, in spite of being beyond conventional retirement age. In his private papers, Dulles has claimed that he accepted reappointment only for a year or so in order to complete his existing projects. In any event, it would have been difficult—even secretly—for Kennedy to repudiate Dulles's program, with or without Dulles in charge, so soon after the President's closely contested election victory. In fact, the President-Elect was deeply concerned over both his marginal electoral victory and Republican criticism of him.

Eagerly exploiting both Kennedy's ignorance and apparent approval, not to mention Eisenhower's last-minute desire to expedite the project, Dulles stepped up recruiting and began to remold the original plan for small-sized guerrilla operations into a single-thrust amphibious invasion of about 600 to 750 or more well-equipped men (20 percent of them veterans) to land at Trinidad on the south coast of Cuba. Should the number of invading troops be increased to 1,500, these would require several months longer to be raised and trained. This significant surfacing of Operation Pluto was no longer dependent upon a coordinated uprising by the fragmented Cuban underground, deemed both too radical and too unreliable by the CIA. Instead, it would be aided by preinvasion and purportedly unidentifiable air strikes from Nicaragua against military targets in Cuba, strikes considered safe since Castro had not yet received up-to-date combat planes from the Soviet bloc. A Special National Intelligence Estimate for December 1960 had recently described Castro's navy as poor and his army as not much better. This same estimate was doubtful that the Soviet Union would seek military bases in Cuba.

Less cheerful was Dulles's report to the President at the meeting on November 29, in which Dulles complained that the 184 different Cuban refugee groups could not be gotten together for a proposed government; Dulles was also afraid to expand the Brigade to 2,000 or 3,000 men, as William Pawley was advocating, because so many unpopular rightists would have to be included. For the State Department, Undersecretary Dillon pointed out that the Cuba operation was known all over Latin America and even within the United Nations, although the Department was also beginning to favor rapid expansion of the Brigade. To another question, Eisenhower replied that he did not share the State Department's fear of "shooting from the hip" and that the United States should take greater risks and be more aggressive.[17]

Unfortunately, it was not yet obvious that the CIA representatives, who talked to the 5412 Special Group supervising the Cuba project on December 3, were already ardent advocates of the agency plan rather than objective appraisers of it. What was worse, in their need, Bissell and Jake Engler, supervisor of planning for Cuba, were attempting to dominate the increasingly radical and independent recent Cuban refugees, such as Manuel Ray, to a point where morale of the refugees, far from being superb, as their CIA advisers were informing the dubious Special Group, was instead becoming shaky and bitter against overweening American tutelage.

Apart from the usually prudent Dillon, another figure with great prestige within the Defense Department, Colonel Edward Lansdale, had told Undersecretary of Defense James Douglas that the CIA plan would require 3,000 men and that its logistics were inadequate. Fearing that the Defense Department would be saddled with the blame for a fiasco, Douglas defended Lansdale against Dulles in the Special Group in December. Lansdale then protested that the Cuban people would not rise against Castro in the event of a landing. Defense Secretary Gates informed Eisenhower himself that the project appeared impractical, and, consequently, his department stalled on delivering training personnel to aid Bissell.

As Secretary of State Christian Herter explained to Whiting Willauer, who had now been appointed overall coordinator for all Cuban actions, there was still considerable doubts within the Eisenhower administration about the CIA plan, including the much-debated question of its timing. With Thomas Mann, who had replaced Roy Rubottom as the latest, and presumably more activist, Assistant Secretary of State for Latin America, Willauer was assigned to investigate the plan. Both men lost little time in concluding that the new plan should not be undertaken unless there was almost no chance for failure. But failure was also a considerable risk, given what old CAT-hand Willauer emphasized was the planned absence of any jet fight cover for the proposed B-26 bombers. Jets, it seemed, smacked to much of open American intervention. In fact, Thomas Mann already wanted to move the ever-growing air component of the Brigade out of Guatemala entirely, but training them in the United States was deemed still more conspicuous. Eventually, after intensive study, Thomas Mann, although a Republican, would try to warn Kennedy's Secretary of State Designate Dean Rusk of the seriousness of the whole problem. As so many would discover in the future, Rusk was not available for discussion of the matter. As for Willauer, along with Tracy Barnes of the CIA, he was confined to keeping the President informed of the Cuba project during the difficult period of transition to the new Democratic administration.[18]

Parallel to and probably reflective of these often-none-too-covert activities were the reactions of Fidel Castro. In late November, even though the sugar harvest was approaching, Castro ordered a partial mobilization of his reasonably loyal 200,000-man rural militia (in addition to his 32,000 regular army men) against an imminent invasion, a possible final fling of the now openly hostile Eisenhower administration. On January 1, 1961, Castro publicly warned the CIA and what his aides called its "Cuban mercenaries" that they could not take over Cuba in a weekend operation. The next day, Khrushchev contributed to the Communist panic by announcing in Moscow that "alarming news is coming from Cuba at present, news that the most aggressive American monopolists are preparing a direct attack on Cuba. What is more, they are trying to present the case as though rocket bases of the Soviet Union are being set up or are already established in Cuba." On the same day Castro paraded thirty-five of his new Russian tanks down the streets of Havana before the foreign press.[19]

On January 2, Castro called the large American embassy in Havana a nest of spies and ordered the expulsion of most its members forthwith, including its six-man CIA contingent. Employing this limitation on the size of the U.S. embassy as his official reason for action, Eisenhower finally broke diplomatic relations with Cuba on January 3. Actually, Philip Bonsal had kept CIA activities to a minimum against Allen Dulles's wishes, but with the reluctant departure of the CIA team from the embassy, Bissell's harassed planners lost their best contact with the already confused and largely abandoned underground in Cuba. Of course, other CIA agents under deep cover remained on for intelligence purposes of the most essential type. When informed of it, Dean Rusk immediately approved of this total break with Cuba on behalf of President-Elect Kennedy.

In the revelatory National Security Council meeting of January 3—so like those of the subsequent Kennedy administration—Secretary Herter said that he suspected that the Cubans might forge a document charging the United States with planning an invasion on January 18. Herter then went so far as to suggest a Hitlerian technique, such as staging a fake attack on Guantánamo, to be used as an excuse for U.S. intervention. The angry Eisenhower said that if the Cubans started shooting the 2,000 to 3,000 Americans still in Cuba, we would then, of course, go in with our own forces, assuming the United States knew about it. Otherwise, we should intervene in March with an already discussed larger Cuban force than at present or quit entirely. Dulles warned that time was running out for the United States because Castro's militia was being strengthened, but Thomas Mann of the State Department still maintained that only 10 percent of Castro's 200,000 militia would actually fight for him. However, Mann also believed that it would be necessary to back up any invasion forces with U.S. troops. General Lemnitzer declared that the anti-Castro Brigade was the "best army in Latin America," not the first such U.S. Army claim for its weak protégés abroad and one implicitly contradicted by Richard Bissell. At least Eisenhower's cooler aide General Goodpaster made some sense; he pointed out that the operation was building up an almost irreversible momentum. The President, however, denied that he was committed.[20]

The actual status of the CIA planning for Cuba in January 1961 was decidedly less advanced than that claimed by Communist propaganda being leveled against it. In appealing for policy guidance from their confused superiors on January 4, Bissell and other agency planners stated that "a small lodgement on Cuban soil" by an all-Cuba force of about 750 men was to be preceded by air strikes, first against enemy air targets and then against heavy army matériel, with air support for the invaders from D-Day on. The goal of the small force was solely to seize an airfield with access to the sea and "try to survive and not break out" unless there was a general uprising or U.S. intervention. Even should "widespread popular support and general uprising" not materialize, "other Latin American countries" might intervene. With the establishment of a provisional government on Cuban soil, the way would then be paved for United States military intervention "aimed at pacification of Cuba and thus will result in the prompt overthrow of the Castro government." At the very least, if Castro did not fall, the force "would continue guerrilla operations" after being driven from the beachhead.

Air support for this already ambitious program consisted only of 15 B-26 bombers against 12 Castro operational planes, which were said to include 6 B-26s, 4 T-33s, and 2 to 4 Sea Furies, "a fairly accurate estimate," as it turned out. The only five anti-Castro Cuban pilots currently available for the B-26s were poorly qualified and "inadequate" in number, although the CIA had recruited eighty American crew members from the Alabama National Guard as a backup. The training of the ground forces in Guatemala was also "not going satisfactorily." This was a great understatement, considering the incipient mutiny of almost half the 550 troops then in Guatemala. It could be suppressed in January 1961 only by the rigorous imprisonment of the ringleaders, leaving their commanders mostly selected by the CIA and sometimes including old Cuban army conservatives (for instance, their controversial commander in chief José [Pepe] San Román himself).

With the assistance of U.S. Army Special Training Force, the anti-Castro Brigade should have been ready for combat by late February, "as planned and desired." Thus, "the question of whether the incoming Administration of President-elect Kennedy will concur" in the current agency plans "needs to be resolved at the earliest possible time." Delay after March 1, 1961, was "inadvisable" because the Guatemalan government could become "unmanageable" after that date, morale among the Cuban recruits there would decline, and Castro's controls were growing in Cuba.

At the time, the agency said that if the Cuban planes and ships resisting the invasion were not "knocked out or neutralized," the invading force would "be courting disaster." Furthermore, "the spectacular aspects of the air operations [over Cuba] will go far towards producing the uprising in Cuba that we seek." Consequently, Bissell's planners recommended that air action against Cuba "commence not later than dawn of D

Minus 1," that "any move to curtail the number of aircraft to be employed from those available be firmly restricted," and that "the operation be abandoned if policy does not provide for adequate tactical air support." To emphasize this essential conclusion, the planners stated that, given the inexperience and paucity of anti-Castro pilots available, "highly skillful American contract pilots" be employed "as flight leaders against the more critical targets" in Cuba.

Furthermore, American flight crews were needed for the C-54 cargo planes employed to supply the invading Brigade at its captured airstrip, wherever that might be. For this reason, Puerto Cabezas in Nicaragua would be essential as an air base for the CIA planes, since it was near central Cuba, unlike the somewhat more distant bases in Guatemala. Puerto Cabezas would also serve as a better embarkation point for the Brigade since the local population at Puerto Barrios in Guatemala had many hostile observers sympathetic to Castro. The Opa-Locka air base in Florida would, of course, be still more efficient as a logistic support base than Puerto Cabezas because "supply by the sea cannot be relied upon, for the Brigade may be driven by superior forces from the beach area. Such a situation could lead to the complete defeat of the Brigade and failure of the mission."[21]

Not surprisingly, on January 5 the 5412 Special Group overseeing the project reported to Eisenhower that "there should be a total reassessment" of the U.S. covert-action policies. Because the Special Group had already expressed doubt that the proposed small invasion force of about 750 men could succeed, recruiting for Guatemala was to be greatly stepped up, as Eisenhower and others had urged, to sustain a larger and thus more open invasion. Special Forces officers from the reluctant Pentagon were at last sent to Guatemala to train the mutinous but still anti-Castro guerrilla units into a regular

striking force. As usual, in the words of the Special Group,
much influenced by Allen Dulles's critic Robert Lovett: "We
have been unable to conclude that, on balance all the covert
action programs undertaken by the CIA up to this time have
been worth the risk or the great expenditures of manpower,
money and other resources involved."[22]

At the same time, a reporter for *The New York Times* finally
revealed the location and substantially the function of the
Retalhuleu camp in Guatemala on January 10 in a page-1 article that the President conceded, in private, was generally
accurate. In order to avoid committing Pesident-Elect Kennedy, Eisenhower decided to say nothing at all about the article, probably hoping that, if possible, Kennedy would go ahead
anyway with the CIA project. Indeed, the Cuban Foreign Minister Raúl Roa had denounced the imminent military aggression against Cuba by the United States, again making it more
difficult for the President-Elect to shelve the project quietly,
should he want to do so. Of course, Roa's and Castro's strident
invasion scare may have been promoted as much out of a need
for an excuse to purge their recently reorganized armed forces
of dissidents as from their agents' reports that 2,000 anti-Castro
Cubans were about to land at three points in Cuba. In any
event, Castro's agents may have penetrated the CIA's Retalhuleu camp and certainly could find out almost anything known
there among the teeming Cuban refugee colony of Miami.

Indeed, Guevara had already complained about Castro's
supposedly exaggerated preparations against invasion as dis
rupting his economic plans. But, on January 11, to substantiate Castro's fears, Ambassador Willauer of the State Department,
Tracy Barnes of the CIA, and representatives of the Joint Chiefs
of Staff met to set up a working committee to coordinate future
activity on the Cuba project. On January 13, the Special Group
of the National Security Council supervising the Cuban proj-

ect approved of the current plans to get rid of Castro, since the State Department now agreed with the CIA in principle.[23]

In Washington, under these circumstances, the Joint Chiefs of Staff were finally brought into planning. Their few permissible military planners consulted naturally began to consider the possibility of more open American military intervention in support of the one-shot CIA amphibious operation, an operation still aimed at Trinidad on the south coast of Cuba. Only in this way could success be guaranteed, General Lemnitzer, Chairman of the Joint Chiefs of Staff, was informed. Trinidad's good dock facilities and remoteness from Castro's reserves, while still near the Escambrays, did much to recommend it for a prolonged, Anzio-type, logistical build-up, with military attrition rather than civilian revolution or internal defections from Castro forces providing the principal method of wearing down the enemy. But in presenting the military plan to the Joint Chiefs of Staff, General Lemnitzer warned them that it still was not a U.S. military operation or even a proper invasion. Therefore, it should not be regarded as such, because the greater secrecy, the necessary nonattributability, and the lack of a written plan within the CIA had precluded either the usual military staffing or various annexes. As his expert on psychological warfare, C. D. Jackson, explained to Eisenhower on January 18, "Real guerrilla training and operation seems to fall somewhere between CIA and Defense and, as JFD [Dulles] had said, 'there exists an unfilled gap in our machinery to handle guerrilla activities.' "[24]

Finally, on January 19, Eisenhower told Kennedy that it was Kennedy's responsibility to do whatever was necessary to overthrow Castro because the United States could not let the present government there go on. To complicate matters further, said Eisenhower, the OAS constantly relayed to him private messages from various Latin American government heads urging us to do something about Castro, while publicly declaring their opposition to U.S. policy. Nevertheless, Eisenhower recommended that Kennedy accelerate the training of the anti-Castro forces and expressed his regret that the United States had not yet recognized any refugee front as the legal government of Cuba. Kennedy's first job, Eisenhower told the President-Elect, would be to find a rebel leader who was both anti-Batista and anti-Castro, even before Kennedy's own specific plans for invasion were completed. Adolf Berle, however, had warned Kennedy that the present CIA-sponsored Frente Revolucionario Democrático was not impressive and that Kennedy should replace it with a younger and more idealistic group from among the recent Cuban exiles. In conclusion, Eisenhower urged Kennedy to keep his mouth shut about the whole operation.

Whether wittingly or not, Eisenhower had complicated his case for intervention in Cuba by telling the already nervous President-Elect that he (Eisenhower) had also been prepared to intervene in Laos without the support of Britain and France, but only if absolutely necessary. Of course, Eisenhower was afraid that a unilateral American action anywhere would cause the United States to be labeled imperialist throughout the world. He was also fond of sharing his heavy burdens with as many allies as possible. But, as Kennedy would soon learn for himself, Defense Secretary Gates had to admit that two large limited wars fought at the same time would present the United States with difficulties possibly leading to the use of nuclear weapons. Eisenhower tried to explain that his policy in the Far East was "like playing poker for tough stakes"—that there was no easy solution. Eisenhower pointed out that the Communists were able to boost morale among underdeveloped peoples higher than the Western Allies could, although he did not choose to speculate over the cause of this problem. But the

President had learned a lot in his eight years in the White House, notwithstanding his amazingly greater readiness to intervene in Laos than in Cuba. To Eisenhower, Laos was already the "cork in the bottle," preventing the loss of most of the Far East.[25]

Despite his own extreme caution regarding overt intervention abroad (with the single limited exception of Lebanon in 1958), Eisenhower, while he was President, had been afraid as early as 1954 that a lasting Communist regime anywhere in Latin America—Guatemala, for instance—would compel the United States to dominate the entire Western Hemisphere by force in order to keep most of South America from going Communist. Thus, from the beginning to the end of his administration, Dwight D. Eisenhower bequeathed to his eager successor a policy both in Asia and Latin America more worthy of Theodore Roosevelt than of a twentieth-century Democrat of supposedly liberal persuasion. Whatever subsequent Republican denials regarding Eisenhower's plans may claim to the contrary, in the words of Admiral Dennison, Eisenhower had certainly left the Cuban "hot potato" in the new President's hands because it was a "very risky and probably . . . unsuccessful operation." Unfortunately, his untried successor thought with good reason that the already protean Cuban project had been fully staffed and approved by everyone concerned in the previous administration. Now Kennedy had either to run with his Cuban hot potato or drop it as quickly and quietly as possible.[26]

IV
A Golden Age

For there is little question that should any Latin country be driven by repression into the arms of the Communists, our attitude on nonintervention would change overnight. . . . We know . . . or surely ought to know . . . that Latin America is certainly as essential to our security as Southeast Asia.[1] —*John F. Kennedy, 1958*

There is a call to life a little sterner,
and braver for the earner, learner, yearner.
Less criticism of the field and court
And more preoccupation with the sport.
It makes the prophet in us all presage
The glory of a next Augustan age
Of a power leading from its strength and pride,
Of young ambition eager to be tried,
Firm in our free beliefs without dismay,
In any game the nations want to play.
A golden age of poetry and power
Of which this noonday's the beginning hour.[2]

—*Robert Frost on Kennedy's inauguration*

ON JANUARY 20, 1961, the day of the inauguration of President Kennedy, Fidel Castro ordered a demobilization of the Cuban militia. As the greatly alarmed Ché Guevara had warned earlier in the month, sugar commitments to Cuba's new Soviet suppliers could not be kept without the prompt release of unnecessarily mobilized farm hands for the harvest. Castro openly expressed hope that the new administration in Washington would suspend the "insane" imperialist projects being developed in the American-sponsored anti-Castro guer-

rilla camps in Florida and Guatemala. To be sure, in announcing that "the moments of greatest tension are past," Castro
also warned that Cubans must "be prepared to return immediately to the trenches, should the nation be endangered." The
Maximum Leader concluded: "We are now on uncertain
ground, filled with imponderables."[3]

Just how uncertain the ground beneath Castro had become
is illustrated by President Kennedy's State of the Union message on January 30, in which he warned that "this Hemisphere intends to remain the master of its own house" and
that "we should prepare ourselves now for the worst." In a
news conference on January 25, the new President had already
said that he had no plans for the resumption of diplomatic relations with Cuba since it was a country whose revolution had
been seized by external forces.[4] While Kennedy now obviously
recognized that Castro's government was Communist, he was,
as a result, falling into the opposite or conservative trap—
namely, believing that a Communist government could thereby
no longer be truly native in character. This was an American
propagandistic inversion of the equally useful Soviet myth for
the avowed protection of eastern European nations from the
insidious wiles of capitalism. To be sure, Kennedy was now
reading the CIA *Current Intelligence Summaries,* replete with
accounts of the assassination of Castro opponents and of supposed guerrilla success in the Escambrays against Castro's
forces.

On January 22, only two days after the inauguration, the top
men of the new administration met Brigadier General David
Gray of the Joint Subsidiary Activities Committee of the Joint
Chiefs of Staff to hear the whole range of possible actions against
Castro. Gray headed a liaison committee to coordinate the secret
actions of the government among the various agencies involved
in paramilitary activities, the Joint Chiefs of Staff, the CIA,

and the FBI. So far, the Gray committee had not been officially informed of CIA planning for Cuba, but it had produced a variety of alternatives ranging from the existing economic war up to an all-out American invasion of the island. The committee had concluded that the minimum action commensurate with success required the employment of a Cuban guerrilla force with U.S. backup, a conclusion that with little coincidence would fit in neatly with subsequent CIA plans.

From January 22 on, General Lemnitzer for the Joint Chiefs of Staff, Robert McNamara for the Defense Department, Robert Kennedy for the President, Dean Rusk for the State Department, and Allen Dulles for the CIA studied the Gray committee options in detail. A Joint Chiefs' memorandum of January 27 summarized the basic consensus that developed: "Unless the United States takes immediate and forceful action, there is great and present danger that Cuba will become permanently established as a part of the Communist Bloc, with disastrous consequences to the security of the Western Hemisphere. Cuba provides a Communist base of operations for export of similar revolutions to an already unstable and potentially explosive Latin America. The Joint Chiefs of Staff believe that the primary objective of the United States in Cuba should be the speedy overthrow of the Castro government, followed by the establishment of a pro-U.S. government. . . . The current Political–Para-Military Plan does not assure the accomplishment of the above objectives, nor has there been detailed follow-up planning to exploit the plan if it succeeds or for any direct action that might be required if the plan is found to be inadequate." The Joint Chiefs of Staff concluded that "an overall U.S plan of action for the overthrow of the Castro government should be developed by an Inter-Department Planning Group."[5]

At a large meeting of the National Security Council on January 28, at last before the new President himself, Allen Dulles said without dissent that Cuba was "now for [all] practical purposes a Communist-controlled state." "The two basic elements in the present situation" were "a rapid and continued build-up of Castro's military power, and a great increase also in popular opposition to his regime."[6] Wary and reserved, Kennedy ordered the Joint Chiefs to review the military aspects of a guerrilla invasion with American support. The State Department was told to prepare the isolation of the popular Fidel Castro from Latin America through the generally pliable Organization of American States. At the same time, the President authorized continued U-2 overflights of Cuba, as well as sustaining the CIA sabotage operations already undertaken by the Eisenhower administration.

Admiral Burke, as Chief of Naval Operations, was rightly irritated that the Joint Chiefs were ordered only to advise on the proposed operation and were forbidden, like so many others involved, to talk about it in a rational military fashion with the subordinates who would provide the staff work. In any case, Lieutenant General Earle G. Wheeler, Director of the Joint Chiefs of Staff Intelligence Joint Staff, ordered General Gray to form a small committee with four other military specialists to study the current CIA plan for the Joint Chiefs. Although agency planners admitted that the matter was urgent because of the threat of imminent completion of the Cuban MiG pilots' flight training, Gray's staff had great difficulty getting the still incoherent plan out of the poorly organized agency.

Upon receiving the CIA's plan for a landing at Trinidad dating from the last three months of the Eisenhower administration, Gray's committee was informed that the Brigade was really just a cadre of leaders for future expansion from the presumably sympathetic Cuban population of the Trinidad region and the nearby Escambrays. With a few bridges leading to the port from the mountainous interior scheduled to be blown up by parachute troops, the Brigade was expected to double in four days and survive Castro counterattacks for at least a week. With defections on such a scale and assuming complete surprise and air supremacy, under General Wheeler's prodding for a favorable report, the Gray committee could only come up with an assessment of a "fair chance of ultimate success [which] . . . even if it does not achieve immediately the full results desired, could contribute to the eventual overthrow of the Castro regime." The committee stressed that the plan was ultimately dependent upon a "substantial popular uprising or substantial follow-on forces." A "fair chance" was later modestly defined by General Gray as about a 30-percent chance of success.

On February 7, upon receiving this notably cautious evaluation from the Gray committee, the Joint Chiefs followed in kind, offering their tepid approval to Defense Secretary McNamara. The proposed airborne assault should succeed, they said, since no opposition was expected, and the amphibious attack should go through against light opposition. The landing logistics, "marginal at best," would be "inadequate" against even moderate opposition. Castro's forces should appear in two to four days, but their lack of training in offensive warfare would enable the invaders to hold out for an unestimated time. Agreeing with the Gray committee, the Joint Chiefs felt that ultimate success depended upon a sizable popular uprising or substantial follow-up forces. An independent appraisal of the CIA plan should be made by a Pentagon team, but at this stage the Joint Chiefs of Staff agreed that there was a fair chance of eventual success, not "necessarily" requiring overt U.S. intervention. Such intervention, in fact, might be required "regardless of international consequences" only in the event of formal U.S. recognition of a provisional Cuban government on the beachhead itself.[7]

At a less official level, General David Shoup, Commandant of the Marine Corps and one of the Joint Chiefs, told his occasional colleagues caustically: "If this kind of operation can be done with this kind of force, with this much training and knowledge about it, then we are wasting our time . . . [with] our [regular] divisions; we ought to go on leave for three months out of four." Shoup had been induced to go along on tentative approval with his fellow Joint Chief of Staff members, who lacked his bitterly earned knowledge of risks of amphibious war from Tarawa, on the theory that arms packs for 30,000 men were included in the build-up to equip the uprisings in Cuba whose chances were allegedly increasing. The fact remains that the Joint Chief of Staff report admitted that the shipping for the landing allowed no margin for miscalculation or unforeseen contingencies, including even moderate opposition. Shoup also pointed out to a startled Kennedy that Cuba was 800 miles long.

Shoup's superior, Admiral Burke, felt that the eminently civilian CIA plan—if that is how it can be described—was "weak" and "sloppy" and without proper military logistic or communications annexes.[8] Nevertheless, like the other Joint Chiefs, he gave his approval, although subsequently, on February 7, his colleague General Lemnitzer told the alarmed Admiral Dennison at Norfolk that Dennison's naval forces were not expected to aid in any evacuation of the Brigade should the situation arise. Ominously, the well-informed Havana radio announced that on January 30 the new President had taken off his mask and was now following the old Eisenhower-Dulles line, but even Havana could not guess what a ghastly travesty of an amphibious raid was being prepared in Washington.

Nevertheless, on February 8, National Security Adviser McGeorge Bundy informed the President that the CIA and the Pentagon were enthusiastic, arguing that an invasion could evoke a civil war in Cuba, thus giving the United States cover for more open support for the Brigade. Bundy also warned that the State Department would still be afraid of the consequences in Latin America. Thus, in his first official review of Cuba, upon being briefed by Richard Bissell in the spottiest manner to the great embarrassment of Generals Lemnitzer and Gray, the President said no more than that he reserved the right to cancel the operation up to the end. Eisenhower could not have phrased it better. But, like Eisenhower, Kennedy did not kill this operation, which seemed to have a life of its own. Also, like Eisenhower, Kennedy again had to postpone what Bundy called the invasion adventure to a new projected date of March 5, a target that would leave little enough time for the demoralized Brigade in Guatemala to recover its morale, let alone for preparation of the additional logistic support now demanded by the Joint Chiefs of Staff.[9]

Another man who could not stop the plan was Sherman Kent, Chairman of the CIA Board of National Estimates and an old friend of Richard Bissell since Yale. Kent estimated that time was not on the side of the United States, since Castro was growing stronger rather than weaker in Cuba. For that matter, other men in the agency feared Castro's success in several Latin American countries in the near future. But, like presidential advisers Arthur Schlesinger and Roger Hilsman, Director of the State Department's Bureau of Intelligence and Research, Kent was not yet officially informed of the Cuban plan. As soon as they heard it, all three men opposed any version of the CIA's plan.

On February 11, President Kennedy abolished both the Planning Board and the Operations Coordinating Board of the

National Security Council on the grounds that these lax Eisenhower controls over cold-war activities reflected undue military influence. Long desired by the powerful Democratic Senator Henry Jackson, the abolition of the Operations Coordinating Board was favored in Kennedy's circle by at least two of the President's more activist civilians: his increasingly powerful National Seurity Adviser McGeorge Bundy and Walt Rostow of the State Department. This dismantling of Eisenhower's institutional brakes was observed by the former President with alarm, and Eisenhower's former Defense Secretary Thomas Gates would conclude later that Kennedy's preference for casual telephone directives over the formal machinery of the National Security Council was a serious mistake. Kennedy's own Secretary of the Treasury Republican Douglas Dillon would say later that the loss of the checks and balances inherent in the Eisenhower National Security Council procedure was the chief reason for the Bay of Pigs fiasco.

The National Security Council itself was to meet only irregularly hereafter, with the general responsibility for leadership and the vital coordination of foreign policy with military strategy avowedly handed over to the State Department, but actually handed over to nobody. This dangerous tendency to weaken the National Security Council was accentuated by the inadequacy and excessive secrecy of State Department leadership under Dean Rusk, despite Kennedy's initial hopes for it. This was accentuated by the President's initial lack of acquaintance with most of his own higher officials and by a deliberate tendency to obliterate the distinction between planning and operations within the National Security Council staff. Those same trends were manifest in the lack of close institutional supervision over the Central Intelligence Agency, since the 5412 Special Group of the National Security Council was allowed to fade away from its position of responsibility for agency actions.

Before his election, President Kennedy had been carefully introduced by reporter Joseph Alsop to Alsop's old friend Richard Bissell. During the fall 1960 campaign and again in February 1961, Kennedy urged that Bissell, rather than taking a top post in the State Department, stay on as Deputy Director for Plans with the expectation of eventually becoming Director of Central Intelligence. Within the CIA, Bissell's role as an important Democrat from the days of the Marshall Plan and as a bitter opponent of communism in Latin America, would not hurt him in his still more ambitious plans to expand the already overweening clandestine activities of the agency, especially with regard to Cuba.[10]

Not surprisingly, just before its brief suspension at this same juncture, the always-too-remote Foreign Intelligence Advisory Board never learned that a freewheeling member of CIA's Foreign Intelligence Staff, William K. Harvey, famous within the agency for the premature exposure of the Soviet mole Kim Philby, had been chosen in January 1961 to head a "research" group for Cuba. This group was to investigate various methods of disabling foreign leaders, including assassination "as a last resort." Harvey testified that Bissell informed him that the latter's authority came "from the highest level," and Richard Helms has testified that "there were no limitations put on the means" employed to "get rid of" Castro by the administration, presumably before or at least coincident with the Bay of Pigs.

Eventually, Bissell's authority in 1961 came from an approving McGeorge Bundy, Kennedy's eminently flexible new National Security Adviser from Harvard. Before the Bay of Pigs, Bissell discretely discussed with Bundy the development of a CIA "executive action" capability. Possibly, honoring the doctrine of plausible presidential denial of awareness, he did not mention that under his euphemism an attempt to assassinate Castro was already under way. In any event, Bundy raised no objection and, in fact, may have twice urged the creation of such a capability. How much Allen Dulles had informed President Kennedy "in rather general terms" of these possibilities remains uncertain, although Helms would testify before the House Select Committee on assassinations in 1978 that the President did indeed know of CIA plans to kill Castro. In any event, Richard Bissell, in 1984, would finally admit that the CIA's plan to assassinate Castro was intended to parallel and supplement an invasion rather than simply provide an alternative to it, as was previously believed.[11]

At this time, Arthur Schlesinger first heard of the plans for Cuba and, before leaving on a mission in South America, carefully sent President Kennedy a memorandum warning him about violently adverse reactions in all of Latin America to his first, dramatic foreign-policy initiative. More important, on February 17 in a meeting at the White House, Adolf Berle, who was in charge of a Kennedy task force for Latin America, told the President that Latin support might be generated for an operation against Cuba, but not by March 31, the CIA's current deadline. Secretary Rusk then attempted to stall on any action in the hope of building up support in the Organization of American States. Rusk was also worried about reactions in the United Nations. The President indicated that he preferred mass infiltrations of guerrillas to any open invasion.

On February 18, in a memorandum to the President, a cooler McGeorge Bundy agreed with Rusk that "diplomatic and public opinion are surely not ready for an invasion, but Castro's *internal* strength continues to grow. The [anti-Castro] battalion's dispersal would be a blow to U.S. prestige, but we should have a hard time at the U.N. if it goes in [to Cuba]." Given another three months, Bundy added, "Bissell's battalion" (the supposed Brigade) could be built up. Then, better to cover an invasion, "the color of civil war would be quite a lot stronger" and allow the United States a better case for intervention.[12]

On February 23, the Cuban Foreign Minister, Raúl Roa, publicly complained to the United Nations that his hopes that Kennedy's administration would reverse the aggressive plans of his predecessor were beginning to evaporate. Instead, the only-too-well-informed Cuban Foreign Minister said that Kennedy was seeking pretexts with which to justify indirect military aggression against Cuba. Four days later, Roa informed sympathetic fellow Latin Americans that the North Americans were planning to establish a provisional Cuban government on a beachhead on Cuban soil with the complicity of the right-wing regimes of Nicaragua and Guatemala. And Castro himself declared that at least 4,000 U.S.-supported mercenaries were almost ready for action from their Guatemala bases. It is likely that either by that time or shortly thereafter Adolf Berle, now the official State Department coordinator for the Caribbean, had inadvertently tipped off the almost unanimously hostile Latin American governments to what was up when he attempted to gain their support for the forthcoming and only slightly ambiguous United States action against Castro.[13]

On a lower level of action, as early as October 1960 Kennedy had discussed with his conservative friend Senator George Smathers of Florida the likely reaction of the American public to an attempt to assassinate Castro. Alternatively, Kennedy and Smathers had considered provoking a Cuban assault upon the base at Guantánamo to provide an excuse for a U.S. invasion of the island. Although, like his brother Robert Kennedy after the Bay of Pigs, he believed that it would be easy to kill Castro, the President always officially disapproved of such efforts, both because the responsibility could be so easily pinned on the United States and because of the moral issues involved.

For example, in the spring of 1961, when Kennedy was already President (but before the Bay of Pigs), the eager

Smathers again tried to bring up the assassination issue. Kennedy then cracked his plate on the dinner table to indicate his displeasure with the now too touchy subject. The President's anxiety on this matter may have been accentuated by the fact that he was having an affair with Judith Exner, who was also seeing Sam Giancana, one of the CIA's Mafia chieftains involved in the proposed assassination of Castro. Indeed, the President's connection with the lady in question would cease only after a discreet visit to the White House from J. Edgar Hoover of the FBI in March 1962.[14]

On March 4, Castro himself recklessly offered the proponents of assassination within the Kennedy administration an excellent pretext in the form of a speech taunting the Cuban exiles to invade the island and boasting about the mountains of arms Cuba was obtaining from Communist countries, including 104,000 automatic rifles and submachine guns, 80 antiaircraft guns, and 55 tanks, as well as 8 still-undelivered MiG fighter planes. Not mentioned by Castro were between 200 and 300 Soviet-bloc military advisers for his growing forces or some 50 Czech-trained Cuban pilots soon to return home, possibly in time for an invasion of Cuba.

At the same time, embarrassed by the growing publicity about the anti-Castro training camps in his country, President Ydígoras for the second time asked President Kennedy to have the Cubans removed from Guatemala by the end of April. The presence of an estimated 120 local Communists living near the CIA's training camp at Retalhuleu in Guatemala could not have helped the Ydígoras government (or the problem of leaks to Castro), notwithstanding the gratitude the President of Guatemala may have felt for the support of the CIA and the anti-Castro Cubans against the local uprising of the previous year.

The rainy season was now imminent in the Caribbean. Allen

Dulles and Richard Bissell added to the pressure by warning the Kennedy administration of the impending arrival in Cuba of Soviet MiG fighter planes along with Czech-trained Cuban pilots. Their presence would automatically abort any marginal operation such as an invasion by Cuban exiles alone. As Bissell put it to Kennedy again and again: "You can't mañana this thing." Moreover, the Cuban exiles in Miami and elsewhere were becoming increasingly restless, and CIA fears that demoralization would spread from the Guatemala camps to Florida grew apace.[15]

At the end of February, General Gray's visiting team of officers at last reported back to the Joint Chiefs of Staff the results of their inspection of the training and morale of the anti-Castro recruits in Guatemala. Most doubtful about achieving surprise at the fairly conspicuous port of Trinidad, Gray's team estimated the Brigade's chances at 85 to 15 against success at this location. Thereafter, the officers told the Joint Chiefs of Staff, the ultimate success of the invaders depended upon the landings' effectiveness as a catalyst for a general uprising on the island. Unhappily, on March 3, the CIA had privately estimated that only 25 percent of Cubans opposed Castro. Even more dolefully, the air-evaluation members of Gray's team emphasized that, even with the most unlikely advantage of total surprise, any attack against Cuba would fail, since a single Castro plane armed with .50-caliber machine guns could sink all or most of the invading ships, an appraisal still more pessimistic than the eventual reality. To complicate matters still further, Admiral Dennison of the Atlantic Fleet was told by the President himself that there would be neither any overt U.S. intervention nor even a rescue bailout, should the operation go wrong. At least the worried Admiral was permitted to send a cruiser, some planes, and a Marine battalion to reinforce his obviously threatened base at Guantánamo.

After some frantic adjustment of such flagrantly negative conclusions to the more traditional American "can do" philosophy, by March 10 the Joint Chiefs managed to cough up another grudging approval of the Trinidad plan. Now, apparently of their own accord, they estimated Trinidad's chance at about 50 percent, although more depressing figures continued to be bandied about beyond the President's orbit. Two of the three regular members (excluding the Marine Commandant) of the Joint Chiefs of Staff had disagreed with General Gray's team on the need for more effective air support, but the Joint Chiefs at least did send an officer experienced in logistics to Guatemala to remedy some of the many Brigade deficiéncies observed in that too-often-underestimated facet of war.

In accordance with the President's reiterated desire, the Joint Chiefs now dropped their prior alternative condition of a large-scale U.S. military operation. Apart from the small invading Brigade, this left the hope of expanding the thousand-odd surviving anti-Castro guerrillas in Cuba as the principal basis on which the Joint Chiefs could foresee the eventual defeat of Castro's military forces, estimated at 32,000 regulars and between 200,000 and 300,000 militia. Perhaps to compensate for this new dependence on the more leftist underground in Cuba, the conservatives controlling the Cuban exiles in the United States set up Operation Forty, by which, in the event of a successful invasion, their own people would establish CIA-like intelligence, control, and, if necessary, assassination groups in Cuba before either the underground or the more liberal Miró Cardona might be able to dominate a new government.[16]

On March 11, the day after the Joint Chiefs nominally approved the Trinidad plan, President Kennedy met the full National Security Council to hear Bissell report on his proposed operation against Cuba. Recommending Trinidad over four other landing beaches, Bissell favored this target as a small port with a friendly population and near the refuge of the Escambrays. With initial success at Trinidad, a provisional Cuban government could be flown in to provide a legal basis for more open American logistics, maintenance, and support. Assuming effective B-26 bombing strikes from Nicaragua before the actual landing and tactical air cover from the Trinidad airstrip thereafter, Bissell, agreeing with General Gray's Pentagon team, felt that it would be possible to keep Castro forces from getting into the beachhead area. Should the shock of the landing not detonate a major revolt, the assault forces could always turn guerrilla in the nearby Escambrays. Dulles chimed in with a stiff warning to the National Security Council that, should it choose to forgo the operation, it would leave the embarrassed Kennedy administration with the frustrated and angry Brigade wandering around the United States, venting its disappointment on many sympathetic ears. But should the operation succeed, as Bissell seductively pointed out, there would be no necessity for overt American intervention.

With the vigorous support of his highly experienced Republican Assistant Secretary for Inter-American Affairs, Thomas Mann, the President firmly resisted such CIA blandishments and threats. While willing to go ahead, Kennedy refused to endorse so spectacular a landing as that at Trinidad. Mann claimed that the airstrip at Trinidad was inadequate to land B-26s and thus would not serve to conceal external U.S. support from the suspicious Latin Americans. The President then asked for a new plan for a less conspicuous landing, preferably at night without any appearance of a Second World War–type of invasion.

Unhappily, the shock effect of an open invasion was precisely what original CIA plans had needed to provide uprisings in Cuba. As Dulles subsequently put it in his private papers, the invasion "required a well-publicized landing so that the people of Cuba . . . could have a clear knowledge of what was in progress," and "the very fact of a quiet landing" rendered both an uprising and defections" impossible."[17] The CIA obviously went along with those new conditions in order to obtain any invasion at all, despite the Joint Chiefs' belief that the absence of any Cuban urprising would almost certainly kill the chance of a successful invasion.

In any event, notwithstanding its modest virtues from a military point of view, the Trinidad plan was finally dead. Two days later, on March 13, with a presumably somewhat clearer conscience and to the great disgust of such hard-headed realists as Thomas Mann, Kennedy proclaimed his Alliance for Progress in Latin America in another effort to don the shining mantle of Franklin Roosevelt's liberal foreign policy. As other Presidents have discovered, the Good Neighbor policy was not, after all, based upon invading Latin America.

V

An Orphan Child

I feel it is most important that if any bloodshed occurs, it should be between Cubans and Cubans, not Americans and Cubans. Please have the strictest instructions issued.[1] —*President Theodore Roosevelt to William Howard Taft, 1906*

We must realize that any bluff will be called. We cannot tell anyone to keep out of our hemisphere unless our armaments *and the people behind these armaments* are prepared to back up the command, even to the ultimate point of going to war. There must be no doubt in anyone's mind, the decision must be automatic, if we debate, if we hesitate, if we question, it will be too late.[2] —*John F. Kennedy, 1940*

I find to my surprise a weakness in decision at the top in all but Bob McNamara, who impresses me as first class. The decisions are incredibly hard, but they don't, like bourbon, improve with age.[3] —*Dean Acheson, July 1961*

COLONEL JACK HAWKINS and the CIA paramilitary staff promptly started to work again on finding a new beachhead to meet President Kennedy's latest political requirements. Considered were the Preston region on the north coast of Cuba, islands near the large Isle of Pines (now Isle of Youth), and other sections of the south coast of Cuba, both east and west of Trinidad. By March 14, they had convinced General Gray's Pentagon review committee that the almost roadless Zapata Peninsula next to the obscure Bay of Pigs, thirty to forty miles west of Trinidad, best filled the new bill. With little likelihood of opposition to a landing in this thinly inhabited swamp region, less air cover would be required and the appearance of a guerrilla type of infiltration preserved. Zapata had a poor airstrip, just large enough to accommodate the vital B-26 bombers flown in from Guatemala and thus make it look more like an internal Cuban operation. Although it lacked Trinidad's docks, so that most supplies would have to come across open beaches, Zapata afforded only arduous access from the interior to the Bay of Pigs, through swamps almost as difficult to cross as the roads to Trinidad through the Escambrays were to travel. Finally, if the hoped-for civilian uprisings of the Trinidad region might be lacking, the Zapata swamps might allow as convenient an initial refuge for the survivors of a defeated Brigade as the Escambrays. In fact, the last of the exhausted guerrillas operating in the Escambray chain had just been flown out of Cuba, leaving that now more distant region a still less viable refuge for survivors of an unsuccessful landing, if they ever got there at all.

Sprung rather abruptly upon the Joint Chiefs of Staff on March 14, the CIA Zapata–Bay of Pigs plan was hurriedly considered by them after they scrutinized several previously rejected alternative sites for invasion. Admiral Burke deemed the new plan's chance of success at less than 50 percent— slighter than that of the previous plan—but was relieved to find that at least there was no more talk of Rusk's suggestion for employing the navy's precious Guantánamo as the *point d'appui* for a Cuban invasion.

Not even permitted the brief military staffing given the earlier Trinidad plan because of the new emphasis on speed and secrecy, on March 15 a disturbed General Lemnitzer submitted the Joint Chief of Staff's acceptance—not approval, it must be emphasized—of the Bay of Pigs as the best alternative to Trinidad with a fair chance of success. When Secretary of Defense McNamara, who knew little about military affairs, conveyed this dubious acceptance by the Joint Chiefs to the President, neither he nor Kennedy realized that the real pref-

erence of the Joint Chiefs was still Trinidad. This became a
source of much subsequent recrimination. Burke thought that
the Joint Chiefs had simply been overruled, while Lemnitzer
believed that from then on the responsibility was no longer
theirs.

On March 15, the President and his assembled aides were
informed of the new plan. The previously skeptical Bundy had
prepared the ground well for Kennedy's acceptance of the new
modifications in a most revealing memorandum on administration ignorance regarding amphibious war. Describing Bissell's "remarkable job" of reframing the landing plan so as to
make it "unspectacular and quiet, and plausibly Cuban in its
essentials," Bundy still recognized that "at some stage" Castro's "sketchy" air force had to be "removed." Colonel Hawkins, "Bissell's military brain," believed that this could be done
with an attack by only six to eight Castro-labeled B-26s against
what Bundy was told was still Castro's "Achilles heel," although
this would constitute "the only truly noisy enterprise" that
remained. Then a "quiet landing of patriots" as an entirely
"separate enterprise" would give Castro no excuse for bringing matters to the United Nations. Landings now only at night,
with parachute operations only at dawn on D-Day to block the
causeways through the Zapata swamps, would reduce the noise
factor to a level satisfactory to the State Department. The President was also left with the impression, which he still shared
with Bundy, that in the event of a defeat, a substantial number
of survivors of the Brigade could disappear into the Zapata
swamps and quietly reappear in the now-too-distant Escambrays, 60 to 80 miles from the Bay of Pigs and beyond the
enemy-occupied city of Cienfuegos. In any case, Kennedy still
would have preferred scattered uprisings all around Cuba to a
politically risky, if militarily more effective, concentrated thrust
anywhere.[4]

Far more aware of the dangers of the new changes, several

of Gray's and Bissell's leading planners for a time threatened resignation, but their furious objections to Zapata's absence of docks and of an unfriendly population at the new beachhead were papered over in Bissell's description of the plan to Kennedy on March 16 as offering less risk, if less decisive results, than the Trinidad plan. In reality, the Bay of Pigs offered more risks as well as fewer opportunities than Trinidad, and in his private papers, Allen Dulles maintains that he told the President that, at best, the Brigade now had only a good fighting chance. Bissell, at any rate, was conscious that only military defectors might be expected from among the sparse population of the Zapata region, and he and his planners did not feel that a landing in the region without major external support would hold out as long as the projected week at Trinidad. Still fewer could anticipate what the President would do in the event of a well-coordinated or swift reaction to the landing on the part of Castro's forces, let alone grasp the implications of the helicopter revolution for catching fleeing Brigade members in the foodless swamps.

Finally, as in Guatemala, the CIA continued to rely upon successful U.S. radio interference with Castro's microwave internal-communication network to force his military units into open voice conversations which the agency could then overhear. In reality, the agency did not even succeed in jamming the microwave set at the Bay of Pigs–Zapata beaches. Last, but not least, only one B-26 raid from Nicaragua on Castro's major airfields—but that fortunately still on D-Day—was currently scheduled. This raid alone, the Joint Chiefs of Staff were informed, was to fulfill the heavy reliance upon strong air support at the crucial moment of landing. The new hope for an unopposed landing at Zapata was supposed to compensate for this latest limitation on the number of raids.

Under a sufficiently optimistic impression of not having to accept Admiral Dennison's earlier offer of a naval bailout in case of failure, Kennedy authorized the CIA to go ahead under the supervision of a new interdepartmental task force consisting of Daniel Braddock for State, General Gray for Defense, and Tracy Barnes for the agency. Although believing in the repeated assurances that a defeated Brigade could transform itself into guerrillas in favorable terrain, Kennedy would still not go so far as to give the revised Cuban invasion his formal approval. But in reiterating his injunction against any open American intervention, on March 16 the President carefully reserved for himself the final decision on the landing up to twenty-four hours before it was to take place. The new target date was now postponed to April 5; later it would have to be reset for April 10 and, ultimately, April 17. So, to the great anxiety of the agency, Kennedy again had gained time for further "second" thoughts.

In a message that came too late and probably would have been ineffective in any event, Arthur Schlesinger wrote the President on March 15 that the political risks of the operation had been underestimated and that the United States might be "rushed into something because CIA has on its hands a band of people it doesn't quite know what to do with." Politely, Schlesinger concluded that, while this was "a genuine problem, it can't be permitted to govern U.S. policy." A rather more sympathetic observer, British Prime Minister Harold Macmillan, noted later on that Kennedy was evidently unaware that he had settled for an untenable compromise between the original Eisenhower project of a small guerrilla landing and the large and open American invasion still covertly favored by the Joint Chiefs of Staff.[5]

Another important reason for the President's reluctance to commit himself even to a comparatively noiseless Cuban operation, let alone an overt American invasion, was that he was simultaneously under great pressure from the Joint Chiefs of Staff and the CIA to intervene in distant, if fortunately almost inaccessible, Laos, where the Communists had recently scored an advance. Dismayed to have discovered, contrary to the assurances of the Eisenhower administration the previous November, that if he sent even 10,000 men to southeast Asia, he would have practically no Strategic Army Reserve left in the United States, Kennedy was naturally stalling for time in both theaters to see which should have priority. Ominously, the enthusiastic Joint Chiefs was pushing for putting nuclear weapons as well as two or three whole divisions against possible Chinese intervention into the Central Intelligence Agency's previously private Asian bailiwick of Laos. As in the subsequent evacuation by sea from Cuba, General Lemnitzer was also concerned with the difficulties of taking men out of Laos by air, should that prove necessary.

Although the Defense Department and the Joint Chiefs advocated either an all-out American intervention in Laos or no action at all, and while elaborate military preparations were being made, Prime Minister Macmillan, then visiting in Florida, was bullied into accepting a limited intervention in Laos. As in earlier British policy, Macmillan had previously favored opening negotiations with the Russians as an alternative. While determined not to accept any visible humiliation over Laos, Kennedy, under Rusk's more cautious influence, failed to see why the United States alone should be responsible for fighting in forbidding terrain for a faraway people who had no interest in fighting for themselves. In addition, the new President was eager to reduce American responsibilities overseas rather than to increase them. So, notwithstanding his grim public and private assertions of firmness over Laos, by late March Kennedy actually welcomed a Soviet peace initiative.

Thus, the essentially artificial issue of Laos was eventually allowed to subside to the trivial dimensions it deserved. Nevertheless, the whole affair illustrated both the severe current limitations of U.S. military resources and the difficulty of backing down before either military or Republican pressure at home. Undoubtedly, Laos served to harden Kennedy's uncertain resolve over Cuba, just as the Cuban fiasco would serve initially to deny the still greater folly of American intervention in Laos, a point that Kennedy himself came to recognize in time.[6]

Meanwhile, during March 18 and March 22, in accordance with the President's desire to make the Bay of Pigs operation as Cuban as possible, the CIA in Miami again tried to reconcile—and seemingly to liberalize—the refugee factions among the anti-Castro Cubans. Briefly concealing the presumptuous Bender (i.e., Droller), the Central Intelligence Agency coerced Manuel Ray's liberal Movimiento Revolucionario del Pueblo (MRP) into joining with the conservative Frente Revolucionario Democrático, under the leadership of the moderate Miró Cardona, formerly Premier of Cuba under Castro. Fobbed off with only a fairly liberal front, now called the Cuban Revolutionary Council, the MRP naturally resented continued CIA dominance of the operation as well as the supposed favoritism and promotion of well-trained but pro-Batista conservative officers from the earlier period, when Bender had still shared power with Howard Hunt as political action officers for the Cuban project.

Bender's far-right-wing political-action colleague Hunt was now relieved of his responsibility for recruiting and indoctrinating Cuban refugees. Under the more liberal influence of White House advisers Arthur Schlesinger and Richard N. Goodwin, Bissell and Barnes continued to favor Bender in his disputes with Hunt on the grounds that they did not intend to be responsible for setting up a right-wing or Batistiano government in Cuba. To Hunt's still greater disgust, he was succeeded by one of his many enemies within the agency: the more liberal former Havana Station Chief James Noel. Finally, on March 18, the arrest of the CIA's Cuban underground chief inside Cuba, Rafael Díaz Hansom, left Díaz's still more demoralized successors confused and ignorant of the agency's new plans for invasion. Consequently, they were quite incapable of carrying our their previous elaborate preparations for a revolt, which, in any case, the CIA no longer expected—at least at the start. At the same time, however, the CIA initiated a report in Washington to the effect that Castro was losing his popularity and the Cubans were expecting an imminent invasion. Unfortunately, in whatever disarray the underground might be, Castro himself was not confused at all. In a speech on March 25, although mentioning the possibility of fighting U.S. Marines, Castro warned that Cuba was too well-armed to permit any mercenary government sustained on Cuban soil by anti-Castro Cubans to last more than twenty-four hours. At the same time his Foreign Minister, Raúl Roa, told the United Nations that a full U.S. invasion was imminent.

On March 28, Arthur Schlesinger went to see the President regarding the liberal-sounding white paper on Cuba, which he was preparing at the President's insistence, notwithstanding resistance from Eisenhower holdovers in the generally uninformed United States Information Agency. During their discussion, Schlesinger asked Kennedy what he thought about "this damned invasion." The President replied that he thought about it as little as possible, meaning that, like the State Department, he did not like the smell of it.[7] Kennedy may have distrusted the argument that a landing would precipitate a popular insurrection against Castro, although Dulles and Bissell were currently asserting that at least a quarter of the population of Cuba would eventually support any invasion that had succeeded in establishing a stronghold on the island.

In his own defense later on, Allen Dulles admitted in his

private papers that, at this time, he "did not wish to raise those issues in a discussion," "which might *only harden the decision against the type of action we required. We felt when the chips were down*—when the crisis arose in reality, *any action required for success would be authorized rather than permit the enterprise to fail.*" In retrospect, Dulles also admitted that the CIA plan for Cuba was "a sort of orphan child JFK had adopted— he had no real love and affection for it [and] proceeded uncertainly towards defeat—unable to turn back—only half sold on the vital necessity of what he was doing, surrounded by doubting Thomases among his best friends." Of these doubting Thomases, Dulles would eventually conclude bitterly but honestly, "There were enough . . . to dull the attack but not enough to bring about its cancellation."[8] And there in a nutshell lay the gist of Kennedy's military failure at the Bay of Pigs.

Notwithstanding subsequent claims that Dulles had never led the President to expect immediate uprisings, it should be noted that, in their reserve supplies, the Brigade now had extra equipment for some 30,000 or more anticipated Cuban recruits. Also included were some 15 million leaflets calling for a revolt against Castro. And in his subsequent investigation of the agency's failures, Lyman Kirkpatrick, Inspector General of the CIA, listed excessive reliance on deserters from Castro's militia as a serious failure in intelligence. Finally, in 1974, William Colby, then Director of the CIA, accounted for its various misestimates in 1961 by blaming it on the agency's overcompartmentalization for security reasons. Said Colby: "We didn't let the analysts in on the act . . . we tried conducting intelligence and action operations through two separate units," with the result that on the lower levels the agency's intelligence branch was not adequately consulted by its operations branch on precisely what the operations people needed to know.[9] Thus, the same committed men in Bissell's Plans Division who planned and pushed for the invasion also ensured that only relatively ignorant men informed it, a common enough failing in amateur military enterprises.

A further source of subsequent confusion in planning for the Bay of Pigs invasion lay in the impression—frequently fostered by the CIA—given to many of the anti-Castro invaders that the United States itself would openly provide air cover for the operation. As we have seen, probably implicit in the acquiescense of the Joints Chiefs of Staff to the revised invasion plan lay their almost automatic assumption that, if necessary, the United States Air Force and Navy would make up for any deficiencies in the marginal air cover entirely based in distant Nicaragua. This assumption—simply a hope for the CIA—was vigorously denied in 1963 by President John Kennedy and his brother, Attorney General Robert Kennedy. Indeed, this issue and the closely allied question of how many air strikes the CIA and the anti-Castro Cubans themselves had planned, or would be permitted, have only muddied the water. Both the Second World War and the Vietnam War have made clear that a force estimated as high as 240,000 regulars and militia who really intended to repel a small invasion could do so very effectively regardless of the intensity of the air cover. In short, the ultimate failure of the Cuban plan lay not merely in the usual overestimation of air power or the amphibious problem of simply getting ashore. As in the Vietnam War, it was, above all, a failure to estimate accurately the enemy's will to fight.

On March 29, in another meeting in the White House with his advisers, President Kennedy was informed by Dulles that the latter felt more confident of success over the Bay of Pigs than he had during the marginal Guatemala operation in 1954. On the former occasion, Dulles had not exhibited much confidence, but Kennedy could not be expected to know how misleading this analogy was.[10] Perhaps influenced by such a seemingly optimistic opinion, Kennedy again vowed that he wanted all American forces kept out of the operation—hardly a practical logistic notion in any event. Kennedy's real hope probably appeared in his repeated questions regarding the opportunities for the invading forces to fade hurriedly into the bush or to be diverted at the last minute elsewhere, without allowing the whole operation to look like a failure.

To encourage the faltering President, the CIA continued to foster Kennedy's erroneous impression that the small and supposedly quiet invading force landing at night in a deserted region consisted of trained guerrillas who, if unsuccessful in provoking an uprising, could easily melt away into the nearby mountains. As Robert Kennedy said later, had his brother known the truth, he might not have approved the operation. With enough hindsight, Bissell, like the reluctant Rusk, would come to realize that the agency had underestimated the possibility of denying American responsibility for the operation. But as early as 1967, Bissell felt that the chances of even establishing a lasting beachhead—to say nothing of conquering the whole island—had only been about 50–50. Unfortunately, in March and early April 1961, he had told John and Robert Kennedy that the chances of success were about 2 out of 3, although Defense Secretary McNamara, General Lemnitzer, and Admiral Burke thought success pretty marginal even then.

The double-talk policy of the facets of the CIA plan here is apparent, since the invasion leaders themselves were not told that, as guerrillas, they could easily flee in the event of failure. After all, as Cubans they would have readily recognized that flight through eighty miles of largely roadless swamps and then around the city of Cienfuegos to the Escambrays was hardly a practical proposal for a defeated and demoralized group of survivors, most of whom had not been trained as guerrillas. Moreover, the Zapata swamps had not been employed as a base for guerrilla activity for many years, most recently because of the effective employment of the helicopter as a search-and-destroy weapon against guerrillas. In this instance, the CIA could claim that it was necessary to protect the shaky morale of the invading Brigade by saying nothing depressing to its lower-ranking members, but no such extenuation can be found for witting or unwitting misrepresentation of fact to the President.

That weekend, traveling with President Kennedy to Palm Beach, Senator Fulbright, Chairman of the Foreign Relations Committee, gave the President a memorandum on the Cuban issue. Agreeing with others of his committee in his opposition to the project, the liberal Fulbright argued that covert American support for an invasion of Cuba constituted a policy of such cynical hypocrisy as to be worthy of the Soviet Union rather than the United States, a policy that, even if successful, Fulbright warned, "would be denounced from the Rio Grande to Patagonia as an example of imperialism." The Senator further feared that, rather than allowing the Cuban operation to fail, the United States would progressively increase its aid until the United States was openly committed, a fear of which Kennedy was already very conscious. Advocating instead the eventual policy of merely containing Cuba, Fulbright concluded that the whole project had been poorly evaluated and was already anything but a secret.[11] A recent admonition of President Figuéres of Costa Rica to the effect that any invasion of Cuba was madness is illustrative of even pro-American Latin opinion, although Dulles may not have relayed any such unwanted warnings to the President.

In retrospect, at any rate, the still more influential and far more conservative Chairman of the Senate Armed Services Committee, Richard Russell, has claimed the while he had known in general of the plan for the invasion, he "would have strongly advised against this kind of operation," had he been

aware that it was imminent.[12] Considering the lengths to which
Russell went to keep his jolly friend Allen Dulles from being
annoyed by indiscreet questions posed by fellow members of
the Armed Services Committee, the threat of the Senator's
opposition could not have been very serious for the agency.
Moreover, Russell was rarely inclined to ask Dulles any difficult questions in private, as the CIA Director has admitted
himself. Even the hawkish former Secretary of State, Dean
Acheson, who offended the President because he (Acheson)
was so "much alarmed" by the Cuba invasion, also dismissed
the "wild idea" of invasion from his mind as patently absurd,
since to Acheson, at least, it was obvious "that 1500 Cubans
[invading] were not as good as 25,000 Cubans" awaiting them.
Also unappealing to a realist such as Acheson was the notion
of invasion as a catalyst for possible uprisings, so much beloved
by Berle as the theory and by Bissell and Dulles as a method
to encourage a reluctant President to intervene without seem-
ing to have to employ the U.S. armed forces.[13]

While those inhabiting the lower echelons of the State
Department were deliberately excluded from knowledge of the
Cuba plans, when the indiscreet and liberal Undersecretary of
State Chester Bowles heard of the operation during Rusk's
absence overseas, he was horrified. Nevertheless, Bowles's
memorandum of March 31, opposing the operation, proved
ineffective, since upon Rusk's return the Secretary asserted
that the Cuban project had been watered down to a mere infiltration along the lines Bowles and Schlesinger had so zeal-
ously urged. With a temperament incompatible with that of
the passionate Bowles, Rusk discouraged his Undersecretary
from seeing Kennedy personally with objections. In all probability, even had he seen Kennedy on this occasion, Bowles would
have had little impact, since like most Stevenson liberals, he
had badly slipped in the President's esteem. As President,

Kennedy no longer needed the left wing of his own party, and he had previously excluded Bowles from knowledge of his Cuban plans.

Painfully aware of the danger of a Latin American explosion in the OAS owing to the failure of Berle's mission there (not to mention the adverse effect of a Cuban invasion upon America's NATO allies), Rusk simply fobbed off the alarmed Bowles with vague and optimistic promises. In retrospect, Rusk has admitted that he had been a little naïve in hoping to conceal the American role in the Cuban operation to any serious degree—at least in its repercussions within the United States. A harsher description of Rusk by Walter Lippmann some years later depicted Kennedy's Secretary of State as "a very intelligent stupid man. He doesn't examine his premises."[14] At least, unlike the more aggressive Berle, who may have further alerted Castro by futile attempts to win support in Latin America, Rusk did not believe that the Organization of American States could be disregarded by the United States simply because Castro had done so. But, then, unlike Berle, Rusk did not believe that great powers could do almost anything they wished.

Bowles, estimating the Cuba project's chances for success as only 1 out of 3 had also suggested to Rusk an open American naval blockade around Cuba, a strategy much less offensive to world opinion than covert action and one partially adopted by Kennedy in 1962. In this deliberately ignored memorandum, Bowles had concluded with words of permanent value: "A great deal of time and money has been spent and many individuals have been emotionally involved in its [the project's] success. We should not, however, proceed with this adventure simply because we are wound up and cannot stop." What bothered the idealistic Bowles most about the new administration was how far astray a man "as brilliant and well-intentioned as President Kennedy," could go in his lack of "a genuine sense of conviction about what is right and what is wrong."[15] The same criticism of Kennedy would be made regarding his Vietnam policy, as Bowles and other liberals would discover.

Thus, the old idea of relying upon either the State Department or congressional committees as watchdogs over the Central Intelligence Agency had been well discredited as early as 1961. That this hope died hard, however, may be seen in a statement by Congressman Michael Harrington as late as 1974. In his commentary on the then-recent activities of the CIA against the Allende government in Chile, Harrington observed: "When you look at the [Central Intelligence Director William] Colby testimony, you'll see that the notion of Congressional oversight of the C.I.A. is a fiction, and the role of the State Department when it comes to the C.I.A. is passive, by-standish [and] totally ineffective." The conclusions of the House Select Committee on Intelligence two years later simply reiterated those of Congressman Harrington.[16]

On April 3 the State Department released Schlesinger's white paper, which articulated the revolution-betrayed-by-Castro thesis of the liberal supporters of the Kennedy administration. Calling upon Castro to sever his links with international communism, the white paper declared that the Cuban regime offered "a clear and present danger" to what Kennedy and Schlesinger claimed was the real revolution in the Americas.[17] In reality, the amount of revolution that the CIA and its Batista-minded invasion leaders were capable of bringing to Cuba was not such as to arouse much support among the Cuban masses, had the CIA even intended to call for such support. But there is little doubt that many of the Cuba operation's advocates in the CIA, such as Bissell and Barnes, sincerely believed in the liberalism of their policy for Cuba compared to that of the right wing, either at home or in Cuba.

As Schlesinger noted on March 29, the final decision on the Bay of Pigs invasion, now rescheduled for April 17, would have to be taken at the meeting of the National Security Council set for April 4. Schlesinger hoped that the decision would be adverse, but he soon discovered that Kennedy had returned from Palm Beach in a more militant mood, although the President had asked Fulbright to attend the climactic meeting on April 4. It is possible, although unlikely, that both the President's father Joseph Kennedy and Senator Smathers influenced the President in this shift. Except for the significant omission of Adlai Stevenson, still carefully kept uninformed at the United Nations in New York, all principal civilians involved were present, including the presidential advisers on Latin America Adolf Berle and Arthur Schlesinger, Robert McNamara and Paul Nitze of the Defense Department, and Dean Rusk and Thomas Mann of the State Department; General Lemnitzer alone represented the Joint Chiefs of Staff.

Bissell and Dulles spoke again for the CIA, declaring that the invading Brigade would land and hold some territory until the Cuban Revolutionary Council had proclaimed itself a government and had rallied internal support behind it within Cuba. The Brigade's own planes, based in Nicaragua, would destroy Castro's small air force before the invaders had landed. To drive their case home, the CIA chiefs stressed that the history of Cuba was one of small insurrections triumphing over the larger forces of established order. Moreover, there was little time to lose, for the arrival of Soviet MiGs and Czech-trained Cuban pilots to fly them was supposedly imminent. To their credit, the CIA spokesmen opposed the President's desire for small scattered landings, averring that the invading forces would merely alert Castro without being able to defend themselves.

Speaking in an emphatic and incredulous manner, Senator Fulbright, an unofficial but still a civilian participant, then denounced the whole operation as both absurdly dispropor-

tionate to the threat Castro currently represented and the kind
of immoral action that an open society such as the United States
could not carry off well. Moving around the council table, the
President next asked Berle his opinion. Among the most bel-
licose, Berle argued that a confrontation with the Communists
in Latin America was inevitable anyway and that it should be
precipitated now. Furthermore, as Chairman of the Inter-
Agency Task Force for Caribbean Contigency Planning, he was
only too well aware of the refusal of Latin American governments to support the Cuban operation and doubted that any
alternatives to the current plan were much good anyway. Berle
had similarly, if not as openly, favored the risky action in Guatemala in 1954, since he had then thought that the chances of
success had been only about 50–50.

Although opposed, Rusk, the perfect organization man, went
along with the operation, as did the skeptical Mann of the State
Department, Bissell's most persistent opponent in the Cuba
project. Like Rusk and McNamara, Mann's acceptance of the
project was on the half-hearted grounds that it was probably
the last opportunity that the administration would have without using Americans. Like his unhappy predecessor as Assistant Secretary of State for Inter-American Affairs, Mann had
undergone much soul-searching over the legality of United
States interventions in Latin America, but he was hooked on
the Bay of Pigs operation since he had so effectively killed its
somewhat more effective Trinidad alternative. In 1965, skeptical or not, Mann would also favor Lyndon Johnson's unnecessary occupation of the Dominican Republic.

Secretary Rusk later complained with good reason about
having to make crucial decisions too hurriedly in a room filled
with large numbers of people. Defense Secretary McNamara,
Paul Nitze, and William P. Bundy of the Defense Department
gave their assent with none of the Joint Chiefs, except General
Lemnitzer, there to gainsay them. Nitze felt the chances of

success were less than even, but hoped that at least the Cubans might rise; otherwise the United States could wait forever for a better opportunity. For the Joint Chiefs of Staff, Lemnitzer said somewhat ambiguously that if Dulles's assumptions were correct, the plan was militarily feasible. Lemnitzer had left himself an enormous escape hatch, if one not too visible to the eager or acquiescent civilians in and out of the Defense Department. But the fact remains, as the often brutally candid Secretary McNamara would finally concede to the Taylor committee later on: "It was not [just] a C.I.A. debacle; it was a U.S. Government debacle." Subsequently, McNamara would testify that the administration was hysterical about Castro at this time.[18]

To ensure that the Bay of Pigs invasion was a full U.S. government debacle and not solely that of the Kennedy administration, the uneasy President would take care to obtain the written, however unfelt, approval of General Lemnitzer and Admiral Burke for the Joint Chiefs. So disapproving and relatively insignificant a figure as Arthur Schlesinger was not asked his opinion in the presence of his superiors. To his regret, neither did he volunteer it, thus giving Robert McNamara the impression that nobody in the room, except Senator Fulbright, opposed the plan. Afterward, Schlesinger was given a private opportunity to explain to the President his continued opposition. For his covert but utterly unavailing efforts, Schlesinger was later firmly rebuked by the President's loyal brother, the Attorney General. He was told to desist in his efforts thereafter.[19]

As a result, while it was substantially true, as President Kennedy would complain a year later, that the advice to the executive branch of those who were brought in was unanimous and wrong regarding Cuba, it is also true that Kennedy had been careful not to consult the many liberal opponents of his policy on the matter. These included the soon-to-be-victimized Adlai Stevenson, the dangerously prominent U.S. delegate to the United Nations, and the soon-to-be-fired Undersecretary of State Chester Bowles. Moreover, neither Dulles nor Bissell had dared make clear the grave fears of their planners regarding the lack of any open American aerial backup for the invasion, and they would not do so until it was almost too late—at the actual moment of landing. Nor had the Joint Chiefs directly informed the President or his Defense Secretary of their preference for a landing at Trinidad rather than for the more improvised project at the Bay of Pigs. As Admiral Burke, in his own defense, subsequently put it, you had to pound on the table to be heard in the Kennedy administration. Instead, Kennedy could console himself with General Gray's assurance that the now-planned night landings over several beaches would reduce the noise factor of the invasion to reasonably inaudible levels.[20]

A year before the whole affair, another subsequent presidential adviser on national security affairs, Henry Kissinger, had written that American pragmatism saw "in consensus a test of validity," since it sought "to reduce judgment to methodology and value to knowledge." The result, Kissinger pointed out, was "a greater concern with the collection of facts than with an interpretation of their significance. . . . Disagreement is considered a reflection on the objectivity or the judgment of the participants. . . . Even very eminent people are reluctant to stand alone. . . . The obvious insurance against the possibility of error is to obtain as many opinions as possible. And unanimity is important, in that its absence is a standing reminder of the tentativeness of the course adopted. The committee approach to decision making is often less an organizational device that a spiritual necessity."[21]

VI
Day of Dupes

I know from experience that failure is more destructive than an appearance of indecision. ... When we go, we must go to win, but it will be better to change our minds than fail.[1] —*President Kennedy, August 29, 1963, before the overthrow of President Diem*

I don't want any more of this crap about the fact that we couldn't hit this target or that one. This is your chance to use military power to win this war, and if you don't, I'll hold you responsible.[2] —*President Nixon to the Joint Chiefs of Staff, 1972*

If we do not succeed at the very onset in surprising the Egyptians and knocking out their planes while they are still on the ground, our plan will fail.[3] —*General Moshe Dayan, 1956*

*A*S IT TURNED OUT, Adolf Berle, eager advocate of the Cuba project and long-time professional anti-Communist who had urged the National Security Council on April 4 to let 'er rip, was closer to the still-uncertain President's opinion than to the opinion of his fellow intellectual at the seat of power Arthur Schlesinger. To be sure, the latter had written yet another memorandum on April 5 in an effort to resist the accelerating slide into the Bay of Pigs. In this new memorandum to the President, Schlesinger emphasized that he would be for "the highly beneficial result of getting rid of the Castro regime," could this be achieved "by a swift, surgical stroke." Unhappily, *"no matter how 'Cuban' the equipment and personnel, the U.S. will be held accountable for the operation, and* *our prestige will be committed to its success.*" Furthermore, "*since the Castro regime is presumably too strong to be toppled by a single landing, the operation will turn into a protracted civil conflict.*" Schlesinger continued: "If the Landing fails to trigger uprisings behind the lines and defections in the Militia (and the evidence that it would do so is inconclusive), the logic of the situation could well lead us, step by step, to the point where the last step would be to dispatch the Marines." In conclusion, the perceptive Schlesinger wrote too tactfully: "On balance, I think that the risks of the operation slightly outweigh the risks of abandonment. These latter risks would be mitigated somewhat if we could manage a partial rather than a total abandonment [i.e., if we could put the men into Cuba quietly]." As an aside, Schlesinger noted that he shared Senator Fulbright's "doubts as to the competence of the exile leaders."

In reply to this half-hearted memorandum, the President simply shrugged off his adviser's fears, saying that as President, he had reserved the right to halt the invasion up to twenty-four hours before the landing. Meanwhile, Kennedy added, "I'm trying to make some sense out of it."[4] Evidently, at this juncture, Kennedy simply wanted to get rid of the embarrassing Brigade by dumping it on the coast of Cuba, where, as he ironically remarked, its members so much wanted to be. How much the President was actually the prisoner of events, as Schlesinger apologetically describes him at this stage, or was just evading unwanted advice is debatable, but Schlesinger himself had concluded by April 6 that the show was finally going ahead, although, as was hoped for by the Kennedy liberals, only as a large-scale infiltration rather than as a resoundingly flamboyant invasion.

In fact, the liberals' influence during April 5 and 6 may have contributed to Kennedy's and Bissell's planning a false defec-

tion for a Cuban pilot just before D-Day, along with a premature air strike and a bona-fide guerrilla landing elsewhere before
D-Day. Although pleased with such dangerous modifications,
Rusk was worried about the invading Brigade calling for U.S.
help and about Soviet counteractions. As he so often had done
in the past, Kennedy asked how the operation might be canceled at the last minute and was reassured by Bissell that it
could be diverted to Vieques in Puerto Rico with little notice.
The President settled for doing everything to make the landing
appear as Cuban as possible, "the objective being to make it
more plausible for U.S. denial of association with the operation."[5]

Meanwhile, in a press conference on April 5, the President
publicly discounted proposals for a blockade of Cuba on the
grounds that such an action was too slow, too risky, and would
give the Russians an excuse for a counterblockade of West
Berlin. At the same time, Edward R. Morrow, head of the United
States Information Agency, asked Allen Dulles, with little success about the line the unprepared Information Agency should
take in the event of invasion. On April 7, another liberal Kennedy adviser, Richard Goodwin, tried to stiffen Rusk's backbone against open invasion, as did Schlesinger on April 8.
Reverting to an earlier idea of Admiral Burke's, Rusk now suggested an invasion of easternmost Cuba instead of the Bay of
Pigs in order to have the support of the U.S. naval base at
Guantánamo. But, as the Secretary remarked sourly after the
event, the U.S. Navy still did not want to spoil the virginity of
Guantánamo.

During the previous two weeks, the difficult naval rules of
engagement for Admiral Dennison at Norfolk had been ham-
mered out by the Pentagon and the CIA to meet the President's ever-more-exacting demands. Finally, by April 6/7,
Dennison was notified that, except at night, he could not openly
convoy the ships of the invading Brigade—only area covering

could be given. Dennison, who had previously been forbidden to use the base at Guantánamo for air cover for the invasion, was now told to keep his destroyers twenty miles offshore during the landing. He could fire only if he were about to be attacked: and should he have to protect the ships of the Brigade in this way, the whole operation would be automatically canceled. General Cabell, Deputy Director of the CIA, was particularly concerned about this point, fearing that Kennedy could use it to escape from the unwanted operation entirely.

Aside from protecting Guantánamo at any price, the U.S. armed services wanted to win regardless of the political consequences and could hardly say, as did Rusk, that "if you have failure it's very nice if the United States is not involved."[6] Rusk also offered the farfetched suggestion that someone other than the President should make the final decision in Kennedy's absence so that this unnamed subordinate's head could "later be placed on the block if things go terribly wrong." Supporting this particular evasion of Rusk in order to protect the President further, Schlesinger proposed that when "lies must be told they should be told by subordinate officials."[7]

That Kennedy's head was inescapably on the block as far as publicity over the forthcoming invasion of Cuba was concerned was brutally apparent by this date. For example, on April 7, Tad Szulc in *The New York Times* wrote that between 5,000 and 6,000 men had already been recruited to liberate Cuba and that their training in Florida, Louisiana, and Guatemala was almost complete, although experts still doubted that even this number would be enough for an invasion. According to his Press Secretary, Pierre Salinger, Kennedy became livid over such leaks. He told Salinger: "I can't believe what I'm reading. Castro doesn't need agents over here. All he has to do is read our papers. It's all laid out for him." In a counterleak of his own, imbued with the currently chic mythology of paramilitary operations, on April 7 Kennedy told

Chalmers Roberts of *The Washington Post* that there would
be no large invasion and certainly no American troops, in spite
of Eisenhower's alleged plans for such an operation in 1960.
The President also denied that there was any intention of using
President Betancourt's Venezuelan army to do the job.[8]

An appeal from the President through an unhappy Schlesinger killed a most revealing piece in *The New Republic*.
Administration sympathizers next contributed to watering down
The New York Times reports between April 6 and April 14 to
eliminate references to the CIA's role in the imminent invasion, to the invasion date, and to the invasion's fundamental
importance to the United States. Instead, somewhat misleading accounts of multiple small-scale landings involving a total
of 4,000 to 6,000 men were printed in *The Times*, red herrings
that the President would profess to regret having planted two
weeks later, when he informed Turner Catledge, *The Times*'s
managing editor, that if more had been printed on the operation, "you would have saved us from a colossal mistake." But
a year later, Kennedy again successfully pressured *The Times*
into silence during the missile crisis over Cuba. Gilbert Harrison, managing editor of *The New Republic,* similarly confessed
regret at having gone along with the administration's desire
for silence over the Bay of Pigs before it was too late.[9]

While it is highly unlikely that at this point leaks could have
thwarted the invasion, Kennedy's growing realization of the
risks inherent in the operation impelled him to send Schlesinger with the thoroughly evasive Barnes, Bissell's deputy, to
brief Stevenson at the United Nations on April 8 regarding the
forthcoming operation. Notwithstanding the President's
expressed desire to protect the integrity and credibility of his
unsuccessful rival in the Democratic party as "one of our great
national assets," Stevenson and his aides were left with the
wishful but erroneous impression that there would be no open
American participation in the project. Consequently, Barnes

and Schlesinger departed, leaving the still only partially informed but strongly opposed Stevenson with his head, too, on the block, ignorant of both the control and the logistic bases of the invasion as well as the Nicaraguan origin of its proposed air strikes.[10]

Better informed, José Miró Cardona, head of the new Cuban Revolutionary Council in New York, issued an inflammatory call to arms for Cubans on the same April 8. Proclaiming "We must conquer or we shall be choked by slavery," Miró Cardona concluded that "duty calls us to war against the executioners of our Cuban brethren." Miró Cardona's rebellious subordinate in the council, Manuel Ray, however, sensed disaster in the appointment of Captain Manuel Artime as the council's civilian representative with the invaders. An experienced candidate for the post, a strongly anti-Batista figure, and a professional soldier—Colonel Ramón Barquín—had also been passed over by the CIA on the ostensible grounds that he had warned against the folly of risking an all-or-nothing invasion of Cuba. But, as the President told Harold Macmillan that same day, Kennedy preferred to have the Cuban exiles inside Cuba rather than outside,[11] so they were going to go there, ready or not.

On April 10, as the anti-Castro Brigade began loading the six old ships leased by the CIA in Nicaragua, Schlesinger sent the President another memorandum warning against allowing American troops to be sucked into Cuba in support of an unsuccessful operation by the invaders. Instead, the Cuban leaders should be told "clearly and emphatically" that American recognition of their provisional government would come only after they had achieved "a better than 50–50 chance of winning under their own steam." Since Schlesinger's continuing fear was precisely what the freewheeling paramilitary types running the CIA operations at the training camps had evidently been encouraging the Brigade leaders to believe as their final hope, his last-minute effort to keep the invasion primarily

a Cuban operation was indeed timely, however ineffective this
would render it as a military project. In justice to Schlesinger,
he warned the President in this same memorandum not merely
that the United States would "be held accountable" for the
Cuban operation "before the bar of world opinion" through the
American press, but also that a *great many people simply*
did not regard Cuba as presenting *"so grave and compelling a
threat to our national security as to justify a course of action
which much of the world will interpret as calculated aggression against a small nation in defiance both of treaty obligations and of the international standards we have repeatedly
asserted against the Communist world* [Schlesinger's empha-
sis]."[12]

As Kennedy was reluctantly becoming aware, the political
sine qua non of the invasion—no overt American support—
would remain to the end incompatible with its military *sine
qua non*—large-scale and open American backing. Whether
the paramilitary officers of the CIA on the spot would actually
have ignored the Kennedy administration and allowed the
Cubans to go ahead with the invasion regardless of Washington's approval is questionable, since no CIA low-level subordinate on the spot could commit a significant amount of
supporting American forces without the President's eventual
knowledge. Indeed, later on, the President's watchdog over the
CIA, Robert Kennedy, would term such action as virtually
treason.

Certainly at this delicate juncture, two of Bissell's most
important planners, Jake Engler and Colonel Jack Hawkins,
reported to Bissell that they wished to resign, since their original plan for the operation had already been pulled apart at the
seams in every possible way. Bissell talked his two planners
into going along with the now sadly revised plan, possibly on
the strength of his and Dulles's continued hope that at the

final moment Kennedy's hand would be forced through a sufficiently resounding commitment at the Bay of Pigs. If hardly noiseless, with failure the code name for the naval side of the operation, Bumpy Road, might actually become noisy enough to force a reversal of Kennedy's adamant policy against open American intervention. Bissell has deemed this explanation as an unprovable allegation as to his motives, although he later regretted not having demanded better equipment in the hope of concealing the U.S. hand.[13]

Although only reasonably optimistic regarding the chances of the invasion, at a press conference on April 12 in a statement subsequently much criticized by the contemptuous Republicans, the President announced defiantly that there would not be "under any conditions an intervention in Cuba by the United States Armed Forces. This Government will do everything it possibly can, and I think it can meet its responsibilities, to make sure that there are no Americans involved in any actions inside Cuba. . . . The basic issue in Cuba is not one between the United States and Cuba. . . . It is between the Cubans themselves."[14] Apart from lack of veracity, such a statement could hardly help the morale of the Cuban opposition to Castro. But Kennedy had left little ground for illusions about his policy for those who wished to hear.

According to Chester Bowles, however, on this same April 12, Kennedy's competitive spirit was aroused by the successful orbiting of the earth in outer space by a Soviet cosmonaut. But, according to Walt Rostow, as late as this date, it was McGeorge Bundy's opinion that the President was still keeping his options open. Another option only too open to Kennedy was Rostow's advice of the same date to gear up for an intervention in Laos as well. But, then, Rostow was the hawk of all hawks.

Later that day, the President ordered Berle and Schlesinger

to go to New York to see the Cuban Revolutionary Council and stress the necessity for no open American intervention, and to explain further that the council would receive no American recognition as a provisional government until it was fully established in Cuba by the purported military efforts of Cubans alone. Neither the Joint Chiefs of Staff nor CIA representatives present in the cabinet room of the White House registered any open objection to these explicit presidential instructions, and Richard Bissell then outlined the latest revision of the Bay of Pigs plan. Why General Gray of the Joint Chiefs did not plead for still another postponement of the invasion, given the appalling logistic tangle he had just been informed of during the Cuban Brigade's embarkation in Nicaragua, is speculative. Possibly, like Dulles and Bissell, Gray feared that if he now reported that the operation was marginal even without any resistance on the beachhead and quite impossible with it, a vastly relieved President and Rusk would have simply canceled it outright. It seems unlikely that these principal proponents of the plan believed, as Bissell may have told Robert Kennedy at this time, that failure was almost impossible, since, at the worst, the Brigade could always fade away into the Escambrays. To be sure, Bissell has recently admitted that the agency light-heartedly assumed that the Zapata swamps around the Bay of Pigs could also support fading-away and defeated guerrillas. Presumably, the operation could still then be called a success by some, if the United States openly intervened to bail out the defeated Brigade.

Contrary to Gray's hopes, none of his superiors stressed the need for complete air control; and, like the other good soldiers, sailors, and airmen, he remained silent. Instead, Bissell again gave way to administration's desire for less conspicuous (i.e., not in the Havana area), less powerful, and less indentifiable air strikes. As a result, the original Joint Chiefs of Staff–approved plan for two air strikes on D-Day minus 1 (D − 1) to take out

Castro's air force was replaced with a single light air strike of only eight planes on D − 2, timed to coincide with a diversionary landing in Oriente Province. Bissell and Gray still preferred, however, to mount a full-scale attack by all sixteen B-26 bombers available on D-Day itself to protect the landings at their most crucial moment. The weak attack of D − 2—the only one actually undertaken, as it turned out—was now intended principally as a diversionary strike to give credence to a fictitious defection of Castro Cuban pilots. It was not, testified General Gray to the Senate Foreign Relations Committee later on, intended to destroy the Cuban air force. Unfortunately, this absurd latest political red herring would give Castro a full forty-eight hours' warning, following the weak initial raid on D − 2, with which to patch up or disperse his surviving planes against the all-out D-Day attack that never came.

While Kennedy did not give even this last-minute plan his final approval, he was informed that his official decision could not be delayed after April 14 because the operational phase of Zapata had already begun on April 12. Apart from the chaotic loadings at Puerto Cabezas in Nicaragua, Operation Southern Tip for the air defense of the southern United States had commenced, and the United States Navy's frustrating rules of engagement for Operation Bumpy Road were going into effect. The CIA was now so furiously racing the clock against its final April 17 invasion date that there was not time left for even a single day's war gaming of the operation. Sunday, April 16, was now set as the final Go–No Go day for Kennedy's decision with regard to the main landing at the Bay of Pigs. By this date, as Robert Kennedy would imply subsequently during the Taylor post-mortem, his brother had slid so far down the slippery slope toward the Bay of Pigs that for all practical purposes his approval for the operation had already been given.[15]

As before, during their visit to New York on April 13, Berle and Schlesinger encountered open incredulity on the part of Miró Cardona that American military support for the invading Brigade would cease at the beachhead. Berle did offer some additional rifles for the 10,000 or more defectors Miró Cardona expected. To convince further the dismayed Cuban leader, Kennedy next sent Barnes to New York to inform Miró Cardona that without the latter's acquiescence, the invasion would be canceled. Whatever grudging ackowledgment Barnes may have extorted from Miró Cardona, in the latter's wishful recollection, these conversations became an administration promise of American troops sooner or later, particularly if matters went badly rather then well. Thereafter, the leak-prone and squabbling Cuban Revolutionary Council was incarcerated at Opa-Locka airport in Florida to prevent any more independent actions or statements without CIA permission.

As a separate transaction, the agency and the Joint Chiefs had already assembled some 35,000 arms packs for Castro defectors for D + 3 onward. Showing signs of still more personal initiative, Admiral Dennison at Norfolk had readied the carrier *Essex* to provide possible aerial cover over Cuba. Without informing the President, Dennison (and Admiral Burke) had already loaded the Marine Battalion, officially only to reinforce Guantánamo, if that proved necessary. Of course, such a battalion would be equally available for the Bay of Pigs, should that be permitted.

Although Dennison had received his naval rules of engagement, he was still not shown the CIA invasion plan and, thus, was unable to make proper arrangements for a subsequent naval rescue of the Brigade in the event of disaster. Not surprisingly, in common with other orthodox military men, the alarmed Admiral concluded that the whole Cuban project should have functioned directly under his own centralized control rather than that of the CIA in Washington. Of course, in peacetime, President Kennedy neither would nor could have risked accepting the transfer of so much authority to a subordinate military figure in what, after all, was an inherently political-military operation. Obviously, transfer of such authority would serve to commit further a President who did not want to be committed at all.[16]

As the last moment for canceling the recently arranged $D-2$ air strike approached, on April 13, CIA's Jake Engler called his fellow planner Colonel Hawkins, then inspecting the restless and insufficiently trained Brigade in Central America, for the Colonel's official evaluation of the Brigade's current condition. In his famous and effectively misleading reply, Hawkins answered: "My observations have increased my confidence in the ability of this force to accomplish not only initial combat missions, but also the ultimate objective, the overthrow of Castro. The Brigade and battalion commanders now know all details of the plan and are enthusiastic. These officers are young, vigorous, intelligent and motivated by a fanatical urge to begin battle. Most of them have been preparing under rugged conditions of training for almost a year. They say they know their own people and believe that after they have inflicted one serious defeat upon the opposition forces, the later will melt away from Castro. . . . I share their confidence. . . . The Brigade officers do not expect help from U.S. Armed Forces. They ask only for continued delivery of supplies. This can be done covertly. [The] Cuban Air force is motivated, strong, well-trained, armed to the teeth, and ready."[17]

A less misleading officer, also engaged in training the Brigade in Guatemala at this time, observed, like General Shoup of the Marine Corps, that sending the Brigade to Cuba was like pitting Boy Scouts against Marines with less than a 15-percent chance of success, however generously success might be defined. Shown to the wavering President on April 14, the

Hawkins cable did the trick, according to Robert Kennedy. The President gave the order for the air stage of the invasion to commence the next day, although he made sure that Admiral Dennison's naval escort for the Brigade was prepared to halt the actual landings, scheduled for April 17, up to the last minute. Even Dulles has admitted that it took courage for Kennedy to overrule some of his advisers and order the invasion to proceed.[18]

As Secretary McNamara would concede after the event, although there had been a gradual erosion of the Zapata plan, it had not been bad enough to call off the operation entirely. On the morning of April 15, the diversionary plan in Oriente Province—Operation Marte—was mounted by Niño Díaz's 170 men to distract Castro's attention from the subsequent main landing at the Bay of Pigs. The next erosion in the CIA plan promptly appeared when Díaz's men refused to land amid the rough breakers and rocks of the diversionary landing site at Baracoa, east of Guantánamo, because of what they called too much enemy activity in the area (among other excuses). The following night, Díaz's men again refused to land because of what the CIA bluntly labeled bad leadership. The abortive Díaz mission was then recalled to Puerto Rico, since it was too late to give any assistance at the Bay of Pigs. Its brief last-minute guerrilla training by the overoptimistic agency would seem to have been a better explanation for its failure than any other.

At dawn on April 15, eight old B-26 bombers from Nicaragua flew over Castro's three most important airfields near Havana and Santiago to destroy as many of his planes as possible. The bombers had the enormous advantage of surprise over a country with no early air warning system, although Castro now had numerous antiaircraft guns. At last, Castro hastened to order a mass roundup of the unprepared and demoralized underground opposition in Cuba, although the CIA planners were not relying upon any uprising of the opposition to make the initial phase of the operation practical. In the next stage, Castro's crippling of the underground, of course, would have further enervated a successful and sustained landing of the Brigade.[19]

Following its release by President Kennedy in the late afternoon of April 14, the Brigade sailed without delay from its temporary maritime base at Puerto Cabezas, Nicaragua, its CIA mentors fearing the imposition of still more limitations and delays, if not outright cancellation, by the half-hearted American President. By no means uncertain regarding his own policy toward Castro, Luis Somoza, the reactionary and corrupt dictator of Nicaragua, appeared at the dock to wave farewell to the departing Cubans. Somoza sent the 1,400-odd men of the Brigade off with the cry: "Bring me a couple of hairs from Castro's beard," almost the last straight statement the Cubans would hear for some time. In 1962, Somoza would unjustifiably assume blame for not having been able to get through to the White House to protest the predating of the first air strike to D − 2, thus losing the advantage of surprise for the actual landing.[20] Obviously, the White House, in disclaiming all responsibility for the operation, wanted to hear nothing from Somoza of his eminently sensible protests.

The American advisers now informed the still trusting Brigade that 700 guerrillas would be waiting near the Bay of Pigs beachhead and that weapons for the anticipated immediate defection of as many as 4,000 or 5,000 of Castro's forces had been loaded on the invaders' ships. Actually, some 15,000 arms packs had already been loaded in the logistic chaos at Puerto Cabezas. Only the Brigade leaders were told of possible sea and air evacuation in the event of failure, and they were antagonistic to the idea.

Guerrilla action in the Escambrays was considered a last resort, perhaps because the CIA feared a new revolt by the Brigade if the latter were ordered to return to that long-since-discarded chestnut once again. The Brigade's six old ships, two procured through Robert Kennedy from the García Line of Cuba and manned with former Cuban naval personnel or American contract crews, were also overloaded with 30,000 to 40,000 gallons of aviation gasoline to sustain the air cover from the airfield at the Bay of Pigs, which, it was hoped, would be occupied immediately. Signals and coded messages between the ships were reduced to a bare minimum because experienced Americans were not allowed to be employed for this vital task. With air cover and numerous armed defectors purportedly assured, all that the invaders would have to do, they were cheerfully told by Frank Bender, was to go straight into Havana. After all, intelligence had officially predicted defectors rather than opposition to greet the landing Brigade.[21]

The CIA plan for minimal air cover over the landing had been more fully developed after the invasion beachhead was shifted from Trinidad to the Bay of Pigs, although, on the whole, the two plans were almost identical, since the same B-26s from Nicaragua would first hit the same three essential interior Cuban fields. While certain CIA planners favored preinvasion air strikes because these strikes would look more like the activity of Cuban defectors, the Joint Chiefs of Staff had replied with greater validity that any minor preinvasion air strikes either on $D-1$ or, still more, $D-2$ would be indecisive and would prematurely alert Castro's forces. The argument that such strikes would set off Castro's countermeasures, such as dispersion of Castro's planes or a roundup of the Cuban underground, was partially met by the CIA's private distrust of and lack of reliance upon the underground in any case.

Although Bissell himself had stated on April 6 that, like the Joint Chiefs of Staff and the U.S. Air Force, the agency had sensibly preferred an all-out strike on D-Day alone, the political advantages of concealing the American hand had led to the State Department's and Bundy's preference for premature and purported Cuban-based air strikes against Castro's air force. While a smaller $D-2$ strike would offer a more convincing cover for fraudulent Cuban defectors in order to account for an anti-Castro air force at all, the main air attack, even without the napalm which the CIA planners had realistically desired, was still scheduled for D-Day itself, but against enemy airfields and microwave communications only. Probably too few within, let alone outside of, the agency recalled the fiasco in Indonesia, when, to Eisenhower's great chagrin, the CIA's air support for the local rebels had turned out to be both inadequate and too obviously American for concealment. In any case, despite Bissell's recent claim that the agency had repeatedly made clear to the administration the essential importance of effective air cover, the point remains that the administration never understood until too late that effective air cover should include a major air strike on the Havana and Santiago fields on D-Day itself. Air cover over the beachhead alone simply would not be enough.

Thus, when on Saturday, April 15, or $D-2$, only six Cuban-manned planes out of the seventeen old B-26 bombers initially available at the Nicaragua base (excluding the two supposed defectors to Florida) staged their first strike without napalm on the three main Cuban airfields, not surprisingly their success was incomplete. The subsequent debriefing of their crews and a U-2 reconnaissance flight indicated that between 50 percent and 70 percent of Castro's air force had been taken out but that he still had left three or four of his T-33 jet trainers, three or four British Sea Fury fighters, and one or two of his own B-26 bombers. Of course, without any early air warning system and insufficient dispersion of his remaining planes, an all-out second strike could have taken out the survivors even without the advantage of surprise. But the American planners did not yet know how effective Castro's T-33 jet trainers, unexpectedly armed with 20-mm cannon, would prove on

D-Day, two days later.[22] Unfortunately, with this premature and weak $D-2$ air strike, the U.S. government would achieve many of the anticipated disadvantages of a new Pearl Harbor without gaining the decisive strategic advantages of that infamous surprise attack.

Moreover, as the State Department had feared, adverse publicity regarding the origin of the first air strike broke out immediately in the United Nations. There, with Soviet aid, the long-forewarned Cuban Foreign Minister Raúl Roa immediately set up an emergency session of the UN Political Committee on the same day as the raid. Roa promptly charged the United States government with "this act of imperialistic piracy" and went on to declare that the dawn air raid "undoubtedly" was "the prelude to a large-scale invasion attempt, organized, supplied and financed by the United States with the complicity of satellite dictatorships of the Western Hemisphere."[23]

Following frantic queries to the State Department, Adlai Stevenson, the principal American delegate to the United Nations, answered Roa in accord with both the CIA cover story and President Kennedy's argument that the CIA's Cuba project should appear to be no more than a struggle strictly between Cubans. Holding up photographs of the markings on two of the planes that had landed in Florida, Stevenson asserted—at this juncture in all innocence—that these two planes had "apparently defected from Castro's tyranny." No American planes or pilots had participated, Stevenson added with only slightly greater accuracy. Roa promptly rejoined that Cuba was expecting another air raid at any moment.[24]

As the CIA cover story began to crumble at its first exposure to daylight, Stevenson, on the advice of his professional Foreign Service deputies, began to sense that he had been betrayed. His efforts to find out from Rusk what actually was happening were further complicated by the temporary confusion of the equally mortified Secretary of State because of the fact that, in

addition to the two fraudulent defector planes provided by the
CIA, a third plane that had landed in Florida was that of a most
unexpected genuine defector. What was worse, differences
between the fraudulent CIA planes and the real Cuban plane
soon became apparent to the press, leaving Stevenson's shock
and Rusk's humiliation to be shared by President Kennedy and
the United States government in general. Not yet a bona-fide
liar on April 15, 1961, and belatedly briefed on the realities of
invasion only the next morning, Stevenson now became angry
and indignant. He would tell an aide that he had been deliberately tricked by his own government, thus leaving the
embarrassed Rusk in a position from which Rusk was unable
to justify further air strikes over Cuba.[25]

Although profoundly doubtful about his first major presidential decision, two hours after Bissell's official deadline for
the final Go–No Go deadline, Kennedy, with a heavy heart,
released the invading fleet approaching the Bay of Pigs. He
had been informed by Bundy that the planners saw no reason
to cancel the operation, perhaps because, with the landing craft
from Vieques, Puerto Rico, having joined the Brigade ships
from Nicaragua only thirty miles south of Cuba, it was almost
too late to call a halt without detection. But, contrary to Bissell's and Dulles's claims in retrospect, the whole operation
could still have been diverted to Puerto Rico even after the
final deadline. Indeed, this was Bissell's greatest fear.

Whether the President had heard Castro's speech delivered
at fever pitch on this same April 16 over the corpses of those
killed in the first strike remains doubtful. In that speech, Castro
called the raid Cuba's Pearl Harbor and accurately predicted
that its purpose was to destroy his air force as a possible prelude to an invasion by what he called American mercenaries—
that is, the volunters of the Cuban Brigade. Simultaneously,
he ordered mobilization of his 200,000-man revolutionary militia.
In his peroration, Castro concluded sanctimoniously: "If Pres-

ident Kennedy has one atom of decency, he will present the planes and pilots before the United Nations. If not, then the world has a right to call him a liar."[26]

Determined that, from that time forward at least, Stevenson should not have to lie before the United Nations, and recognizing the threat of the disintegrating CIA cover story to America's reputation at large, Rusk and Bundy resolved that any additional air attacks from outside Cuba beyond the beachhead area had to be stopped. And the two so informed the politically, if not militarily, aware Kennedy at Glen Ora, Virginia, where he was staying to play down the significance of the occasion. As Bundy put it long after the event, he himself did not know enough yet to go beyond a "beginner's credibility" and ask the CIA estimators below the level of the top agency advocates of the operation for their own personal judgments.[27]

Trusting his more moderate advisers, the President agreed to drop the second air strike scheduled to complete the destruction of Castro's air force on the morning of the landing, April 17. Bundy then went to New York to calm down the dismayed Stevenson, who was still discovering how badly he had been used. Stevenson did not resign, possibly because he was assured by both the President and Bundy that there would be no further conspicious air strikes on the Havana or Santiago fields.

Stunned by this abrupt and unexpected presidential decision, Bissell, on the evening of April 16, took General Cabell, Deputy Director of the CIA, with him to the State Department to protest Rusk. To the fury of the CIA air controllers, Cabell, though an air-force officer himself, at the very last minute had carefully refused to allow the planned D-Day strike to go through without Secretary Rusk's expressed approval. Like the President, Dulles was away from Washington, the better to be able to disclaim public responsibility for the operation; but, unlike Kennedy, Dulles was purportedly out of touch with his desperate subordinates in the Central Intelligence Agency on a cover speaking-trip to Puerto Rico. In reality, as he would put it in his private papers, during his official absence, "we believed that in a time of crisis we would gain what we might lose if we [had] provoked an argument earlier."[28]

Arguing through the night of April 16–17 with Rusk, Cabell and Bissell were unable to persuade the Secretary of State that the old freighters and landing craft could not be fully unloaded before dawn or that the Nicaraguan-based planes might not be established upon the beachhead airstrip before a serious air attack could take place on the invading ships. At the same time, it was too late to cancel the operation already unfolding on the shore. Rusk simply told Cabell and Bissell that overriding political factors transcended their military arguments. Stevenson had insisted that further air strikes would wreck the U.S. reputation at the United Nations. Instead of appealing directly to the President (as Rusk offered to permit from his office and as Bundy later claimed would have been effective), because they were impressed by the difficulties of Stevenson's position at the United Nations, a bitter Cabell and Bissell returned to CIA headquarters to disallow the second air strike, which was about to take off from its Nicaraguan base. By their impassioned arguments, Cabell and Bissell at least won the right to transfer the B-26 strikes from the major airfields to the beachhead, where the strikes were also essential to isolate the battlefield from Castro's tanks and artillery.

Bissell's appalled operations staff rightly considered this decision a disaster, as did the long-silent Admiral Burke when he learned of it the next morning. With some evidence from CIA records to substantiate him, Rusk consoled himself with the thought that the CIA still expected to pull off the invasion

and hold the beachhead for a time anyway, without nearly as
public a strike as one against the main Havana or Santiago
airfields would have been. In any case, the Rusk-Kennedy
decision did not prevent thirteen air missions from Nicaragua
by the B-26 bombers from providing inadequate air cover on
D-Day over the beachhead itself. After all, the top political figures of the administration could hardly be expected to know
of the deficiencies of an obsolete B-26 against even a prop fighter
plane. What was worse was that the old B-26s were operating
without even their usual tail gunners because of the gas
requirements for the long flight from Nicaragua. Thus, the
Brigade's B-26s were just sitting ducks against even the slower
prop fighters such as the Sea Furies, let alone jets like the T-
33 trainers. But the fact remained that the CIA attempt to whittle
down Kennedy's still-firm resolve against open American action
badly backfired against the whole operation when the agency
was faced with the brutal realities of the actual invasion. Other
last-minute damage-control measures by the CIA included
warning the Brigade ships to unload as much as possible at
night and then sending the now seriously endangered ships
fifty miles to sea during the next day. Unfortunately, owing to
the operation's weak logistics, this would prove only partially
possible.

It is more probable that Cabell and Bissell also feared that
when the President and Rusk woke up to how marginal affairs
actually were, they might still cancel the whole operation at
the moment of debarkation. In fact, later on Kennedy was to
regret not having done precisely this once it had become clear
to him that the original premises for the operation had been so
fundamentally altered by his own actions. In retrospect, Dulles
eventually came to regret having pushed the reluctant Kennedy into an operation that the President would drop at the
first opportunity rather than do what was necessary to make it
succeed. Significantly, unlike his desperate, lower-echelon

planners at the time, Dulles did not condemn Cabell or Bissell in either his private papers or public statements for not having gone far enough in pleading with the President at this decisive moment; but he did blame himself. After all, whatever his feelings, Dulles was a gentleman.

Thus, when at 4:30 A.M. on the day of the invasion General Cabell finally decided to appeal directly to the President at Glen Ora, Kennedy turned down a pathetic, last-minute suggestion by Bissell and General Lemnitzer for U.S. naval fighter cover (CAP) for the invasion while the Navy was still within international waters—from three miles offshore, if possible, to up to twelve miles offshore. Therefore, the naval air cover from the carrier *Essex* remained bound by the prior State Department restriction of air cover from the U.S. Navy up to only twenty miles offshore—in other words, too far out to protect the six unloading invasion ships offshore, let alone the landing craft at the vulnerable moment of beaching.

Nonetheless, these futile appeals to the President did signify the eagerness of the CIA, General Lemnitzer, and the U.S. Navy to overcome the inherent inadequacies of a covert scheme with the open commitment of American naval power, embodied in the *Essex*, in order to provide a substitute air cover against Castro's now more probably surviving air force. At least the seven American destroyers accompanying the *Essex* were authorized by the President to give the Brigade early warning of an aerial attack, as long as the destroyers and the *Essex* remained thirty miles offshore. But the further humiliation to the proud U.S. Navy in trying to conceal the nationality of U.S. crews, ships, planes, and pilots operating beyond the State Department's severe territorial limits simply compounded the hopeless incompatibilities of the whole operation.

In retrospect, Bissell has staked out an unofficial apolgia with the argument that he was mistaken only in not insisting upon all-out bombing of Cuban airfields. Like General Thomas White,

Chief of Staff of the Air Force during the secret official investigation by the Taylor committee in 1961, Bissell publicly
declared in 1965 that a second bombing strike might have made
a critical difference for the invasion attempt and added that, if
he had been able to dump five times the tonnage of bombs on
Castro's airfields, the agency would have had a damned good
chance for victory in the landing. General Taylor, however,
would not personally subscribe to this opinion in the future.
In Bissell's most optimistic scenario, with two B-26s based on
the captured Girón (Bay of Pigs) airfield, Castro's extensive
troop communication and transport system might be effectively halted. Here, the CIA theory was that, once their microwave transmission system was bombed out, Castro's troops
would be forced into voice communication, which the Americans could then overhear.

On the other hand, in 1967, Bissell privately was less certain
and more honest about the decisiveness of a second air strike,
if only because of the weakness of the sixteen- or seventeen-
plane Brigade air force, its insufficiency of pilots, and the more
than 600 miles between Nicaragua to Cuba, which required
about a seven-hour B-26 turnaround time for about one hour
over the target area. In 1967, Bissell conceded that such basic
factors had reduced the aerial striking force to the equivalent
of only one-and-a-half B-26s over the landing beachhead at
any given moment, as opposed to the much shorter turnaround time for Castro's planes from their Havana bases 100
miles away. In these circumstances, according to Cuban-based
testimony, the Brigade's weak air force did a remarkably good
job, a job sustained by U.S. General Dossiter's excellent ground
maintenance and armaments men in Nicaragua. Of course,
after the D-Day landing itself, the agency had accurately estimated that Castro would be down to only four or five operable
planes; but by then the damage had been done to the invasion
fleet.[29]

Bissell's second thoughts on the efficacy of air power may also have been prompted by the disappointing results of the Vietnam War between 1965 and 1967. In any case, even in 1961, that long-time admirer of American air power and more open advocate of American intervention, Vice-President Lyndon Johnson, had urged Kennedy to employ the U.S. Air Force to aid the Brigade. At that time, anticipating his future views on Vietnam, Johnson had said that the United State must "will the means" to victory over Castro.[30] In Vietnam, Johnson, too, would learn the inherent limitations of an infinitely greater air force against large and determined land forces.

A final argument on behalf of greater air support for the Cuba project remains in the CIA hope that such support would serve to commit the reluctant Kennedy sooner and more seriously to the project, when he realized both the impossibility of concealing such an open American hand and the enhanced chances of gaining enough time to set up a U.S.-recognized anti-Castro government on the beachhead. Such a government would then have to be rescued by open American intervention even before the risky three or four days on its own that were contemplated in the agency plans.[31] After all, to the CIA and perhaps to the United States Navy, if not to the State Department, the difference between their open intervention on $D+1$ and $D+4$ or $D+5$ must have seemed slight at best, and they could see little reason why an embarrassed but fighting President could not go along with it. Should this have been the true intention of Dulles and Bissell, they failed in their endeavor through being too clever by half. Any such deceptive scheme, based upon simultaneously outwitting both Kennedy and Castro, was too inherently ambitious to succeed, apart from its many other grave deficiencies.

VII
Bumpy Road

The [American] plan was to launch a force of . . . volunteers . . . as a rallying-point around which the Cuban people would rise. The first attempt was made in May of 1850; unfortunately, the Cuban people showed no inclination to rise, and it ended in a ludicrous fiasco![1] —*Walter Millis*

They will end up by putting me ashore with inadequate forces and get me in a serious jam. Then, who will take the blame?[2] —*General John Lucas before Anzio, 1944*

Frankly, I don't know how to conduct an amphibious operation in which the [Chinese Nationalist] troops fight and [the American naval] ships don't.[3] —*Admiral Forrest Sherman, 1951*

APART FROM their disappointment at discovering on the night of their landing, April 16–17, that their American destroyer escort would not be accompanying them after they were within twenty miles of Cuba, the invading Brigade members soon encountered other unpleasant surprises, aspects of the operation whose naval side was code-named "Bumpy Road." Fortunately for its self-respect, the Brigade never learned that in the event of detection and attack while still at sea, the U.S. Navy had orders to abandon the whole operation and convoy the would-be invaders willy-nilly to Puerto Rico. Although contrary to normal amphibious practice—or, for that matter, to the original Trinidad plan—the disembarkment now began at night in an obscure region for the sake of greater security; the invaders were detected even before landing, probably by a lighthouse on a key far offshore. Worse still, very bright lights bathed the landing beaches in a brilliant glare, although there were only a few militia in the immediate vicinity. Contrary to wishful anticipations, most of the local militia of poor charcoal workers proved both active and hostile, as did an unexpected regular infantry battalion recently placed nearby. Indeed, intelligence concerning the location of Castro's militia units had been poor, since the landing area was not, as hoped, virtually empty. The CIA was fairly accurate, however, with respect to Castro's two main regular forces, each of which comprised about 6,000 men. One of these units was about eighty miles east at Santa Clara and was armed with tanks and artillery. The CIA had estimated with some precision that the other unit, the Combined Force Occidente, could arrive at the beachhead within about ten hours from its base at Camp Libertad, over one hundred miles away in the vicinity of Havana.

Possibly by microwave radio from the beach militia, Castro was aroused sometime after 1:00 A.M. on April 17 with the news of the Brigade's arrival in the region of the Bay of Pigs. This, of course, may have contradicted CIA assurances that Castro had no direct communications with the beachhead. Still uncertain that this was to be the sole landing site, for several hours Castro held back some of his T-45 tanks and other higher-grade reserves at Camp Libertad, but a stream of unarmored convoys began heading for the beachhead from Havana. Only after he had received reports of parachute landings did Castro or his numerous Soviet bloc military advisers decide that Girón (as the Cubans called the Bay of Pigs) was the target for the main assault. Up to 100,000 suspects were in the process of being rounded up throughout Cuba to thwart any rising of the anti-Castro underground well before instructions for action could reach them from the CIA. According to both Dean Rusk and CIA Inspector General Lyman Kirkpatrick, with this hardly improbable action by Castro, the basic premise of the original Cuban invasion plan, which was meant to precipitate uprisings by its shock action, now lost its point. Consequently, the whole Cuban operation now should have been called off as rapidly as possible.

Unexpected coral reefs, which the CIA had not cared to hear about from either the better-informed U.S. Navy or Marine Corps, delayed or thwarted the inefficiently run, old landing craft and their thirty-six badly maintained small aluminum boats in their attempts to approach the Blue Beach at Girón, where there was immediate resistance. At least the landing beaches were fairly well marked by specially trained CIA teams. Like much of the heavier matériel employed by the CIA, the landing craft had been procured at the last minute in any which way and were old, in order to help conceal the American hand in the invasion. In any event, all but one of the smaller boats broke down, notwithstanding initial American maintenance. Logistically, the lack of proper amphibious control or planning—including the provision of only one crane for unloading supplies without the benefit of the Trinidad docks, the lack of floodlights for night operations once Castro's own beach lights were destroyed, and failure to assign landing officers to establish truck control on the beaches or to provide any bridging capacity for an advance inland through the swamps—proved so disastrous that one expert had stated in the original Joint Chiefs of Staff evaluation that the operation was likely to collapse for these reasons alone. Almost as serious, the failure of one of the parachute drops to land near enough to cut the main road to the Playa Larga at Palpite left this vital route wide open for Castro's immediate counterattack with several thousand militia and regulars. Castro was well aware of his urgent need to wipe out the beachhead before a provisional government could be established there. Not unusually, the parachutists had been fired upon by their own trigger-happy Brigade while dropping up to sixteen miles inland as highly essential blocking forces and, as is also customary in such operations, had lost much of their parachuted ammunition in the surrounding swamps.

Most shocking of all, from shortly after dawn, the slow old ships of the invaders, protected only by machine guns that were grudgingly granted to their alarmed crews by the originally optimistic CIA planners and loaded to the gunwales with green men, ammunition, and high-octane aviation gasoline in incompatible juxtaposition, came under repeated aerial attack from the few but vigorous aircraft that had survived the small B-26 raid on D − 2. Under Vice-Admiral Dennison's and Rear Admiral John Clark's current rules of engagement, U.S. naval air cover was still twenty miles offshore. Castro—or his Soviet-bloc advisers—thus could make the courageous and correct decision to concentrate Cuban planes against the vital enemy ships and landing craft rather than to cover his poorly protected infantry in the vicinity, infantry that initially lacked the antiaircraft guns still in Havana. Before the largely untrained and badly commanded Fifth Battalion of the Brigade could be induced to disembark, the *Houston* was crippled by several attacks by Castro's few still-undamaged, rocket-equipped T-33s and Sea Furies, but managed to ground only about sixty yards from shore. Fortunately, the machine guns were now in place on the invading ships, contrary to the original CIA plan that none would be needed since Castro was not supposed to have any planes left on D-Day. Less fortunately, those demoralized men of the Fifth Battalion who could be persuaded to swim ashore without their weapons found themselves several miles from the Second Battalion, already ashore at the Red Beach at Playa Larga, and thus were unable to reinforce it before Castro's counterattack. Without most of its ammunition and heavy supplies, the Second Battalion was left alone with only 270 men and two days' supply of ammunition to meet a desperate assault, supposedly ordered by Castro himself. This took place with 800 soldiers and 12 tanks at about 3:00 P.M., or the time estimated by the CIA for the arrival of Castro's estimated 12,000 regular troops stationed in the nearby Havana and Santa Clara regions. Unhappily, the poor fire discipline characteristic of the untried Brigade resulted in such an excessive consumption of what ammunition remained that the Second Battalion actually ran out of ammunition on D-Day itself.

Less than three hours after the sinking of the *Houston* at about 9:00 A.M., a ship on which all the vital enciphering equipment had been placed, the *Rio Escondido*, off the Blue Beach at Girón, blew up under air attack. Consequently, orders in the clear arrived from distant Washington at about 2:00 P.M., permitting the *Atlantico*, which held the remaining communication equipment, and the other surviving ships and landing craft to retire from the beach area to a safe haven about fifteen miles offshore, where carrier aircraft now were allowed to protect them. Although Washington had only poor direct communications with the beachhead, there could be neither a command ship nor a fully empowered commander on the spot, since such decisions might necessarily involve more open American intervention without the distant President's knowledge, let alone consent.

Although some of the Brigade's ships finally did halt at about twice the authorized distance from the landing beaches because they lacked Americans on board with enough authority to stop them earlier, the *Atlantico* and the *Caribe*, unbeknownst to Washington, fled without answering radio calls so much farther south in to the Caribbean than authorized that the U.S. Navy could not round them up in time to unload the supplies of the *Caribe* during the second night of the invasion. Still worse, the reluctant *Blagar* and other ships, which did turn about when ordered to do so by the navy, steamed so slowly that they were unable to reach the beaches before dawn and thus were also unable to supply the Brigade in the darkness before they were again withdrawn far offshore. Finally, the contract skipper of the *Blagar* reported something of a mutiny aboard ship unless he could obtain an American destroyer escort or air cover, since his crew had been demoralized by the rebellious survivors of the sunken *Rio Escondido*, whom they had picked up earlier. The *Escondido* survivors were finally subdued by force after they had stopped the *Blagar*'s engines. Unable to extort either an escort or air cover from the White House, the CIA finally gave up all attempts to bring in the desperately needed ammunition by sea, although inadequate and widely dispersed air drops made during the night largely benefited Castro's troops in the vicinity.[4]

As Secretary Rusk was firmly informing a press conference on the morning of April 17 that the United States had no intention of intervening in the Cuban affair, Schlesinger was telling the Washington Bureau of *The New York Times* that the landing force consisted only of 200 or 300 men who were there solely to bring supplies to the Cuban underground. Under the growing influence of the tougher Robert Kennedy rather than that of Dean Rusk, however, the President began to modify his stop order against more air raids on the interior airfields. Because of the rapid loss of four planes, trying vainly to cover the beachheads, to Castro's fast T-33 jet trainer fighters, Kennedy now permitted three B-26s to bomb at dawn on the morning of April 18 the dangerous San Antonio de los Baños airfield near Havana in an effort to destroy the no-longer-underestimated T-33s and the British Sea Fury bombers. Castro's remaining planes had been concentrated at only the two fields near Havana to maximize their time over the Bay of Pigs and, therefore, constituted better targets. But the Brigade air headquarters in Nicaragua was distracted by conflicting calls for aid to the embattled beachheads at the same time.

Obviously, as Dulles would admit after the event, Castro's air force had turned out to be far more efficient in its deployment, if not larger, than expected. Its courageous and skillful pilots may have already been drawn from the 50 or more being trained in Czechoslovakia for the dreaded Soviet MiGs. On the other hand, unknown to the President, when some of the exhausted Brigade air crews refused to fly again, the CIA in Nicaragua began planning to replace them with American contract pilots for the last desperate flights over Cuba.

Unfortunately, heavy morning haze aborted the April 18 mission over Castro's interior airfields, and thus his rapidly diminishing but aggressive air force was left active for another day of bombing, hereafter directed at the poorly supplied invaders themselves rather than at their now-distant ships. On the afternoon of April 18, the Brigade's B-26s encountered and claimed to have destroyed some twenty enemy tanks. But the Red Beach had already been wiped out, while the remaining Blue Beach was being attacked by twelve tanks and four jet planes. As the *coup de grâce,* Castro's effective Soviet-supplied field artillery was at last in action. According to Castro's own account, at least, he was personally shelled by his own armor while trying to get a tank in position to fire on one of the already abandoned ships of the invaders. At any rate, unlike the administration in distant Washington, Castro was not attempting to mastermind operations without much idea of what was actually happening on the spot.

At a dismal luncheon with his unhappy sympathizers—James Reston of *The New York Times* and Arthur Schlesinger—Kennedy observed that he had probably made a mistake in retaining Allen Dulles as Director of Central Intelligence on the grounds that, as a new President, he could not correctly estimate the true meaning of such a legendary figure as Dulles. In fact, to get the exact pitch on CIA, the President now claimed that his brother Robert would be the right man to head the agency. A bitter Kennedy concluded, taking a line his administration would after repeat: "It is a hell of a way to learn things, but I have learned one thing from this business . . . McNamara has dealt with Defense; Rusk has done a lot with State, but no one has dealt with C.I.A."[5] At least the dismayed President was right in the last part of his lament—no one had yet dealt with the Central Intelligence Agency.

Part of Kennedy's exploding rage was, no doubt, evoked by a strong note that he received that morning from Premier Khrushchev of the Soviet Union. With a good case, the Soviet Premier laid it on the line: "It is not a secret to anyone that the armed bands which invaded that country [Cuba] have been trained, equipped and armed in the United State of America. The planes which bomb Cuban cities belong to the United States of America, the bombs they drop have been made available by the American Government. . . . We shall render to Cuban people and their Government all necessary assistance in beating back the armed attack on Cuba."

Hastily dictating his answer himself, Kennedy stated that he planned no direct American military intervention in Cuba, but that should the Soviet Union do so, the United States would immediately honor her "obligations" to protect the Western Hemisphere against "external aggression." The President went out of his way to express the hope that Khrushchev would not employ the invasion as a pretext "to inflame other areas of the world" (such as Berlin, in particular) in order to thwart the United States on Cuba.[6] How much more Kennedy's statement committed him not to intervene with U.S. forces as long as the Soviets did not do so remains a matter of conjecture.

Late on the evening of April 18, after the annual congressional reception of the White House, matters came to a head.
Representing the now thoroughly discredited agency in Dulles's continued absence, and fully aware that this crisis could
lead to open American intervention, Bissell made a plea for
what had always been inherent in his and Dulles's interpretation of the CIA plan—namely, direct American air support from
the U.S. naval detachment offshore. Like Bundy, the more
cautious General Lemnitzer now openly joined Admiral Burke
in supporting Bissell's last effort to take out Castro's air force.

Burke also begged for the employment of a large 1,500-man
U.S. Marine battalion on the aircraft carrier *Essex* offshore,
along with a single American destroyer to help the embattled
Brigade. Unfortunately, as Lemnitzer later conceded, it was
no longer just a question of saving the invasion with American
intervention; it was now a question of whether the U.S. Navy
could hope to rescue the defeated invaders alone. In Kennedy's subsequent aside to an intimate, the Joint Chiefs of Staff
may have also hoped that the inexperienced President would
panic and try to save his own face with a last-minute open
intervention. Kennedy then concluded that if that were the
case, the Joint Chiefs "had me figured all wrong."[7] They were
certainly not the only people to underestimate the new President.

Opposed by Rusk and McNamara, Bissell, Burke, and Lemnitzer had to settle for another weak compromise by the President, a one-hour, six-plane U.S. naval air cover over the
disintegrating beachhead to protect the Brigade's B-26s by
interposing the American planes between the two contending
Cuban air forces. Kennedy did not even grant this so-called
naval CAP the right to fire at Castro's planes unless the American planes were attacked, but the CIA still told the Brigade

commander, Pepe San Román, that air cover would be for the duration of the whole operation. Rusk opposed even allowing unmarked amphibious craft with U.S. naval crews in dungarees to go close inshore to pick up the uncaptured remnants of the escaping Brigade from their widely scattered beachhead pockets stretching over 36 miles. At this point, as fed up with Rusk's denial of U.S. participation in the invasion as Admiral Burke was with Kennedy's restraints, the President raised his hand to just below his nose and said that the United States was already involved up to that particular part of his anatomy. Kennedy then authorized Bissell, but not the U.S. Navy, to help the Brigade to escape in any way it could, either by land or by sea. Unfortunately, for fear of discouraging the Brigade, the CIA had not really told Brigade leaders any of the supposed plans for escape to the Escambrays, leaving only the sea route as a way out.

Even though well before the invasion the increasingly pessimistic CIA planners had discussed, but not made plans for, the sticky possibility of a primary evacuation by sea, they had done so without informing Admirals Burke or Dennison, whose naval forces would have to do the work. Although the prescient Dennison had made some unofficial preparations for this notoriously difficult operation of war, Burke was still under the impression that the guerrilla option in the Escambrays remained the primary escape option. Nonetheless, even under Kennedy's latest relaxation of the naval rules of engagement against the exposure of the American hand on April 19, at the end only two U.S. destroyers were authorized to go closer than two miles offshore at night or five miles in the daytime. In pursuit of their new so-called humanitarian rescue mission, the destroyers might return fire on Castro's field artillery with its range being three miles from the beaches. Consequently, only a few men from the escaping Brigade could be picked up by boats, and these were mostly from the small uninhibited keys off the coast. Fortunately, Castro and his subordinates were equally careful not to allow either Cuban planes or artillery to fire at the unidentified but only too obviously American destroyers offshore, however fiercely they pounded the small boats plying to and from the beachhead.

As usual, without realizing it, Kennedy had gone further in his latest commitment than he had sought, because most of the seventeen demoralized and exhausted Cuban Brigade pilots of the surviving B-26s now refused to fly over the vanishing beachhead without bona-fide American air support. Instead, and without the President's knowledge, four of their places in two B-26s were taken by American volunteers from the air base at Nicaragua. Because of poor coordination and communication among the several divided commands of General Gray and the CIA in Washington, the Brigade's base in Nicaragua, and the U.S. Naval Command off Cuba and in Norfolk, the few B-26s still attacking Castro's most effective Soviet howitzers on the morning of April 19 arrived ahead of their brief naval air cover from the *Essex*. In another humiliating occurrence, the four volunteer American airmen were shot down and killed, probably by Castro's now numerous and accurate antiaircraft guns, thus invalidating the administration's last pretense that the United States was not involved in the invasion. By this stage, the Brigade's air losses had amounted to nine B-26s, or more than half of its total. No wonder its Cuban pilots were refusing to fly.

Not surprisingly, one of the conclusions reached by the Taylor commission was that only a unified U.S. task-force commander in a well-equipped command ship on the spot could really have conducted any effective amphibious operation—a truism of the Second World War. As it was, communications between the U.S. ships offshore and the Cuban invasion ships in their immediate vicinity were conducted only with the greatest difficulty, owing to the different and unknown radio circuits used by the CIA and the Navy.[8]

With little ammunition or air support, the virtually abandoned men of the demoralized Brigade began to surrender in the late afternoon of April 19 in the face of incessant attacks by about 20,000 well-armed Castro militia and regular troops. By now even the airstrip near the beachhead was under artillery fire, thus cutting off the previous locally based B-26 air defense, normally of two planes. At last the original order for the Brigade, which had forbidden heading for the swamps in the event of defeat, was rescinded, although the previously unprepared men who had fled there were soon captured despite the original training of about 25 percent of the Brigade in guerrilla warfare. This came as a great shock to the President and Lemnitzer, and may explain some of the otherwise absurd restrictions on Dennison's rescue efforts.

In the end, of approximately 1,300 men who had actually landed on the beaches from the Brigade, almost 1,200 were captured and about 100 killed in combat. The last-minute claim of the Cuban Revolutionary Council in Miami that most of the invaders had fled to the Escambrays was clearly exposed as fraudulent as most of the other strident proclamations made in its name by the New York public-relations firm engaged by the CIA during the landing.[9]

That night in Washington, the President personally broke the news of the defeat to the indignant and confused members of the Cuban Revolutionary Council, whose leader, Miró Cardona, still demanded the force of 10,000 to 15,000 Americans he felt had been promised to him in support of the invasion. For the moment, Kennedy agreed to sustain the council with the resources of the United States government only in noninvasion activities. Perhaps this would eliminate the council's embarrassing public complaints in the future. Liberated at last from their house arrest by the CIA in order to prevent leaks during the actual landing in Cuba, the distraught members of the council would eventually come to believe that, in the misleading words of Castro, "Kennedy was the only President with the courage to change his mind" about invading Cuba.[10]

Meanwhile, however, in a fighting speech the next day to the American Society of Newspaper Editors, Kennedy officially warned the Soviet Union that "we do not intend to be lectured on 'intervention' by those whose character was stamped for all time on the bloody streets of Budapest." Kennedy's blunt warning did not seem to have much effect on Khrushchev, who told his staff that the young President lacked a strong backbone and would not stand up to a serious challenge in the future, whether it be in the Caribbean or elsewhere. More immediate in its implications was the President's admission that "there are from this sobering episode useful lessons for us all to learn. Some may be obscure and wait further information. Some are clear today. . . . We intend to re-examine and re-orient our forces of all kinds—our tactics and our institutions here in this community." To Bundy, however, the errors of the Cuban project had been only tactical; Ché Guevara, Bundy told his staff, had learned more from the Guatemala episode in 1954 than had the United States.[11] The point, however, was that Bundy would not learn from the Bay of Pigs to oppose gradual Vietnamese escalation.

That same April 20, appealing for support from Richard Nixon, his recently defeated rival for the presidency, Kennedy was told by the latter to send the U.S. Marines into Cuba under whatever legal pretext he could muster in order to overthrow Castro. Possibly excited by the dismayed confusion of Dulles, who had finally been driven to return to Washington with a bad case of gout to see the President on what Dulles called "the worst day" of his (Dulles's) life, Nixon remained true to his early hard line against Castro, who, Nixon felt, was a "dangerous threat" to the United States. Less eager than ever for any further expansion of the operation, Kennedy answered Nixon, as he would similar pleas by Dulles and Senator Barry Goldwater, by asserting that Khrushchev was in "a very cocky mood" and might compensate for a Castro defeat by going into Berlin as a result. Two days later, upon seeing Kennedy, Eisenhower himself would deny the logic of this particular excuse for inaction, but Kennedy persisted in trying to conceal the American hand long after it could no longer be denied. Dulles could only tell Nixon that he (Dulles) had made the greatest mistake of his life in not informing Kennedy earlier that Kennedy could not afford to fail at the Bay of Pigs.[12] Dulles, indeed, had misjudged his President.

Likewise significant for the future, Nixon was also then willing to push the Democrats into an American military intervention in Laos, as they were still being urged to do this same week by Walt Rostow, Arleigh Burke, and the U.S. Air Force in SEATO Plan No. 5. National communism, at least outside of Europe, was still Richard Nixon's enemy even at the moment of his political rival's profound humiliation on the same issue. But the embittered and disillusioned President replied: "I don't see how we can make any move into Laos, which is thousands of miles away, if we don't make a move in Cuba, which is only ninety miles away." Just the same, still trying to retain Indochina, Kennedy ordered the American military advisers in Laos to put on their uniforms this same April 20.[13] They would not shed them for the next fourteen years.

At last permitted to see the "shattered" President, Undersecretary of State Chester Bowles attended three highly emotional meetings of the National Security Council from April 20 to April 24. There, the idealistic Bowles did his best to resist the various savage schemes of revenge against Castro cooked up by the humiliated hawks. To the fury of Robert Kennedy, Bowles urged that the President not allow matters to degenerate into a personal contest with the Cuban leader. Rusk, however, had already opposed the suggestion of Charles ("Chip") Bohlen of the State Department to send in American troops. Bowles recorded on the evening of April 20: "What worries me is that two of the most powerful people in this Administration—Lyndon Johnson and Bob Kennedy—have no experience in foreign affairs, and yet they realize this is the central question of this period and are determined to be experts at it. When a newcomer enters the field and finds himself confronted by the nuances of international questions, he becomes an easy target for the military–C.I.A.–paramilitary-type answers which can be added, subtracted, multiplied or divided. This type of thinking was almost dominant in today's conference, and I found it damning. The President appeared by all odds to be the most calm, yet it was clear that he had been suffering from an acute shock and it was an open question in my mind as to what his ultimate reaction would be."[14]

An eventual presidential reaction in this era, which McNamara would admit was hysterial about Castro, was the decision by Kennedy and the Special Group in the autumn of 1961 to resume covert "plans to get rid of Castro." As Richard Helms subsequently testified, assassinations would once again become acceptable "because nobody had any stomach anymore for any invasions or any military fiascos" of the Bay of Pigs type. By this period, the President can hardly have been unaware of the CIA plans for assassination, as is implied in his secret interview with reporter Tad Szulc on November 7, 1961. At this interview, Kennedy asked Szulc: "What would you think if I ordered Castro to be assassinated?" When Szulc disapproved of the suggestion, the President professed to agree with Szulc "completely."[15]

At least for some time, however, immediately following the fiasco at the Bay of Pigs, orders went out from Washington to forbid the CIA to assist further in the planned assassination of President Trujillo of the Dominican Republic (Operation Emoth). Hardly by coincidence, agency light arms for this project had already arrived in the Dominican Republic on April 19 during the Bay of Pigs, and the countermanding of the orders by President Kennedy himself on May 29 could not prevent Trujillo's murder by the local opposition on May 30, 1961.

Although all CIA personnel were hastily removed from the Dominican Republic, it goes without saying that no U.S. officials involved were censured in any way by the belatedly alarmed Kennedy administration, let alone by the agency. In fact, the assassination of Trujillo would eventually be resoundingly described in CIA documents as a "success" for Western democracy in its struggle against totalitarian dictatorships.[16] Indeed, Bowles would harm himself with the administration by successfully opposing an open American intervention in the Dominican Republic. At least notwithstanding such alleged successes for democracy, on May 29 President Kennedy had informed the CIA that "as a matter of general policy" the United States "cannot condone assassination."[17] More accurately, Kennedy had feared a Communist takeover in the Dominican Republic in the event of Trujillo's assassination, but the agency had certainly followed its own policy as long as possible here without fully informing or fully obeying its superiors.

VIII
The Perfect Failure

For some time I have been disturbed by the way C.I.A. has been diverted from its original assignment [of centralized intelligence]. It has become an operational and at times a policy-making arm of the government.[1] —*Harry Truman, 1963*

I have made a tragic mistake. Not only were our facts in error, but our policy was wrong because the premises on which it was built were wrong.[2] —*President Kennedy to Clark Clifford after the Bay of Pigs, April 1961*

Not only was top level organization [in Vietnam] diffuse and chaotic to the point that nobody and everybody was in charge, but an entire regular command structure designed for conventional warfare was transplanted into a guerrilla environment for where it was not suitable.[3] —*Martin van Creveld*

*V*ICTORY," observed John Kennedy a few days after the resounding failure of the Cuban project, "has a hundred fathers, and defeat is an orphan." Indeed, as the President would remark dourly in his first post-mortem following the Bay of Pigs: "There is only one person in the clear—that's Bill Fulbright. And he probably would have been converted if he had attended more of the meetings." With his usual candor, Admiral Burke has admitted that at this stage Kennedy did not believe anybody and that he should not have done so.

If the virtual unanimity of the President's carefully selected professional advisers on the Bay of Pigs served to alert Attorney General Robert Kennedy to the need for a devil's advocate opposing established intelligence opinion in the future, the President's bitterness especially welled out against the Central Intelligence Agency. Recognizing that his administration could not survive another fiasco as flagrant as the Bay of Pigs, Kennedy was reported as initially desiring "to splinter" the agency into "a thousand pieces and scatter it to the winds."[4] Calming down, the President decided that he would investigate the causes of the CIA's failure and "get it under control" for the future. In addition to feeling a personal responsibility for the failure, Kennedy had decided to discourage bureaucratic recriminations as much as possible.[5]

A few days later, a sharp critic of compulsive American interventionism abroad, the liberal U.S. Ambassador to India John Kenneth Galbraith wrote of the Bay of Pigs that he hoped Kennedy would not be "too forgiving of those who led him astray." "Unfortunately," concluded Galbraith, "the man who makes a mistake usually has a certain commitment to those who got him into it. He shared their bad judgment; he must, accordingly, share their excuses and apologies and in a measure accept them." Nevertheless, according to the well-informed Thomas Powers, President Kennedy's chief motive in appointing his highly questionable investigating committee was really to find a better method of removing Castro rather than just to ascertain why the operation had gone wrong.[6]

Whatever his reasons, Kennedy chose both Allen Dulles and Admiral Arleigh Burke, Chief of Naval Operations, as members under the chairmanship of the previously uninvolved General Maxwell Taylor. Attorney General Robert Kennedy was the fourth member of what was variously called the Green committee or Taylor's Cuba Study Group. Of the group's members, Dulles had been among the principal advocates of the fiasco. Burke, if critical of the President's casual administrative practices, remained a strong anti-Castro man. Taylor was an intimate of Dulles in the White House and subsequently a hawk on Vietnam. Since the fourth member was his passionately loyal brother, the President was clearly taking few chances of allowing hostile hands to get hold of this exceedingly vulnerable issue.[7] And hostile hands were to be found everywhere, the CIA's office of National Estimates itself commenting savagely on the "widespread conception of confusion and contradiction in U.S. policy and action and some fears of irresponsibility on the part of the C.I.A."[8]

Hereafter, Robert Kennedy would remain as his badly burned brother's only nominal watchdog on the CIA because, in George Ball's phrase, the quickly seduced and hawkish "Bobby . . . always used to go to the 303 [5412 Special Group] Committee; he was fascinated by all that covert stuff, counter-insurgency and all the garbage that went with it."[9] Indeed, according to Admiral Dennison, the Attorney General tried to have the records of the fiasco destroyed. But, notwithstanding his abrupt conversion to agency values rather than to its reform, it was not until May 1962 that Robert Kennedy was officially informed of the agency's attempts to assassinate Castro before the Bay of Pigs. Significantly, by then his only reaction was to complain about the CIA's lack of consultation with him, and the use of the Mafia in these attempts rather than what the Senate Select Committee would later call the impropriety of the attempts themselves. Robert Kennedy's reaction may be accounted for, in part, by the fact that he had himself come to favor renewed covert action against Cuba. Eventually, to be sure, following Lyndon Johnson's involvement in Vietnam, Robert Kennedy, like so many others, confessed: "I have myself wondered at times if we did not pay a very great price for being more energetic than wise about a lot of things, especially Cuba."[10]

Perhaps, in part, for such personal reasons, Taylor's Cuba committee construed its mandate to investigate the operation narrowly, focusing upon the technical rather than the more important political failures of the operation. To his subsequent avowed amazement, Taylor was not informed of the CIA assassination plans, and neither Dulles nor Bissell chose of his own accord to point out this omission any more than each had made sufficiently clear so many other painful but crucial problems to the President before the Bay of Pigs. The Taylor committee concluded that almost all the resources for the Zapata or Bay of Pigs project were inadequate for a contested as opposed to an almost unresisted landing, and further stated that the President should have been made more aware of the significance of the cancellation of the second air strike, since, contrary to his information from the agency, there was no possibility of turning the Brigade into a guerrilla force following a defeat. For the future, the Taylor committee recommended that the CIA be responsible only for covert political action, leaving large-scale and undisclaimable paramilitary activities to the adequately staffed and commanded Pentagon. The President implemented this recommendation on June 28 with results that were none too satisfactory in Vietnam, as his Republican successor Richard Nixon would complain in the future. Nor was it ever applied in Laos, as agency Director William Colby has justifiably observed.[11]

In the last analysis the Taylor committee felt that a combat landing probably could have been pulled off with open American intervention. Failing that, the committee now courageously concluded that it would have been better to have called it off entirely while still in the planning stages. Furthermore, the project suffered both from absentee control from distant Washington as well as from the hopelessly inadequate communications surviving Castro's bombing. Even those had to be improvised by the resourceful but unofficial CIA man at the beachhead, Grayston Lynch. As we have seen, the President would never permit the assignment of a fully empowered American commander to be on the spot, let alone an adequately equipped U.S. command and communications ship. Finally, the Taylor committee observed that, despite their disclaimer of responsibility, the Joint Chiefs of Staff had never made their preference for the Trinidad alternative sufficiently clear because of their too easy acquiescence in the Zapata–Bay of Pigs plan. Apart from this particular criticism, General Taylor had great difficulty persuading Admiral Burke to go along with any blame at all of his fellow colleagues on the Joint Chiefs of Staff. Failures in intelligence, shocking as they were, were not deemed serious, and the committee did not investigate in depth the delicate fact that the anti-Castro underground was being rounded up even before the landing started.

Notwithstanding unwanted efforts by Bowles and Schlesinger to combine the research functions of the CIA and the State Department in a single organization totally separated from the CIA's clandestime operations, both the Taylor and Killian committees, in addition to Dulles and Rusk, successfully opposed such a politically explosive proposal. While no such basic changes were made in the agency's organizational inheritance from General Donovan's Office of Strategic Services, by 1976 the Senate Select Committee on Intelligence Activities would recommend a variation of such a change. Unfortunately, a fundamental criticism of the agency at the Bay of Pigs already was that of excessive compartmentalization for security purposes, and a still wider divorce of intelligence from operations would only accentuate this failing.

To be sure, within a few months, both the State Department and the CIA were to face a new bureaucratic threat when the perennially innocent Defense Secretary Robert McNamara—still smarting over having been first misled by the President and the CIA about Cuba and then blamed for the debacle—on August 1, 1964, set up the politically more acceptable Defense Intelligence Agency, which combined the branches of the three military services. This agency, which consequently embraced most of the intelligence community, now reported directly to the Secretary of Defense rather than being under the control of the no-longer-fully-trusted Joint Chiefs of Staff, thus giving the inexperienced McNamara and President another source for evaluation of any proposed operation.[12] Since the President found the Joint Chiefs frequently in disagreement and in any case no longer respected its Chairman, General Lemnitzer, because of Lemnitzer's role in the Bay of Pigs fiasco, McNamara allowed Kennedy's new military representative in the White House, General Maxwell Taylor, to report for the Joint Chiefs for the time being, pending Taylor's own appointment as Chairman of the Joint Chiefs of Staff the next year. Unhappily, the establishment of a larger but inefficient rival to the Central Intelligence Agency led only to McNamara's disappointment in his new Defense Intelligence Agency and eventual reacceptance of CIA intelligence to alleviate his own future errors in Vietnam. Moreover, this proliferation of the intelligence jungle hardly served to resolve the CIA's failure adequately to sever the evaluation of intelligence from its responsibility for even the small-scale covert operations still permitted it, let alone to compensate for the CIA's failure to exercise minimal centralization of the whole intelligence community.

The President's order of May 29, emphasizing that all CIA activities in the field were subject to oversight and coordination by American Ambassadors abroad, remained in some cases no more than a polite fiction because of the reluctance of both the State Department and many of the politically appointed Ambassadors to implement it. In addition, the Ambassadors were given no direct authority over the agency Station Chiefs in their respective countries. Thus, the only nonagency control over clandestine services overseas remained largely a dead letter, leading to the disastrous renewal of Ambassadors' authority by President Nixon in 1969 in time for the resultant Vietnam evacuation fiasco of 1975. In short, there may be no organizational solution for certain intelligence dilemmas.

As recommended by the Taylor committee, the former 5412 Special Group—now renamed the 303 committee and eventually the 40 committee—would be strengthened by President Kennedy with a permanent membership and staff, and a more vigorous role in planning and reviewing covert operations. It remained, however, at the subcabinet level under the chairmanship of Special Assistant McGeorge Bundy but with the Director of the CIA and the Chairman of the Joint Chiefs as standing members. Unfortunately, if, in the overstated words of the Senate Select Committee in 1976, this committee prevented the agency from getting "out of control"—that is, out of control of the President and the National Security Council—it often met irregularly and remained as deliberately nonaccountable for its actions as the President himself, at least until 1974.[13] Moreover, the frequent bypassing of the 40 committee by both the President and CIA, as well as the continued weakness of its staff, could render ineffective even this active and reasonably powerful watchdog over the agency.

In reality, as Richard Helms, a later Director of Central Intelligence, described a function of the Special Group or of the 303 or 40 committees in the period before 1974, "nobody wants to embarrass a President of the United States by dis-

cussing the assassination of foreign leaders in his presence."
Therefore, according to Helms, the Special Group was "the
mechanism that was set up . . . to use as a circuit breaker so
that these things did not explode in the President's face . . .
[and so] that he was not held responsible for them."[14] The
Operations Coordinating Board of the Eisenhower era, as well
as the Foreign Intelligence Advisory Board, the latter soon to
be revived after having been briefly allowed to lapse by Kennedy before the Bay of Pigs, may also have served as such
circuit breakers to protect the bureaucratic rear of the experienced old Eisenhower. The trouble is that organizations set up
to conceal responsibility, as in the case of those of Eisenhower
or Kennedy, for attempted assassinations or covert invasions,
may themselves be inherently irresponsible.

In one respect, however, there had to be some public change.
With refreshing candor, President Kennedy told his personal
friend, Richard Bissell, that had the United States been run
by a cabinet government as in Great Britain, he would have
had to resign over the failure at the Bay of Pigs. Instead, under
the requirements of a four-year presidential rule, he would have
to demand Bissell's resignation in the next year as well as that
of Allen Dulles and of General Cabell as the three principals
responsible for the operation within the Central Intelligence
Agency. Bissell's Clandestine Operations unit was supposed to
be purged and converted into a support branch for the agency,
no longer starring in its too spectacular role as the all-powerful
action unit. President Ydígora of Guatemala also may have been
forced to resign in 1963 as a result of Kennedy's embarrassment over the Bay of Pigs.

In the uninhibited words of Robert Amory, Deputy Director
of Intelligence of the agency, for the future "a C-team" should
no longer be employed in major operations of this kind. Such
incorrigible romantics as E. Howard Hunt, of sensational

incompetence in the Watergate raid of 1972, are examples of
the type of personnel often used in projects like the Cuban
operation, notwithstanding Allen Dulles's direct orders to employ
a first-class group of men for this project. Still worse, it is probable that Hunt may again have been employed in the Domestic Operations Division on one of several still more absurd minor
projects to harass Cuba under Lyndon Johnson in the mid-
1960s, projects that were finally aborted by the far greater folly
of the Vietnam War after 1965. But, of course, Hunt was even
employed by Dulles to assist him on the in-house agency
investigation of the operation after its failure—as remarkable
an example of Dulles's poor judgment of his subordinates as
can be found. No wonder that, in his own tougher investigation, Kirkpatrick was particularly shocked by this appointment.

In Amory's terms again, it was actually "a strange bunch of
people, roughnecks" of European and Asian background "with
absolutely no sense or feel about political sensitivities of the
people" in Latin America who actually carried out the orders
of the Deputy Director of Plans. Significantly, Bissell's own
deputy and successor, the cautious if equally evasive Richard
Helms, had successfully managed to disclaim any responsibility for the Cuba operation. The disapproving Colonel King had
simply been shunted aside. In accordance with the long-
standing rivalry between the Deputy Director of Plans and the
Deputy Director of Intelligence, Amory himself, Bissell's theoretical equal in the bureaucratic hierarchy of the agency, was
not officially informed or consulted at all, although actually,
like Roger Hilsman in the State Department, he had learned a
good deal about it and had vainly offered his help.[15]

Significantly, the same bifurcation within the agency would
continue to be condoned a decade later during the elimination
of Allende in Chile. As would be observed in the Final Senate

Report in 1976: "The existence of this enforced isolation between the two Directorates negated the potential advantages of having collectors and analysts in the same Agency."[16] In such circumstances, it is less surprising that the available French and British intelligence reports on the effectiveness of Castro's control over Cuba were not employed by the CIA. As Michael Howard has put it, "The security profession . . . suffers in all nations from a *déformation professionnelle* that secrecy can only make worse. Without the scrutiny of critical eyes and independent judgments, security operatives and those who control them, working in their isolated and twilit world, are likely to lose all sense of proportion and become, to put it mildly, pretty odd."[17] Finally, the CIA's military investigator in Guatemala, the eloquent Colonel Hawkins of the U.S. Marine Corps, in reality knew little of the demanding professional art of amphibious warfare, while Amory himself had had far more amphibious experience in the Second World War than Hawkins and was already a prominent member of the agency (although one hostile to the Cuban invasion).

The President was justified, then, in dismissing Dulles, apart from the fact that he and Dulles operated on different wave lengths and never could really communicate effectively. In recent years, Dulles had been very removed from actual operations, weak as an overall intelligence coordinator (especially with the military), and excessively easygoing in his selection and supervision of unsuccessful subordinates. Like Bissell, his fellow scapegoat for the humiliated administration, Dulles had pushed Kennedy too far on an obviously inadequate invasion plan in the hope that the President would then rescue it from failure with the United States Navy and Marines. Moreover, the brilliant and nervous Bissell had been the principal advocate of the operation as well as egocentric and inexperienced in both the complex political factors in Latin America and the technical imperatives of amphibious operations, notwithstanding his belated struggle for more air support in Cuba at the actual moment of the plan's failure.

Significantly, regardless of his repeated efforts to carry out the impractical and contradictory orders of the half-hearted administration at the Bay of Pigs, in the fall of 1961, as the now official scapegoat, the disillusioned Bissell would again be "chewed out" in the cabinet room of the White House by President Kennedy and his brother for "sitting on his ass and not doing anything about getting rid of Castro and the Castro Regime." Indeed, this was to be another excuse for his dismissal, apart from the Bay of Pigs. As for the air force's man in the CIA, General Cabell, whose original appointment had been deemed urgent because of Dulles's administrative incompetence, he had done useful work in obtaining air force support for the CIA as well as congressional backing from the vital committees of that unpredictable body. He was dismissed anyway, perhaps as much to please the outraged agency over its last-minute loss of air cover as to meet the need for more top-level scapegoats. Colonel J. C. King, once again in effective power as Chief of the Western Hemisphere Division of the agency, would be spared for another three years before being replaced as ruler over his unsophisticated crew of former FBI men. After all, he had gone to West Point with Maxwell Taylor, and he had reflected doubts about the Bay of Pigs. At a lower level, many men such as Tracy Barnes and Gerry Droller were actually promoted, despite their major roles in the disaster, while the Special Group of the National Security Council was not touched at all. Last but not least, liberal critics of the whole operation such as Fulbright, Schlesinger, and Bowles would not be consulted during the Cuban missile crisis the following year.[18] But if open naysayers were punished, more discreet critics such as Rusk and Helms could prosper.

Like the United States Air Force with respect to practically any war, Bissell's own defense naturally took the line that, with several times the bombing tonnage which Kennedy permitted on Cuban airfields, the Central Intelligence Agency might have pulled off an invasion prolonged enough to evoke American recognition and open military support, notwithstanding the reluctance of the administration to intervene so openly. Bissell's claim for the possibility of such a dexterous victory with only increased aerial strength is opposed not merely by the conclusions of General Taylor's committee, but also by Lyman Kirkpatrick, Jr., the former Inspector General of his own agency, in Kirkpatrick's intra-agency investigation. Kirkpatrick has disingenuously complained that the members of the CIA whom he criticized, such as Dulles, Bissell, Cabell, and Barnes, were unduly shocked and upset by what Robert Amory has called Kirkpatrick's most damaging investigation and what Thomas Powers has considered the only serious investigation of the Bay of Pigs. Since Kirkpatrick, agreeing with Taylor and Amory, concluded that the agency had miscalculated both the quality and the quantity of the forces needed for the operation all along the line, Bissell's argument that more air strikes alone could have achieved victory is at least questionable. Kirkpatrick also decided that Bissell and his operations colleagues lacked objectivity and thus were overoptimistic, especially in anticipating mass defections from Castro's militia, and that Bissell and Cabell should have pleaded earlier for a second air strike. Kirkpatrick was especially critical of Bissell's refusal to ask the CIA's numerous analysts what they thought of his revised plan. Despite his denials to the contrary, Bissell may have surmised the answer he would get and chose instead to try to bluff the inexperienced President with the acquiescence of his superior, Allen Dulles, in this deceptive game. The only explanation for Richard Bissell's behavior is that he was either stupid or an audacious gambler for high stakes—and he was not stupid. Ironically, Bissell, like Dulles, had deeply embarrassed

Eisenhower with his risky and ultimately unsuccessful U-2 operation over Russia in May 1960.

The Kirkpatrick arguments went as far as they could within an in-house agency review—much too far, in fact, for his own future with the CIA. If Kirkpatrick necessarily avoided discussing the motives of Dulles and Bissell, his fundamental conclusion that the operation was "too big to be a raid and too small to be an invasion" is incontestable. In this way, the Bay of Pigs resembles the ill-fated British operation against Dieppe in August 1942, an amphibious fiasco the motives for which still remain shrouded in carefully calculated ambiguity.[19] In any case, for the basic CIA concept of seizing a beachhead long enough to establish an anti-Castro government on it to become viable, at least 10,000 to 15,000 men with full and open American support would have been required. Such a force probably never could have been obtained from the Cuban refugees, let alone sustained by the reluctant Kennedy administration. Furthermore, Castro was raising, training, and equipping troops far more rapidly than could the CIA, whose endeavors in Guatemala and elsewhere were marginal and surreptitious at best.

There is still less doubt that many in both the CIA and the administration were profoundly mistaken in believing that Fidel Castro was a hysteric because of his non–Anglo Saxon behavior, a hysteric who, like Arbenz in Guatemala, could be bluffed into surrendering his large military forces to what in the last analysis amounted to little more than psychological and technical pressures. It was difficult for Americans to accept in Cuba, as it would be again in Asia, that while much of the population would fight hard against native groups associated with the United States, they rarely would fight on behalf of such groups with any real determination. For example, Castro had landed in Cuba in December 1956 with practically no resources, compared to those of the CIA five years later. But at the end of 1958, Castro defeated Batista's nominal forces, estimated at 50,000 men, with only 3,000 guerrillas because the Cubans would no longer fight for America's former man in Havana.[20]

Of course, the Central Intelligence Agency was not alone in being taken in by false and facile analogies between Guatemala and Cuba. According to Theodore Sorensen, President Kennedy was particularly bitter about the seemingly unanimous acceptance by the Joint Chiefs of Staff of the change to the Bay of Pigs from Trinidad. To the new President, acquiescence by the Joint Chiefs spelled approval; to the military, it did not. According to Robert Kennedy, the President had trusted the Joint Chiefs of Staff because Eisenhower supposedly had trusted them, and President Kennedy had also feared the very real political repercussions of turning down the supposed Eisenhower–Joint Chiefs plan. The President finally considered the Joint Chief's preparatory study for Cuba disgraceful, in part because excessive secrecy imposed by the CIA prevented sufficient military staffing. Perhaps unduly influenced by McNamara, the overbearing Secretary of Defense, the Joint Chiefs of Staff had assured Kennedy that the chances of success in Cuba were as great as they had been in Guatemala. Kennedy would say bitterly a year later after the Cuban missile crisis: "The first advice I'm going to give my successor is to watch the generals and to avoid feeling that just because they were military men their opinions on military matters were worth a damn."[21] At the time, even Bundy had believed that the Joint Chiefs actually favored the Bay of Pigs–Zapata operation and were not just going along with it to please the President. But on Kennedy's behalf, the decline of the Joint Chiefs from the glory days of the Second World War had long been manifest and would continue into Vietnam.

McNamara's defense was that with only ninety days in office, few appointive civilians had had time to get on top of their jobs. Furthermore, except for Rusk, they were all inexperienced, and it was only on December 8 that Kennedy had met Rusk and McNamara for the first time. It should also be recalled that, while the original Joint Chiefs of Staff plan based on Trinidad rather than the Bay of Pigs had been overruled by the President himself, the Joint Chiefs did not voice sufficiently strong objections to make any impact upon their inexperienced civilian superiors. After all, however, ignorant of its last-minute modifications, the Joint Chiefs of Staff had acquiesced in the Bay of Pigs–Zapata plan four times between March 15 and April 15, although they were not given a chance to revise the final version because of the shortage of time. Thus, the Taylor committee was justified in concluding that in the future, the Joint Chiefs were to take full responsibility for paramilitary operations, just as they did for conventional military operations, and that they were to bring any objections forcefully to the attention of their civilian superiors. Not surprisingly, on June 28, 1961, President Kennedy formally presented the Joint Chiefs of Staff with such definitions of their duties.

For the past, however, since the necessary illusion that the invasion could still be covert had excluded the Joint Chiefs of Staff from full involvement, the Joint Chiefs could justifiably claim little responsibility for the subsequent fiasco, however much the President and the Attorney General may have sought to shift the blame onto them after the event. But Kirkpatrick's final conclusion, which was also that the the Taylor committee, remains unassailable—namely that, to be seriously and successfully undertaken, the invasion should have been transferred to the Defense Department as early as November 1960. As McNamara would naturally put it in his then-classified testimony after the Bay of Pigs, a military operation should never be conducted except under a military man. Of course, any such

candid recognition before April 17, 1961, of the Cuban operation's essential needs would have resulted in its probable death
at the hands of the exceedingly nervous President and the State
Department, as its sponsors were well aware.[22]

In agreeing with McNamara that the Bay of Pigs was, likewise, his biggest mistake, Secretary of State Rusk has done
himself an injustice for significant reasons. After all, it was
partly his characteristic weakness before the military that made
Rusk, however halfheartedly, go along with the invasion as
much as his relatively optimistic estimate that the operation
stood a 50–50 chance of success. It should also be recalled
that Rusk, as well as Bowles and Bissell, had underestimated
the domestic-publicity aspects of the invasion. Even more
ominous regarding both McNamara's and Rusk's confessions
of error over the operation was their essentially conformist and
conservative belief—shared at the time with Bundy—that it
was only the execution of the Cuba project, not the basic
American policy toward Cuba, which was so fundamentally
mistaken in 1961.

With regard to Vietnam, if all three men would continue to
support this same policy of attempting to suppress national
communism in non-European regions, Rusk would continue
to cripple the military he had so much admired since his air-
force days in China with policy restrictions that made the
strategy the military advocated impossible to carry out successfully. At least, as Roger Hilsman remarked, profiting in
1963 from the fiasco at the Bay of Pigs, Rusk vetoed another
harebrained CIA scheme to sponsor a Nationalist Chinese attack
on the Chinese Communist coastline on the grounds that the
United States could not again hope to disavow its responsibility for supporting such futile pinpricks.

It should be recalled that, in the words of an avowedly activist President, Rusk was a good errand boy who could be counted

upon not to rock the boat. In all probability Kennedy's more liberal alternatives for appointment as Secretary of State—Stevenson, Bowles, Fulbright, and perhaps the more conservative but highly experienced Robert Lovett—would have openly opposed the project and might have been able to forestall it entirely. But, then, it was no accident that a hawk like Dean Acheson had opposed the appointment of Fulbright as Secretary of State. Instead, Acheson had advised Kennedy to choose Dean Rusk for the post on the grounds that Rusk had been "loyal and good in every way" as Assistant Secretary of State for the Far East.[23] A future biographer would conclude that Rusk sometimes had trouble communicating even with his own unruly subordinates, when what Kennedy actually required an "aggressive" Secretary of State "to penetrate the palace guard" of his too numerous advisers on foreign policy. So weak would Rusk be in the ensuing Cuban missile crisis that Robert Kennedy would conclude that Rusk suffered a nervous breakdown from the strain of his responsibility.[24]

Not merely, then, did President Kennedy weaken the State Department rather than strengthen it because, like Franklin Roosevelt, he proposed to be his own Secretary of State. Alternatively, Kennedy may have wished Bundy to be his "*de facto*" Secretary of State, a dangerous anticipation of Henry Kissinger that Bundy wisely declined.[25] In an even more dangerous effort to wipe out another time-tested Eisenhower technique and destroy the distinction between planning and operations, the President had also gutted the National Security Council and its subordinate staffs, although the National Security Council itself had never controlled the secret operations of the Central Intelligence Agency. As Eisenhower described Kennedy after the Bay of Pigs, the young President looked upon administration as a very personal thing and had little idea of its multifarious complexities. Or, as Taylor would put it, the informal methods pursued in 1961 by Bundy's NSC and the

State Department to supervise covert operations failed conspicuously in their greatest test in Cuba. Like McNamara, however, Taylor stressed that at this stage Kennedy still headed a team of virtual strangers who had not yet learned to work together as a successful group. And Bundy has conceded that he himself had had a very wrong estimate of what would happen at the Bay of Pigs and thus could not have acted either as an effective spur or watchdog vis-à-vis the usually passive Rusk.

But the fact remains that having appointed so weak a figure as Rusk to head the State Department—a man incapable of making effective national-security policy—the President had thereby rendered ineffective his preferred alternative to the possibility of working through the subordinate staffs of the National Security Council. While, as he had been warned would happen the previous January by his weaker predecessor, National Security Adviser Gordon Gray, following the Bay of Pigs the undeniably able McGeorge Bundy would again build up the surviving residue of the National Security Council staff for the sake of more effective coordination and review of the various government organs in the future, a newly renamed Eisenhower Board of Consultants on Foreign Intelligence Activities would give him no authority over the CIA or any other intelligence branch of the government. At least the revival of this old board was a result of Kennedy's consulting that longtime critic Dulles, the able and acerbic Lovett.

In June 1961, moreover, in National Security Study Memoranda 55 and 57, President Kennedy in theory assigned the responsibility for all paramilitary projects, excluding very small-scale unattributable operations, to the Chairman of the Joint Chiefs of Staff, Laos excepted. But the President and his brother continued to encourage the CIA to conduct its dangerous and provocative, if useless, raids and sabotage activities in Cuba (Operation Mongoose) until 1963, possible on an even larger scale than Kennedy had envisaged.[26]

A possible distinction between President Kennedy and some of his more liberal and cautious advisers was that Kennedy actually, albeit at first rather ruefully, disapproved of Castro—and not just for electioneering purposes against Nixon. Moreover, in his fighting Irish words to his brother Robert on D-Day for the Bay of Pigs, Kennedy said that he would rather be called "an aggressor in victory than a bum in defeat."[27] There is nothing new in avowed liberals such as Woodrow Wilson or William Gladstone embracing the imperialism that they had condemned in conservative governments; in fact, it was under Wilson that American interventionism in the Caribbean reached its apogee, and at that time without the consoling cover of anticommunism. The fatal weakness in this doctrine as a rationalization for suppressing national communism in Asia or Latin America, if not in most of Eastern Europe, where that ignoble role could be safely left to the Soviet Union, was that, like Russia in Europe, the United States would then find itself opposed by an increasingly popular local nationalism in the course of its increasingly futile endeavors to extirpate bona-fide native communism.

Presumably, it was in part for this reason that Kennedy reflected so fundamental a hesitancy over the Cuban operation that Eisenhower would privately describe him as a profile in timidity and indecision. Determined to subordinate and to conceal as much of the American intervention in Cuba as possible, Kennedy fell into the trap of approving an operation that was too large to be covert even under the auspices of the CIA and too small to be effective, as the Joint Chiefs of Staff had rightly feared. Intelligent, if superficial, as Kennedy might be in George Ball's famous description, nonetheless there was no easy way out of the activist trap, as may be seen in the failure of Kennedy's successor in the open American military intervention in Vietnam in 1965. On the other hand, had the Bay of Pigs succeeded as a consequence of an overt, prolonged, and large-scale American intervention, the result might have been something of the nasty public and prolonged struggle that took place in Vietnam. Unlike Vietnam, however, an open American intervention in Cuba could have succeeded even against a majority of the Cuban population and the almost universal outrage of the rest of Latin America. For this reason alone, General Taylor was mistaken in favoring a still less promising intervention in Indochina in 1961 as a preferable alternative to Cuba.

In defense of Kennedy over the Bay of Pigs, Theodore Sorensen has stressed the difficulty of arresting the momentum of a bureaucratic machine deliberately geared by Kennedy for action; the excessive reliance upon air power, seen before in Korea and obvious again in Vietnam; the innocent belief in the possibilities of secrecy, as far as American participation was concerned; the undue faith in U.S.-sponsored guerrilla warfare, a result of the erroneous information that the great bulk of the population opposed Castro; and the pragmatic overemphasis upon the need for immediate action before it was too late.[28] In fact, it was already too late for covert action in Cuba even during the last year of the administration of the more careful and experienced Eisenhower. But it is still true that the highly ambivalent Kennedy had the courage neither to carry the operation through nor to cancel it outright. To judge less harshly, perhaps as a moderate, the indecisive Kennedy tried to straddle two incompatible courses of action and fell between them, as he would start to do again in 1962–1963 with Eisenhower's other fatal legacy—Vietnam.

Contrary to his more conservative and activist critics, however, Kennedy does deserve praise for resisting the far greater folly of an open and indefinitely prolonged American military intervention, regardless of the immense pressure brought to bear and of the serious political consequences for himself. Such a vast compounding of error would be seen in Vietnam once

Kennedy's distrustful and uncertain hand was replaced by a President who fully believed in his predecessor's ever-more-activist and still-more-mistaken advisers. Like Kennedy, Lyndon Johnson, too, would learn that war is not just politics by other means. In July 1962, fifteen months after the Bay of Pigs, President Kennedy granted an interview to the then-controversial *New York Times* reporter Herbert Matthews during which he said: "He [Fidel Castro] ought to be grateful to us. He gave us a kick in the ass and it made him stronger than ever. However, that invasion did some good. If it wasn't for that we could be in Laos now—or perhaps unleashing [Nationalist] China."[29] More than two decades later, Castro was equally affable regarding the Bay of Pigs when he remarked that, although Kennedy had been too young and inexperienced in politics in 1961, the President was at least very intelligent, presumably because Castro believed that Kennedy didn't really want to invade Cuba.

Kennedy was showing a capacity for learning from his mistakes before his untimely death, a capacity for growth that was most apparent in the closely run missile crisis over Cuba in October 1962. On that occasion, contrary to the desire of most of his professional military advisers, although with some of the usual amateurish Kennedy staffing procedures, the President refused to rely upon American air power or upon the U.S. Marines for action against Castro. Unlike Johnson in Vietnam, he instead chose to rely solely on a then-decisively-strong American naval power against Castro's Soviet suppliers. Regardless of the degree of threat posed for the United States by the medium-range Soviet missiles, in 1962 Kennedy was politically on the spot for some action against Castro in response to aroused American public opinion, independently of essentially the same problem of winning the next election.[30]

But unlike the operation against the Bay of Pigs, if at the time of the missile crisis the President had to act, the decisions he made then were his own and his brother Robert's, however uncertainly his confused advisers had thrashed out their recommendations. Even in the lunatic world of undercover activities against Castro, the half-baked CIA operations against Cuba pushed so feverishly by both Kennedy brothers, whether for assassination or sabotage, were cut back starting at the end of 1963 and abandoned with the Victnam War in 1965. Unfortunately, the gradual abandonment of action against Castro almost certainly was precipitated by President Kennedy's unexpected and embarrassing assassination rather than recognition of the futility of such activities per se, although Lyndon Johnson displayed little of the Kennedy brothers' too personal vendetta against Castro. Johnson was also aware that, shortly after a risky new CIA attempt to kill Castro in September 1963, the Cuban leader had warned an Associated Press reporter that "we are prepared to fight them and answer in kind. United States leaders should think that if they are aiding terrorists' plans to eliminate Cuban leaders, they themselves will not be safe." And Desmond Fitzgerald, Bissell's successor, has been charged with incorporating a highly provocative remark into the President's speech on November 18, just four days before Kennedy's assassination, regarding the necessity for removing Castro. On the other hand, many years later Castro found it expedient to claim that the death of his unsuccessful antagonist was a terrible blow.[31]

For these reasons alone, John F. Kennedy was justified in his growing distrust of his professional experts, however much he may have compounded their errors with his own incertitude. Certainly, his decidedly less sophisticated successor Lyndon Johnson, who plunged into the far greater folly of Vietnam in the name of avoiding the limited failure of the Bay of Pigs, was compelled in 1968 to turn to personal friends in a long overdue attempt to bail himself out of the ensuing stalemate. Following the Tet offensive in 1968, Johnson himself had discovered the

peril of accepting the advice of the once-again-mistaken colleagues whom he had inherited from his younger and similarly too eager predecessor. The more basic reasons for the
failure of almost all American military initiatives since the
Inchon landing in 1950 demand deeper examination of the
fundamental U.S. illusions about both this country and foreign nations during a period of prolonged political and military
irresolution.

As liberals, both John Kennedy and Lyndon Johnson exaggerated their foreign problems in the vain hope of resolving
them. As a most experienced conservative in foreign and military matters, Eisenhower minimized his problems in order to
sweep them under the carpet for as long as possible in the
hope that their seriousness might eventually subside. Nevertheless, Kennedy reluctantly accepted Eisenhower's poisoned
legacy in Indochina as well as Cuba, although in a reversed
order from Eisenhower's priorities of January 1961.

For Cuba, from their conception under Eisenhower to their
almost instant death at their belated birth under Kennedy in
April 1961, all U.S. plans for violent action against Castro were
a total failure. None ever had a real chance at any stage. Indeed,
these plans ran the gamut of failure from the hopeless inadequacy of resources allocated because of the successful CIA
deception of the Kennedy administration (if not entirely that
of Eisenhower) to a final failure of will on the part of the
Eisenhower administration, let alone that of Kennedy. The
eventual result of those blundering means of two administrations were simply to drive Cuba into the arms of the Soviet
Union as a nearby military or even nuclear base against the
United States. Like the similar but greater error in Vietnam,
the Bay of Pigs should remain for all time a shining example
of how not to conduct a fundamentally dishonest foreign policy or to attempt covert war by such a policy's ensuing absurd
strategies and tactics.

Notes

Front Papers and Preface

1. Frank Mankiewicz and Kirby Jones, *With Fidel: A Portrait of Castro and Cuba* (Chicago, 1975), p. 173, cf. Lee Lockwood, *Castro's Cuba, Cuba's Fidel* (New York, 1975), p. 204; Herbert Matthews, *Revolution in Cuba* (New York, 1975), p. 215.
2. "McGeorge Bundy Is Completing One Job, Preparing for Another," *The New York Times* (May 22, 1979), B8.
3. *Foreign and Military Intelligence*, Bk. I: *Final Report . . . Select Committee . . . Intelligence Activities* (Washington, April 14, 1965), p. 551; cf. Daniel Schorr, *Clearing the Air* (Boston, 1977), pp. 151–160, William Colby with Peter Forbath, *Honorable Men: My Life in the CIA* (New York, 1978), p. 386.
4. John F. Kennedy, *Public Papers of the Presidents: John F. Kennedy, 1961 . . .* (Washington, 1962), p. 726.
5. In Benjamin Bradlee's revealing account, *Conversations with Kennedy* (New York, 1975), pp. 127–128; cf. Theodore Draper,
Castro's Revolution: Myths and Realities (New York, 1962), p. 59; Harry Rositzke (in a Brown University symposium), "The C.I.A.: Past Transgressors and Future Controls," *Monograph on National Security Affairs* (Providence, R.I., October 11, 1975), p. 10; Irving Janis, *Victims of Groupthink* (Boston, 1972), pp. 14–49; "Nixon Watergate Tapes," *Time* (August 19, 1974), 9; Richard M. Nixon, *Memoirs of Richard M. Nixon*, Vol. 1 (New York, 1978), pp. 515, 640–642; Arthur Schlesinger, Jr., *Robert Kennedy and His Times* (Boston, 1978), pp. 486–487; John Prados, *Presidents' Secret Wars* (New York, 1986), ch. VI.
6. Theodore Draper, "Journalism, History and Journalistic History—An Exchange," *The New York Times Book Review* (December 16, 1984), 29.
7. *Knowing One's Enemies: Intelligence Assessment before the Two World Wars*, ed. E. R. May (Princeton, 1984), p. 4.

I. Guatemala's "Fortune" and "Success"

1. Walter LaFeber, *Inevitable Revolutions: The United States in* *Central America* (New York, 1984), p. 109.

2. Herbert Matthews, *Fidel Castro* (New York, 1969), p. 179; cf. *United States–Vietnam Relations 1945–1967*, Department of Defense Study (Washington, 1971), Bk. I, first sect., pp. C-1, C-30.

3. Philip Bonsal, *Cuba, Castro and the United States* (Pittsburgh, 1971), p. 173.

4. Robert F. Smith, *The United States and Cuba: Business and Diplomacy, 1947–1960* (New Haven, 1960), pp. 18–29, 106–111, 149–152; A. R. Millet, *The Politics of Intervention: The Military Occupation of Cuba 1906–1909* (Columbus, 1968); Mario Lazo, *Dagger in the Heart: American Policy Failures in Cuba* (New York, 1968), pp. 34 ff.; Ramón Eduardo Ruiz, *Cuba: The Making of a Revolution* (New York, 1968), pp. 24 ff., 86 ff.; Irwin Gellman, *Roosevelt and Batista* (Albuquerque, 1973), pp. 104 ff.

5. *Supplementary Detailed Staff Reports on Foreign and Military Intelligence*, Bk. IV: *Final Report . . . Senate Committee to Study . . . Intelligence Activities* (Washington, 1976), pp. 44–45, 51, 62; cf. *Foreign Relations of the United States [FRUS], 1952–1954*, Vol. IV: *The American Republics*, Department of State (Washington, 1983), pp. 6–10, 1031–1057, 1369; Dwight D. Eisenhower, *The White House Years*, Vol. I: *Mandate for Change, 1953–1956* (Garden City, N.Y., 1963), pp. 421–422; Adolf Berle, MS: *Papers* (Hyde Park, N.Y., March 31, 1953), and B. Berle and T. Jacobs, *Navigating the Rapids: . . . Papers*, ed. B. Berle and T. Jacobs (New York, 1973), pp. 210–221; Spruille Braden, *Diplomats and Demagogues: Memoirs* (New York, 1971), pp. 410–411; Thomas McCann, *An American Company: The Tragedy of United Fruit* (New York, 1976), pp. 5 ff.; Richard Immerman, *The CIA in Guatemala* (Austin, 1982), pp. 94 ff.; Stephen Schlesinger and Stephen Kinzer, *Bitter Fruit* (Garden City, N.Y., 1982), pp. 74–102; Blanche Cook, *The Declassified Eisenhower* (Garden City, N.Y., 1981), pp. 227–234; William Corson, *The Armies of Ignorance* (New York, 1977), pp. 335–336, 342 ff., 355 ff.; LaFeber, pp. 93–108; Stephen Rabe, "The Johnson (Eisenhower) Doctrine for Latin America," *Diplomatic History* (Winter 1985): 96–97; "Memorandum by Thomas Mann for Charles Murphy," MS (Independence, Mo.: Truman Library, December 11, 1952), p. 142.

6. *FRUS 1952–1954*, Vol. IV, p. 42; cf. *Central Intelligence Agency: CIA Information Reports*, declassified 1982 (Washington, April 6–May 14, 1953); Cole Blasier, *The Hovering Giant* (Pittsburgh, 1976), pp. 159 ff.

7. *FRUS 1952–1954*, Vol. IV, pp. 1061–1086; cf. Immerman, pp. 134–136; Schlesinger and Kinzer, pp. 138 ff.; Stephen Ambrose, *Ike's Spies* (Garden City, N.Y., 1981), pp. 222–224; *id., Eisenhower*, Vol. II: *The President* (New York, 1984), pp. 192–197; LaFeber, pp. 109–120; *Hearings:* "Communist Threat to the United States through the Caribbean," *Senate Internal Security Committee* (Washington, November 5, 1959), Pt. III, pp. 865–866; Kim Philby, *My Silent War* (New York, 1968), p. 229; John Ranelagh, *The Agency: The Rise and Decline of the CIA* (New York, 1986), pp. 267 ff.

8. *FRUS 1952–1954*, Vol. IV, pp. 1090–1102; cf. Eisenhower, pp. 421–422; Berle, p. 619; Ambrose, *Ike's Spies*, ch. 16; Immerman,

pp. 136 ff.; Edward Bernays, *Biography of an Idea: Memoirs* (New York, 1965), pp. 744 ff.; Harry Rositzke, *The CIA's Secret Operations* (New York, 1977), pp. 174, 190; William Leary, *Perilous Missions: Civil Air Transport and CIA Covert Operations in Asia* (University, Ala., 1984), pp. 173, 211; Walter Laqueur, *A World of Secrets* (New York, 1985), pp. 74–79.

9. Eisenhower's "unshirted hell" remark may have been made closer to April 26, just before the surrender of Dien Bien Phu, and not necessarily on January 16, as it might appear to be in the record. *FRUS 1952–1954,* Vol. IV, p. 1095, n. 1, pp. 1101–1102; Eisenhower, *Papers:* W. B. Smith, "Memorandum for the President," Department of State (Abilene, Kans.: Eisenhower Library, January 15, 1954), p. 1. Toriello, on January 16, has described Eisenhower as both sympathetic and naïve, which, of course, may have been just another presidential pose. Blasier, p. 165.

10. *FRUS 1952–1954,* Vol. IV, pp. 46–49; cf. Schlesinger and Kinzer, pp. 113–146; *The Central Intelligence Agency: History and Documents,* ed. W. M. Leary (University, Ala., 1984), pp. 23–24; Immerman, pp. 143–151; Tad Szulc, *Compulsive Spy* (New York, 1974), pp. 67 ff.; E. Howard Hunt, *Give Us This Day* (New Rochelle, N.Y., 1973), pp. 112–119; Arthur Schlesinger, Jr., *A Thousand Days* (Boston, 1965), pp. 179, 189.

11. *FRUS 1952–1954,* Vol. IV, pp. 1098–1106; cf. James Hagerty, *The Diary of James C. Hagerty,* ed. Robert Ferrell (Bloomington, Ind., 1983); John Prados, *Presidents' Secret Wars* (New York, 1986), ch. VI.

12. *FRUS 1952–1954,* Vol. IV, pp.

1111–1126; cf. Hagerty, May 14–24, 1954; Schlesinger and Kinzer, pp. 147 ff.; Eisenhower, p. 424.

13. Cook, pp. 267–268; cf. *FRUS 1952–1954,* Vol. IV, pp. 1120–1125; Immerman, pp. 159–160; Sir Anthony Eden, *Memoirs: Full Circle* (Boston, 1960), pp. 151 ff.

14. *FRUS 1952–1954,* Vol. IV, p. 1132; Harrison Salisbury, *Without Fear or Favor* (New York, 1980), pp. 148 ff.

15. *FRUS 1952–1954,* Vol. IV, pp. 1131–1149; cf. W. Leary and W. Stuech, "The Chennault Plan to Save China: . . . Chennault and the Origins of the CIA's Aerial Empire, 1949–1950," *Diplomatic History* (Fall 1984): 349 ff.

16. *FRUS 1952–1954,* Vol. IV, pp. 1152–1174; cf. Paul Kennedy, *The Middle Beat* (New York, 1971), p. 42; *Central Intelligence Agency: CIA Information Reports* (June 15–July 9, 1954).

17. *FRUS 1952–1954,* Vol. IV, pp. 1174–1176; cf. *United Nations, Security Council, Official Records* (New York, June 10, 1954), pp. 29 ff., (January 20, 1954), pp. 2–38; David A. Phillips, *The Night Watch* (New York, 1977), pp. 44 ff.

18. Allen Dulles, *Papers, Articles and Briefings* (Princeton: Mudd Library, 1965), Box 244, p. 14; Eisenhower, pp. 425–426; *Hearings before House Subcommittee . . . on Communist Aggression in Latin America* (Washington, October 8, 1954), pp. 170–178; *Central Intelligence Agency: Current Intelligence Digests . . .* (Washington, June 24–25, 1954); Richard Bissell, *Transcript: Eisenhower Oral History* (New York: Columbia University Library, 1967), pp. 13–21: author's conversation with Jens Jebsen, Allen Dulles's son-in-law

(New York, October 17, 1975);
Thomas Powers, *The Man Who
Kept the Secrets: Richard Helms
and the CIA*, MS (New York:
1979), p. 69.
19. Dwight D. Eisenhower, *Papers:*
"Dulles-Herter Series" (Abilene,
Kans., June 24, 1954), Box 2; cf.
FRUS 1952–1954, Vol. IV, pp.
1180–1185; Robert Murphy, *Diplomat among Warriors* (New
York, 1965), pp. 413–415.
20. Hagerty, June 24–26, 1954; cf.
"Eisenhower-Churchill," *Harkness Memorandum* (Princeton:
Mudd Library, John Foster Dulles
Additional Papers, 1954), pp. 1–
2; Roy Rubottom, Jr., *Transcript:
Dulles Oral History* (Princeton:
Mudd Library, June 12, 1966),
pp. 8–12; *Eisenhower: The Diaries*, ed. Robert Ferrell (New York,
1981), pp. 222–223; Eden, pp.
153–155; John Colville, *The
Fringes of Power* (New York,
1985), p. 694.
21. *FRUS 1952–1954*, Vol. IV, pp.
1188 ff.; cf. Phillips, pp. 47 ff.;
*Central Intelligence Agency: CIA
Information Reports* (August 18,
1954); Victor Marchetti and John
Marks, *The CIA and the Cult of
Intelligence* (New York, 1974), p.
298; Lord Moran, *Taken from the
Diaries of Lord Moran* (Boston,
1966), pp. 599–600.
22. Prados, ch. VI; Phillips, pp. 51–
54.
23. *FRUS 1952–1954*, Vol. IV, pp.
81–86; cf. *Supplementary Detailed Staff Reports on Foreign
and Military Intelligence*, Bk. IV
(Washington, 1976), pp. 29, 52–
55; J. F. Campbell, *The Foreign
Affairs Fudge Factory* (New York,
1971), pp. 106, 155 ff.; Thomas
Mann, *Transcript: Eisenhower
Oral History* (New York: Columbia University Library, February
23, 1968), pp. 14–15; *The Central Intelligence Agency: History

and Documents*, pp. 62 ff.
24. *The Central Intelligence Agency:
History and Documents*, p. 64, n.
9; *Supplementary Detailed Staff
Reports on Foreign and Military
Intelligence*, Bk. IV, pp. 52–54;
cf. Powers, p. 70; *Doolittle Report CIA*, MS (Washington: The
National Archives, declassified
April 1, 1976).
25. Arthur Schlesinger, Jr., *Robert
Kennedy and His Times* (Boston,
1978), pp. 455–456; *The Central
Intelligence Agency: History and
Documents*, pp. 62–75; cf.
Campbell, pp. 10, 153 ff.; *Supple-
mentary Detailed Staff Reports
on Foreign and Military Intelli-
gence*, Bk. IV, pp. 39–55; *Foreign
and Military Intelligence*, Bk. I:
*Final Report . . . Select Commit-
tee . . . Intelligence Activities*
(Washington, April 14, 1965), pp.
63, 114, 429, 447, 480–481;
"House Select Committee on
Intelligence," *The Village Voice*
(February 16, 1976), 10, 153–
160; Lyman Kirkpatrick, Jr.,
"Paramilitary Case Study—The
Bay of Pigs," *Naval War College
Review* (November–December
1972): 37; Ernst Halperin, *The
National Liberation Movement in
Latin America*, MS (Cambridge,
June 1969), pp. 12–56; Charles
Yost, *The Conduct and Misconduct of Foreign Affairs* (New York,
1972), p. 161; Admiral Stansfield
Turner, *Secrecy and Democracy:
The CIA in Transition* (Boston,
1985), pp. 145–150; *The President's Foreign Intelligence Advisory Board* (PFIAB) (Washington,
1981), pp. 1–21.
26. Schlesinger, *Robert Kennedy*, pp.
455–458; *The Central Intelligence Agency: History and Documents*, pp. 62 ff.; Powers, pp.
70–73; Ray Cline, *Secrets, Spies
and Scholars* (Washington, 1976),
pp. 181–183; W. M. Ewald, Jr.,

Eisenhower, the President: Crucial Days, 1951–1960 (Englewood Cliffs, N.J., 1981), ch. XV; R. H. Smith, Spymaster's Odyssey: The World of Allen Dulles, MS (New York, n.d.), ch. 27, pp.

6–30; Joseph B. Smith, Portrait of a Cold Warrior (New York, 1976), ch. XIV; Marchetti and Marks, pp. 26, 101, 122; Prados, chs. VII, VIII.

27. Rabe, 98.

II. Fidel's Cuba

1. Arkadi Shevchenko, Breaking with Moscow (New York, 1985), p. 105.

2. Henry A. Kissinger, The Necessity for Choice (New York, 1961), p. 174.

3. Richard Dunlop, Donovan, American Master Spy (New York, 1982), p. 451.

4. Indeed, Smith's still more conservative predecessor Arthur Gardner may have suggested to Batista that the FBI or CIA should assassinate Castro, an offer that Batista allegedly had rejected. Hugh Thomas, Cuba, or the Pursuit of Freedom (New York, 1971), pp. 866, 947–987, and his "The U.S. and Castro, 1959–1962," American Heritage (October–November 1978); 30; Dwight D. Eisenhower, The White House Years, Vol. II: Waging Peace 1956–1961 (Garden City, N.Y., 1965), ch. XVIII; Lyman B. Kirkpatrick, Jr., The Real C.I.A. (New York, 1968), pp. 157–176; Paul Bethall, The Losers (New York, 1969), pp. 61 ff.; Philip Bonsal, Cuba, Castro and the United States (Pittsburgh, 1971), pp. 22, 28; Earl T. Smith, The Fourth Floor (New York, 1962), pp. 58 ff., 161 ff.; Fulgencio Batista, The Growth and Decline of the Cuban Republic (New York, 1964), pp. 267 ff.; Spruille Braden, Diplomats and Demagogues: Memoirs (New York, 1971), pp. 300–301, 402–413; J. Dorschner and R.

Fabricio, The Winds of December (New York, 1980), pp. 48 ff., 155 ff.; Operation Zapata: The "Ultrasensitive" Report and Testimony of the Board of Inquiry on the Bay of Pigs (Frederick, Md., 1981), pp. 55 ff.

5. Executive Sessions of the State Foreign Relations Committee, 1961 (Washington, 1984), Vol. XIII, Pt. 1, p. 413; cf. Eisenhower, p. 521; Dwight D. Eisenhower, Papers: "Herter Memorandum for the President," Department of State (Abilene, Kans., December 23, 1958), Box 18, and "Memorandums of Conference with the President" (Abilene, Kans., May 16, 1960), Box 50; Smith, pp. 118 ff., 159–162; Hearings: "Communist Threat to the United States through the Caribbean," Senate Internal Security Committee (Washington, August 27, 30, and September 2, 1960), Pt. IV, pp. 687, 737–740; Roy R. Rubottom, Jr., Transcript: Dulles Oral History (Princeton, 1967), pp. 70–81; John F. Kennedy, The Strategy of Peace, ed. Allan Nevins (New York, 1961), pp. 167–168; Thomas, Cuba, pp. 967, 976–977, 991, 1015–1026, 1044–1060, and id., "The U.S. and Castro," 30; Manuel Urrutia Lléo, Fidel Castro and Castro's Cuba: An American Dilemma (Washington, 1962), pp. 202–203; Khrushchev Remembers, ed. E. Crankshaw (Boston, 1970), pp. 488–490;

Bonsal, pp. 17–24, 40, 55 ff.; *Operation Zapata,* pp. 55–56; General Maxwell Taylor, *Taylor Committee Report . . . Memorandum for Record of Paramilitary Study Group Meetings,* Pts. 1 and 2 (declassified June 21, 1978), p. 2; Dorschner and Fabricio, pp. 145 ff., 244–247, 406, 506–509; Arthur Schlesinger, Jr., *A Thousand Days* (Boston, 1965), pp. 200–201, 221; Richard Welch, Jr., *Response to Revolution* (Chapel Hill, N.C., 1985), pp. 30–32.

6. *Executive Sessions of the Senate Foreign Relations Committee, 1959* (Washington, 1982), Vol. XI, pp. 83–126; cf. *Central Intelligence Agency: Memoranda for the Director* (Washington, Office of National Estimates, 1961), p. 3; Eisenhower, *Papers:* "Memorandum for the President," Department of State (Abilene, Kans., January 7, 1959), Box 4.

7. Stephen Rabe, "The Johnson (Eisenhower) Doctrine for Latin America," *Diplomatic History* (Winter 1985): 99.

8. Enrique Meneses, *Fidel Castro* (London, 1966), p. 96; B. Berle and T. Jacobs, "The Cuban Crisis: Failure of American Foreign Policy," *Foreign Affairs* (October 1960): 44–45, and *id., Navigating the Rapids* (New York, 1973), pp. 694–695; Eisenhower, *Waging Peace,* pp. 521–523; Bonsal, pp. 25 ff., and author's interview with Bonsal (Washington, November 3, 1971); Maurice Halperin, *The Rise and Decline of Fidel Castro* (Berkeley, 1972), ch. II, pp. 57–58.

9. Eisenhower, *Papers:* "Memorandum of Conferences with the President" (Abilene, Kans., April 27, 1959), Box 8; cf. *CIA Report on Castro Visit* (Washington, April 27, 1959), pp. 1–2; Richard M.

Nixon, "Cuba, Castro and John F. Kennedy: Reflections on U.S. Foreign Policy," *Reader's Digest* (November 1964), 281–288; *id., The Memoirs of Richard M. Nixon* (New York, 1978), Vol. I, pp. 248–250; *id., Six Crises* (Garden City, N.Y., 1967), pp. 351–352; Eisenhower, *Waging Peace,* p. 523; Bonsal, pp. 28 ff., 62–66, 105–124, 168–169; Carlos Franqui, *Family Portrait with Fidel: A Memoir* (New York, 1984), pp. 32 ff.; Theodore Draper, *Castro's Revolution* (New York, 1962), pp. 62–65; Lee Lockwood, *Castro's Cuba, Cuba's Fidel* (New York, 1967), pp. 147 ff., and *id., Transcript: Castro Oral History* (New York, August 1965), pp. 201–202; Richard Bissell, Jr., *Transcript: Dulles Oral History* (Princeton, 1967), pp. 68–76; *Hearings:* "Communist Threat to the United States through the Caribbean," Pt. III, pp. 162–164; Batista, pp. 267 ff.; Berle and Jacobs, *Navigating the Rapids,* pp. 695, 703, 716; Fidel Castro, "Castro Sees Hope for Better U.S. Ties," *The New York Times* (October 27, 1974), 3.

10. Eisenhower, *Papers:* "Memorandum for the President" (Abilene, Kans., November 5, 1959), Boxes 4 and 5; *Hearings:* "Communist Threat to the United States through the Caribbean," Pt. III, pp. 162–164, Pt. XIII, pp. 844–849; Thomas Gates, Jr., *Transcript: Eisenhower Oral History* (New York, August 1967), pp. 39, 55; Urrutia Lléo, ch. XIII; Rufo Lopez-Fresquet, *My Fourteen Months with Castro* (Cleveland, 1966), pp. 52–62, ch. XIV; Bonsal, pp. 52–62, 100–128.

11. *Alleged Assassination Plots Involving Foreign Leaders: An Interim Report* (Washington, 1975), pp. 92 ff.; cf. Peter Wyden,

The Bay of Pigs (New York, 1979), pp. 19–24; Bonsal, pp. 121–138; Taylor (April 23, 1961), p. 204; Warren Hinckle and William Turner, *The Fish Is Red* (New York, 1981), pp. 33–44; *Central Intelligence Agency: National and Special National Intelligence Estimates* (Washington, December 29, 1949), p. 5; George Kistiakowsky, *A Scientist at the White House* (Cambridge, 1976), pp. 227–337.

12. Eisenhower, *Papers:* Ann Whitman File Diary Series, "Memorandum of Conference with the President" (Abilene, Kans., January 26, 1960), Box 7; *ibid.*, "Memorandum of Conferences with the President" (Abilene, Kans., January 23, 1960), Box 4; *Declassified Documents Reference System:* "Goodpaster Memorandum" (Carrollton, Md., January 25, 1960), p. 209D.

13. *Alleged Assassination Plots,* pp. 13–17, 93, 110, 114, 277–278; cf. Eisenhower, *Waging Peace,* pp. 533–534; Taylor (April 23, 1961), pp. 3–6, (May 2, 1961), p. 12; F. Parkinson, *Latin America, the Cold War and the World Powers: A Study in Diplomatic History 1945–1973* (Beverly Hills, 1974), pp. 74–75; Paul Meskil, "Frogmen Blew Up French Ship in Havana," *Daily News* (April 25, 1975), 18; Edward Gonzalez, "The United States and Castro," *Foreign Affairs* (July 1972): 727 ff.; Kistiakowsky, pp. 266–275; *Declassified Documents Reference System:* "Records of Action by the National Security Council" (March 10, 1961), p. 1610; *Central Intelligence Agency: ... National Intelligence Estimates* (Washington, June 14, 1960), pp. 23 ff.

14. *Declassified Documents Reference System* (Carrollton, Md., 1984), Department of State, February 15, 1961, 943, 1–5; cf. Taylor, *Taylor Committee Report,* Pt. 3: "Program of Covert Action against Castro," Pts. 1 and 2 (Boston, declassified April 1985), and "Memorandum No. 1," pp. 1–2; Eisenhower, *Papers:* "Herter Memorandum for the President," Department of State (Abilene, Kans., March 17, 1960), Box 10; General Nathan Twining, *Transcript: Dulles Oral History* (Princeton, March 16–19, 1965), pp. 40–43; General Maxwell Taylor, *Swords and Plowshares* (New York, 1972), p. 181; John Prados, *Presidents' Secret Wars* (New York, 1986), pp. 177 ff.; Joseph B. Smith, *Portrait of a Cold Warrior* (New York, 1976), pp. 335, 342; H. R. Halderman with Joseph Di Mina, *The Ends of Power* (New York, 1978), p. 27.

15. Eisenhower, *Papers,* "Herter Memorandum ...," Box 10; Bonsal, pp. 136 ff., and author's interview with Bonsal, cited; Smith pp. 140 ff.; Thomas, pp. 1000–1001, 1241 ff.; Rufo Lopez-Fresquet, *My Fourteen Months with Castro* (Cleveland, 1966), pp. 170–173; Karl Meyer and Tad Szulc, *The Cuban Invasion: The Chronicle of a Disaster* (New York, 1962), pp. 43–57; Halperin, pp. 78–79, 89, n. 1; Roberta Wohlstetter, "Kidnapping to Win Friends and Influence People," *Survey* (Autumn 1974): 5–31; Mario Llerena, *The Unsuspected Revolution* (Ithaca, N.Y., 1978), p. 246; *Strategy for Conquest,* ed. Jay Mallin (Coral Gables, Fla., 1970), pp. 294–311; David Rosenberg, *Arleigh Albert Burke, Chief of Naval Operations 1955–1961,* MS (Annapolis, 1980), pp. 86–87.

16. Eisenhower, *Waging Peace,* p. 535; cf. Theodore Draper, *Cas-*

184 NOTES

tro's Revolution: Myths and
Realities (New York, 1962), pp.
78–81; Dwight D. Eisenhower,
Public Papers of the Presidents:
Dwight D. Eisenhower 1960–
1961, Vol. XIII, Pt. 2 (Washington, 1961), pp. 562–563; Ramón
Eduardo Ruiz, Cuba: The Making
of a Revolution (New York, 1968),
pp. 48 ff.; L. H. Jenks, Our Cuban
Colony: A Study in Sugar (New
York, 1928), pp. 78 ff., 188 ff.;
Khrushchev Remembers, p. 490;
Bonsal, pp. 145–165; Thomas
Mann, Transcript: Eisenhower
Oral History (New York: Columbia University Library, February
23, 1968), pp. 51–52; Franqui,
pp. 66–68; Central Intelligence
Agency: Memorandam for the
Director, 1960–1962 (Washington: Office of National Estimates,
February 21, 1961), pp. 6–7.
17. Soviet Relations with Latin
America 1918–1968: A Documentary Survey, ed. Stephen
Clissold (London, 1970), pp. 255–
257; cf. Khrushchev Remembers,
p. 491.
18. Eisenhower, Papers: "Memorandum for the President" (Abilene,
Kans., March 10, 1960), Box 10,
and "Memorandum of Meeting
with President" (Abilene, Kans.,
July 6, 1960), Box 4; Eisenhower,
Waging Peace, pp. 534–536;
"Russia Defies Monroe Doctrine,"
The New York Times (July 13,
1960), 1, 3; L. P. Bloomfield and
A. C. Leiss, Controlling Small
Wars: A Strategy for the 1970s
(New York, 1969), pp. 106–109;

Schlesinger, pp. 226–228; Bonsal, pp. 67, 154, 161; Taylor,
Taylor Committee Report:
"Memorandum No. 1," p. 1; CIA,
"How the CIA Built . . . Network
for Propaganda," The New York
Times (December 26, 1977), 37;
Bernard Diederich, Trujillo: The
Death of the Goat (Boston, 1978),
pp. 40–55; Central Intelligence
Agency: National and Special
National Intelligence Estimates
(NIE) (March 22, 1960), pp. 3–
4. In 1960, McNamara stated that
the United States had 6,300 strategic warheads as opposed to only
200 Soviet equivalents. Michael
Charlton, "Star Wars," Encounter (February 1986): 14; cf. Walter Laqueur, A World of Secrets
(New York, 1985), pp. 144–155.
So much for the famous missile
gap.
19. Alleged Assassination Plots, pp.
71–82, 262–267, 338–339; Paul
Meskil, "C.I.A. Sent Bedmate to
Kill Castro in 1960," New York
Daily News (June 13, 1976), 3;
Steve Dunleavy, "A Cloak or Dagger Duo," New York Post
(November 1, 1977), 16.
20. Taylor, Taylor Committee Report:
"Memorandum No. 1," p. 1;
Eisenhower, Waging Peace, p.
526; Eisenhower, Papers: "Memorandum of Conversations with
the President" (Abilene, Kans.,
April 26, 1960), Box 49, and
"Notes on Legislative Leadership
Meeting" (Abilene, Kans., August
16, 1960), Box 3.

III. The Hot Potato

1. Richard Challener, Admirals,
Generals and American Foreign
Policy, 1898–1914 (Princeton,
1973), p. 118.
2. William Shawcross, Sideshow

(New York, 1979), p. 135.
3. Stephen Ambrose, Eisenhower,
Vol II: The President (New York,
1984), p. 639.
4. John F. Kennedy, The Strategy

of Peace, ed. Allan Nevins (New York, 1961), p. 168. Of course, peace is a policy, a word smacking of politicians, and thus not as patriotic as the significantly military term strategy; cf. Harris Wofford, Of Kennedys and Kings (New York, 1980), pp. 342–343.

5. John F. Kennedy, Freedom of Communications: Final Report of the Committee on Commerce, U.S. Senate Subcommittee on Communication, Pt. I: The Speeches, Remarks, Press Conferences and Statements of Senator John F. Kennedy, August 1–November 7, 1960 (Washington, 1961), p. 87. The tremendous recent shift in American public opinion may be seen in the FBI investigation now launched against members of the State Department such as Richard Rubottom and William Wieland, who had previously opposed action against Castro. B. Berle and T. Jacobs, Navigating the Rapids (New York, 1973), pp. 716, 729; Fulgencio Batista, The Growth and Decline of the Cuban Republic (New York, 1964), pp. 270–271.

6. Kennedy, Freedom of Communications, Pt. I, Speeches, pp. 303, 475, 511–552, 607–608.

7. Allen Dulles, Papers, Articles and Briefings (Princeton, 1965), pp. 4–5; Richard M. Nixon, Freedom of Communications: Final Report of the U.S. Senate . . . Subcommittee on Communications, Pt. II: The Speeches, Remarks, Press Conferences, Study Papers of . . . Richard M. Nixon, August 1–November 7, 1960 (Washington, 1961), pp. 196, 661; Arthur Schlesinger, Jr., A Thousand Days (Boston, 1965), pp. 224, 226; Peter Wyden The Bay of Pigs (New York, 1979), p. 67n.; "Nixon Rebutted by White House," The New York Times (March 21, 1962), 10; William Attwood, The

Reds and the Blacks: A Personal Adventure (New York, 1967), pp. 10–11; Soviet Relations with Latin America 1918–1968: A Documentary Survey, ed. Stephen Clissold (London, 1970), p. 259; Philip Bonsal, Cuba, Castro and the United States (Pittsburgh, 1971), pp. 170–174; Dean Acheson, Transcript: Kennedy Oral History (Boston, April 27, 1967), pp. 6 ff.; Chalmers Roberts, First Rough Draft (New York, 1973), p. 186; Kent Beck, "Necessary Lies, Hidden Truths: Cuba in the 1960 Campaign," Diplomatic History (Winter 1984): 53–59.

8. Nixon, pp. 710–716; Schlesinger, pp. 224–226.

9. The president's son John Eisenhower, William Colby, and General Andrew Goodpaster have all denied President Eisenhower's cognizance of these attempts, while Arthur Schlesinger has speculated that Richard Nixon flashed the "green light" to kill Lumumba. Arthur Schlesinger, Jr., Robert Kennedy and His Times (Boston, 1978), p. 486; William Colby with Peter Forbath, Honorable Men: My Life in the CIA (New York, 1978), p. 428; Supplementary Detailed Staff Reports on Foreign and Military Intelligence, Bk. IV: Final Report . . . Senate Committee to Study . . . Intelligence Activities (Washington, 1976), pp. 138–142; Alleged Assassination Plots Involving Foreign Leaders: An Interim Report (Washington, 1975), pp. 112–115, 262–263. Cord Meyer's appraisal seems the fairest—namely, that Eisenhower authorized the assassination, although, as with Trujillo, the CIA did not actually have to carry it out itself. Cord Meyer, Facing Reality (New York, 1980), p. 218. For a judicious and an exhaustive

discussion of the subject, see Madelaine Kalb, *The Congo Cables* (New York, 1982), pp. 53–196.

10. Wyden, pp. 31–32, 68–73; cf. Admiral R. L. Dennison, *Transcript: Oral Reminiscences* (Annapolis: U.S. Naval Institute, August 1975), pp. 331–333; David Rosenberg, *Arleigh Albert Burke, Chief of Naval Operations 1955–1961*, MS (Annapolis, 1980), p. 87; Haynes Johnson and others, *The Bay of Pigs* (New York, 1964), pp. 53–54; "Guatemala Ex-Chief Says Kennedy Ordered His Ouster," *The New York Times* (April 17, 1964), 2; Schlesinger, *A Thousand Days*, pp. 228–232; Richard Bissell, Jr., *Transcript: Eisenhower Oral History* (New York: Columbia University Library, 1967), pp. 29–30; General Maxwell Taylor, *Taylor Committee Report . . .* , Pt. 3: "Brigade Briefing on Guerrillas" (Boston, May 31, 1961; declassified April 1985), pp. 1–2.

11. Wyden, pp. 31–32, 68–73; Dwight D. Eisenhower, *The White House Years*, Vol. II: *Waging Peace 1956–1961* (Garden City, N.Y., 1965), pp. 536, 612–618; Taylor, *Taylor Committee Report:* "Memorandum No. 1," p. 203, and *id., Taylor Committee Memorandums* (May 2, 1961), p. 12; Lyman Kirkpatrick, Jr., *Transcript: Kennedy Oral History* (Boston, April 16, 1967), pp. 13–15; Charles Murphy, "Cuba—The Record Set Straight," *Fortune* (September 1961): 95–96; Allen Dulles, *The Craft of Intelligence* (New York, 1965), pp. 157–158; David A. Phillips, *The Night Watch* (New York, 1977), pp. 35–38, 87–92; Joseph B. Smith, *Portrait of a Cold Warrior* (New York, 1976), pp. 340–343; *Executive Sessions of the Senate Foreign Relations Committee, 1961* (Washington,

1984), Vol. XIII, Pt. 1, pp. 583–585; Thomas Mann, *Transcript: Kennedy Oral History* (Boston, March 13, 1968), pp. 17–18; William Rust and others, *Kennedy in Vietnam* (New York, 1985), pp. 23–24.

12. *Alleged Assassination Plots*, pp. 99, 116.

13. Dennison, pp. 333–340; Wyden, pp. 78–80; Thomas Powers, *The Man Who Kept the Secrets: Richard Helms and the CIA*, MS (New York, 1979), pp. 100–103; *Operation Zapata: The "Ultrasensitive" Report and Testimony of the Board of Inquiry on the Bay of Pigs* (Frederick, Md., 1981), p. 59.

14. "Editorial," *The Nation* (November 19, 1960): 378–379; cf. Ronald Hilton, *Hispanic American Report* (Stamford, November 1960), p. 58, and author's interview with Hilton (Stamford, Calif., May 3, 1984); Victor Bernstein and Jesse Gordon, "The Press and the Bay of Pigs," *Columbia University Forum* (Fall 1967): 5–7; Harrison Salisbury, *Without Fear or Favor* (New York, 1980), pp. 138 ff.

15. "Guerrilla War Is Stressed in Guatemala Troop Training," *The New York Times* (November 20, 1960), 32; Paul Kennedy, *The Middle Beat* (New York, 1971), pp. 153–167; Richard Bissell, Jr., *Transcript: Kennedy Oral History* (Boston, April 1967), p. 3; Turner Catledge, *My Life and the Times* (New York, 1971), pp. 259 ff.

16. Salisbury, p. 142; Bernstein and Gordon, 7–8.

17. Dwight D. Eisenhower, *Papers:* "Meetings with the President" (Abilene, Kans., November 29, 1960), Vol. II, Box 5, File Folder, 1960; cf. *Central Intelligence Agency: National and Special*

National Intelligence Estimates (Washington, December 6, 1960), pp. 1 ff.; Dulles, *Papers*, Box 244, pp. 2–3; Adlai Stevenson, *Papers* (Princeton: Mudd Library, December 6, 1960), Box 789; *Executive Sessions of the Senate Foreign Relations Committee, 1961*. Vol. XIII, Pt. 1, p. 585; Theodore Sorensen, *Kennedy* (New York, 1965), p. 295.

18. Eisenhower, *Papers:* "Willauer Memorandum to Livingston Marchant" (Abilene, Kans., January 18, 1961), Vol. 2, Box 5; Taylor, *Taylor Committee Report:* "Memorandums" (April 23, 1961), pp. 6–7, and (April 24, 1961, afternoon), p. 506; *Executive Sessions of the Senate Foreign Relations Committee, 1961*, Vol. XIII, Pt. 2, p. 34; Schlesinger, *A Thousand Days*, pp. 232 ff.; Dulles, *Papers*, Box 244, pp. 2–3.

19. Elie Abel, *The Missile Crisis* (New York, 1966), p. 16.

20. Eisenhower, *Papers, Special Assistant of National Security Affairs Records 1952–1961:* "Memorandum of Meeting with the President" (Abilene, Kans., January 9, 1961), Box 5; cf. Eisenhower, *Waging Peace*, pp. 613–614; Bonsal, pp. 166–175; Johnson and others, pp. 51–62. In an interview with the author (Alexandria, Va., March 26, 1985), General Andrew Goodpaster insisted that the operation could have been canceled outright to the end, if there were sufficient determination to do so.

21. Taylor, *Taylor Committee Report*, Pt. 3: "Policy Decisions Required for Strike Operations against Government of Cuba" (January 4, 1961); cf. *ibid.*, Pts. 1 and 2, and "Memorandum No. 121"; *ibid.*, "Memorandums" (April 24, 1961), pp. 2–9, 196; "U.N. Sets Hearings on Cuba's Charge of U.S. Aggression," *The New York Times* (January 2, 1961), 1–2; *Declassified Documents Reference System:* "Memorandum . . . with Dean Rusk" (Carrollton, Md., January 3, 1961), p. 2940; *Central Intelligence Agency: Current Intelligence Bulletins*, declassified September 1976 (Washington, January 3, 1961), p. 42; *Central Intelligence Agency: Memoranda for the Director, 1960–1962* (Washington, January 27, 1961, referring to December 8, 1960), p. 1; *Executive Sessions of the Senate Foreign Relations Committee, 1961*, Vol. XIII, Pt. 1, pp. 445–446; Bissell, *Transcript: Eisenhower Oral History*, pp. 29–30; R. H. Smith, *Spymaster's Odyssey: The World of Allen Dulles*, MS (New York, n.d.), ch. 23, pp. 13–16, ch. 32, pp. 9–10, ch. 34, pp. 16–17; John Prados, *Presidents' Secret Wars* (New York, 1986), pp. 183–185.

22. Schlesinger, *Robert Kennedy*, pp. 457–458; cf. Taylor, *Taylor Committee Report:* "Memorandums" (April 23, 1961), p. 7; *Operation Zapata*, pp. 71–72.

23. Herbert Matthews, *Revolution in Cuba* (New York, 1975), pp. 198 199; Paul Kennedy, "U.S. Helps Train an Anti-Castro Force at Secret Guatemalan Air-Ground Base," *The New York Times* (January 10, 1961), 1, 11; and *id.*, *The Middle Beat*, pp. 221–225; Taylor, *Taylor Committee Report:* "Memorandums" (April 27, 1961), p. 38, and (May 13, 1961), pp. 23–24; Taylor, *Taylor Committee Report*, Pts. 1 and 2 (January 31, 1961), p. 14; *ibid.*, "Memorandum No. 1," pp. 5–6; *Central Intelligence Agency: CIA Information Reports*, declassified 1982 (Washington, January 11, 1961); *Central Intelligence Agency: Current Intelligence Digests and*

Weekly Summaries (Washington,
January 12, 1961), p. 3; *Executive Sessions of the Senate Foreign Relations Committee, 1961,*
Vol. XIII, Pt. 2, p. 66.
24. *Foreign Relations of the United States* [*FRUS*] *1952–1954,* Vol.
XIII: *Indochina,* Department of
State (Washington, 1982), Pt. 1,
p. 982.
25. Eisenhower, *Papers, Post-Presidential, 1959–1961, Kennedy, J.
F.,* recorded by General Wilton
Parsons (Abilene, Kans., January
19, 1961), Box 5; cf. *Executive
Sessions of the Senate Foreign
Relations Committee, 1961,* Vol.
XIII, Pt. 1, p. 585; Schlesinger,
Robert Kennedy, pp. 444n., 528,
702, and *id., A Thousand Days,*
pp. 163–164; Clark Clifford, "A
Vietnam Reappraisal," *Foreign
Affairs* (July 1968): 604; *The
Pentagon Papers,* Senator Gravel
ed., Vol. II (Boston, 1971), pp.
635–643; Admiral Arleigh Burke,
Oral Reminiscences 1955–1961
(Annapolis, 1973), pp. 220–221.
While Eisenhower's own disclaimer of awareness of the new CIA
plan need not be taken too seriously, according to Robert Hurwitch, the State Department
official in charge of the Cuba desk
at this time, in his briefing for
Kennedy's meeting with President Eisenhower, Hurwitch could
not inform the President-Elect of
the current plans for Cuba. Like
almost all other medium-level
officials in the department, he had
been bypassed on information for
any such operation. Robert A.
Hurwitch, *Transcript: Kennedy
Oral History,* Pt. I (Boston, April
24, 1964), pp. 3–12, 29–33.
26. Dennison, p. 335; cf. Berle and
Jacobs, pp. 726, 732; Eisenhower, *Waging Peace,* p. 614;
Phillips, pp. 99–100; Earl Mazo,
*Transcript: Eisenhower Oral
History* (New York: Columbia
University Library, December 7,
1966), pp. 44–46; Gordon Gray,
*Transcript: Eisenhower Oral
History* (New York: Columbia
University Library, December 7,
1966), pp. 257–277.

I V.   *A Golden Age*

1. John F. Kennedy, *The Strategy
of Peace,* ed. Allen Nevins (New
York, 1961), pp. 172–175.
2. Robert Frost, *Of Poetry and
Power,* ed. A. Glikes and P.
Schwaber (New York, 1964), p.
52.
3. *American Foreign Policy, Current Documents,* 1961, Department of State Historical Office
(Washington, June 1965), pp.
282–283; "Castro Suggests Amity
with U.S.," *The New York Times*
(January 21, 1961), 1, 6; Maurice
Halperin, *The Rise and Decline of
Fidel Castro* (Berkeley, 1972), pp.
89–92; *Central Intelligence
Agency: Current Intelligence
Digests and Weekly Summaries*
(Washington, January 26, 1961),
p. 9.
4. Theodore Sorensen, *Transcript:
Kennedy Oral History* (Boston,
April 6, 1964), p. 292; cf. *Kennedy and the Press: The News
Conferences,* ed. H. Chase and A.
Lerman (New York, 1965), p. 5;
Richard Bissell, Jr., *Transcript:
Kennedy Oral History* (Boston,
April 1967), pp. 10–12; *Alleged
Assassination Plots Involving
Foreign Leaders: An Interim
Report* (Washington, 1975), p.
119; *Executive Sessions of the*

Senate Foreign Relations Committee, 1961 (Washington, 1984), Vol. XIII, Pt. 2, pp. 24–44.

5. General Maxwell Taylor, Taylor Committee Report and Memorandum for Record of Paramilitary Study Group Meetings, Pt. 3: "Memorandum of Discussion on Cuba," declassified April 1985 (Washington, January 28, 1961), pp. 1–2.

6. Ibid., "Military Evaluation of the Cuban Plan" (February 3, 1961), pp. 1–36.

7. Ibid.; cf. CINCLANT Contingency Operation Plan (Cuba): "JCS Memorandum of the Secretary," Box CCS37, 3142 (Washington: National Archives, February 1, 1961), 312–61(S); Declassified Documents Reference System: "Memorandum of Discussion on Cuba, Cabinet Room, January 23, 1961" (Carrollton, Md., January 23, 1961), p. 554, 1–2.

8. Peter Wyden, The Bay of Pigs (New York, 1979), pp. 89–93; cf. John Ranelagh, The Agency: The Rise and Decline of the CIA (New York, 1986), p. 364.

9. Declassified Documents Reference System: "Memorandum for the President" (February 8, 1961), pp. 556, 1. Estimates for the number of arms packs vary enormously. Central Intelligence Agency: Current Intelligence Digests and Weekly Summaries (February 2, 1961), Pt. J, p. 3; Taylor, Taylor Committee Report: "Memorandum" (April 24, 1961), pp. 3, 4, 12, afternoon meeting, pp. 8–12, and (May 13, 1961), p. 13; ibid., Pt. 3: "Military Evaluation of the Cuban Plan," declassified April 1985 (Washington), pp. 5, 10, 26–27, 30–32; Operation Zapata:. The "Ultrasensitive" Report and Testimony of the Board of Inquiry on the Bay of Pigs (Frederick, Md., 1981), pp. 66 ff., 103–107; Arthur Schlesinger, Jr., A Thousand Days (Boston, 1965), pp. 238–239; Morton Halperin, "The President and the Military," Foreign Affairs (January 1972): 322; Admiral R. L. Dennison, Transcript: Oral Reminiscences (Annapolis: U.S. Naval Institute, August 1975), p. 337.

10. Lucien Vandenbroucke, "The 'Confessions' of Allen Dulles—New Evidence on the Bay of Pigs," Diplomatic History (Fall 1984): 392; Jean Stern, The Times of Robert Kennedy (New York, 1970), p. 130; "The National Security Council," in Jackson Subcommittee Papers and Policy-Making at the Presidential Level (Washington, 1965), pp. 38–40; Senator Henry Jackson, Senate Subcommittee Hearings and Findings Pts. V and VI (Washington, May 26–June 14, 1960), pp. 668 ff., 725 ff., 761 ff., 789 ff., 881 ff., 905; Thomas Gates, Jr., Transcript: Eisenhower Oral History (New York: Columbia University, August 1967), pp. 34–36, 271–275; Taylor, Taylor Committee Report: "Memorandum No. 1," pp. 4, 7; ibid., "Memorandum" (May 4, 1961), p. 6, (May 8, 1961), pp. 22–28; id., Responsibility and Response (New York, 1967), pp. 67–69; id., Swords and Plowshares (New York, 1972), pp. 196–199; Schlesinger, pp. 209–210; Ellis Briggs, Anatomy of Diplomacy (New York, 1968), p. 17.

11. Alleged Assassination Plots, pp. 83, 117–121, 181–188, 264–265, 275; cf. Vandenbroucke, 374, n. 33; Robert Amory, Transcript: Kennedy Oral History (Boston: Kennedy Library, 1966), File 7, File 17, pp. 19–20; Bisscll, pp. 2, 50–52; Ray Cline, Secrets, Spies

and Scholars (Washington, 1976), pp. 186–187; Arthur Schlesinger, Jr., Robert Kennedy and His Times (Boston, 1978), pp. 478–492; Thomas Powers, The Man Who Kept the Secrets: Richard Helms and the CIA, MS (New York, 1979), p. 106; Charles Yost, The Conduct and Misconduct of Foreign Affairs (New York, 1972), pp. 141–143; and, especially, William Colby with Peter Forbath, Honorable Men: My Life in the CIA (New York, 1978), pp. 186, 213–214, 317, 428–430; H. H. Ransom, Report to the President by the Commission on CIA Activities within the United States (Washington, June 1975).

12. McGeorge Bundy, National Security Files (Boston: Kennedy Library, February 8, 19, 25, 1961), Box 35.

13. American Foreign Policy: Current Documents, 1961, p. 285; Richard Walton, The Remnants of Power: The Tragic Last Years of Adlai Stevenson (New York, 1968), p. 28; Adolf Berle, Diary, MS (Hyde Park, N.Y., December 18, 1960); id. Papers and Diary, MSS (Hyde Park, N.Y., February 16, 1961); Executive Sessions of the Senate Foreign Relations Committee, 1961, Vol. XIII, Pt. 2, pp. 23–24.

14. Alleged Assassination Plots, pp. 123–130, 826; "Kennedy Cover-Up Denied by Church," The New York Times (December 16, 1975), 45; Senator George Smathers, Transcript: Oral History (Boston: Kennedy Library, March 31, 1964), pp. 6B–7B; Bissell, pp. 36–37; Jack Anderson, "Six Attempts to Kill Castro Laid to the CIA," The Washington Post (January 18, 1971), B17; Judith Exner, My Story, As Told to Ovid Demaris (New York, 1977), pp. 210 ff., 251–252; Powers, pp. 121–124.

15. Amory, pp. 128–129; cf. Central Intelligence Agency: Current Intelligence Digests and Weekly Summaries (March 9, 1961), pp. 9–10; Taylor, Taylor Committee Report: "Memorandums" (April 23, 1961, afternoon meeting), p. 20, (April 26, 1961), p. 3, (May 1, 1961), p. 6, (May 3, 1961), pp. 3, 13. The Joint Chiefs also feared that Castro might soon receive two Soviet destroyers, thus complicating further their difficult planning for Cuba. Taylor, Taylor Committee Report: "Memorandums" (May 18, 1961), p. 8; id., Taylor Committee Report, Pt. 3: "Proposed Operation against Cuba" (March 11, 1961), pp. 3–5; ibid., "Evaluation of the CIA Cuban Task Force," p. 18.

16. Taylor, Taylor Committee Report, Pt. 3: "Military Evaluation of the Cuban Plan," pp. 7–8; ibid., "Evaluation of the CIA Cuban Volunteer Task Force" (February 1961), pp. 2–23; ibid., "Memorandum No. 1," pp. 7–8; ibid., "Memorandums" (April 23, 1961), pp. 16 ff., (afternoon meeting), pp. 11–206, (April 26, 1961), pp. 2–5, (May 3, 1961), pp. 3–13; Operation Zapata, pp. 10 ff., 106 ff.; Dennison, pp. 34, 146; Schlesinger, Robert Kennedy, p. 487n., and id., A Thousand Days, pp. 238–240; George Volsky, "Cuba Exiles Recall Domestic Spying and Picketing for C.I.A.," The New York Times (January 4, 1975), 8; Haynes Johnson and others, The Bay of Pigs (New York, 1964), pp. 66–67; Bissell, pp. 10–17; Bissell claims that the Joint Chiefs of Staff deemed the chances of success about 2 to 1. Richard Bissell, Jr., Transcript: Eisenhower Oral History (New York: Columbia University Library, 1967), pp. 26–27.

17. Allen Dulles, Papers, Articles and

Briefings: Conclusions (Princeton: Mudd Library, 1965), Box 244; cf. Operation Zapata, pp. 12–13, 56–57; Taylor, Taylor Committee Report, Pt. 3: "Proposed Operation against Cuba" (March 11, 1961), pp. 1–12; id.,

Taylor Committee Report: "Memorandum No. 1," pp. 9–10; ibid., "Memorandums" (April 26, 1961), pp. 3–5, and (May 3, 1961), pp. 3 ff.; id., Swords and Plowshares, p. 188.

V. An Orphan Child

1. A. R. Millet, The Politics of Intervention: The Military Occupation of Cuba 1906–1909 (Columbus, 1968), p. 123.
2. John F. Kennedy, Why England Slept (Westport, Conn., 1961), pp. 229–230.
3. Walter Isaacson and Evan Thomas, The Wise Men: Six Friends and the World They Made (New York, 1986), p. 613.
4. Declassified Documents Reference System: "Memorandum for the President, March 15, 1961" (Carrollton, Md., March 15, 1961), 556, 1; cf. Allen Dulles, Papers, Articles and Briefings: "My Answer to the Bay of Pigs" (Princeton: Mudd Library, 1965), Box 138, the more revealing earlier version, pp. 15 ff.; Operation Zapata: The "Ultrasensitive" Report and Testimony of the Board of Inquiry on the Bay of Pigs (Frederick, Md., 1981), pp. xiii, 66–67, 177, 344; General Maxwell Taylor, National Security File (Boston: Kennedy Library, February 3, March 11, March 15, 1961), Box 35; Richard Bissell, Jr., Transcript: Kennedy Oral History (Boston, April 1967), pp. 5–10, 24–25; Robert Amory, Transcript: Kennedy Oral History (Boston: Kennedy Library, 1966), pp. 127–180; Robert Murphy, Transcript: Eisenhower Oral History (New York: Columbia University

Library, 1973), pp. 33–34; Thomas Mann, Transcript: Kennedy Oral History (Boston, March 13, 1968), pp. 17–18; Lucien Vandenbroucke, "The Decision to Land at the Bay of Pigs," Political Science Quarterly (Fall 1984): 477–482; General Maxwell Taylor, Taylor Committee Report and Memorandum for Record of Paramilitary Study Group Meetings: "Memorandum No. 1," declassified April 1985 (Washington), p. 13; ibid., "Memorandums" (April 24, 1961), p. 17, (afternoon meeting), p. 15, (April 26, 1961), pp. 2–6, (May 1, 1961), pp 9–10, (May 3, 1961), pp. 8–10, (May 4, 1961), pp. 1–4, 7–9, (May 8, 1961), pp. 11–29, (May 18, 1961), pp. 2–11, (May 19, 1961), pp. 1–3; ibid., Pt. 3: "Evaluation of the Military Aspects of Alternative Concepts, CIA Para-Military Plan, Cuba" (March 15, 1961), pp. 1–10, esp. Appendix C; ibid., "Summary of White House Meetings" (May 9, 1961), pp. 1–2; id., Swords and Plowshares (New York, 1972), pp. 188, 194; David Rosenberg, Arleigh Albert Burke, Chief of Naval Operations 1955–1961, MS (Annapolis, 1980), pp. 90 ff.; David A. Phillips, The Night Watch (New York, 1977), p. 102.
5. Schlesinger, Papers, Memoranda for the President (New York, March 15, 1961); Harold Macmillan, Pointing the Way 1959–

1961 (London, 1972), pp. 353–354. Macmillian would tell the President later on that, had Cubans only shot the Prime Minister's plane, Kennedy then "could have had [his] little invasion." Benjamin Bradlee, *Conversations with Kennedy* (New York, 1975), p. 226.

6. Arthur Schlesinger, Jr., *A Thousand Days* (Boston, 1965), pp. 329–339, and *id.*, *Robert Kennedy and His Times* (Boston, 1978), p. 528; Arthur Dommen, *Conflict in Laos* (New York, 1967), pp. 188–195; Amory, p. 37; David Halberstam, *The Best and the Brightest* (New York, 1969), p. 89; Warren Cohen, *Dean Rusk* (Totowa, N.J., 1980), pp. 127–132; George Ball, *The Past Has Another Pattern: Memoirs* (New York, 1982), pp. 361–363; Roger Hilsman, *To Move a Nation* (New York, 1967), pp. 127–135; William J. Rust and others, *Kennedy in Vietnam* (New York, 1985), ch. II; George M. Kahin, *Intervention* (New York, 1986), pp. 127 ff.

7. Schlesinger, *A Thousand Days*, pp. 244–247; cf. *Central Intelligence Agency: Current Intelligence Digests and Weekly Summaries* (Washington, March 27 and March 30, 1961), pp. 4–11; *Central Intelligence Agency: CIA Information Reports*, declassified 1982 (Washington, April 6, 1961), p. 1; Carlos Franqui, *Diary of the Cuban Revolution* (New York, 1980), pp. 43–44, 105; Nicolas Rivero, *Castro's Cuba: An American Dilemma* (Washington, 1962), pp. 173–179; Richard Bissell, Jr., *Transcript: Eisenhower Oral History* (New York: Columbia University Library, 1967), p. 9; E. Howard Hunt, *Give Us This Day* (New Rochelle, 1973), pp. 142 ff.; Lyman Kirkpatrick, Jr.,

"Paramilitary Case Study—The Bay of Pigs," *Naval War College Review* (November–December 1972): 35–36; Jay Mallin, "The Call to Arms That Never Came," *Tropic, The Miami Herald* (March 10, 1974), 10–44; Joseph B. Smith, *Portrait of a Cold Warrior* (New York, 1976), pp. 340–342.

8. Dulles, Box 244, nn., 2, A; cf. especially Thomas Powers, *The Man Who Kept the Secrets: Richard Helms and the CIA*, MS (New York, 1979), pp. 74–75; Schlesinger, *Robert Kennedy*, pp. 452–453; Bissell, *Transcript: Eisenhower Oral History*, pp. 29–30; Allen Dulles, *The Craft of Intelligence* (New York, 1965), pp. 157–158; "Rusk on the Record," *The Village Voice* (April 16, 1985), 17; Taylor, *Swords and Plowshares*, p. 190; *id.*, *Taylor Committee Report:* "Memorandum No. 1," pp. 16–17; *ibid.*, "Memorandums" (April 24, 1961), pp. 18–19, (May 8, 1961), pp. 9–18, 23–24, 33.

9. "Director Colby on the Record," *Time* (September 30, 1974), 19; cf. Lyman Kirkpatrick, Jr., *Transcript: Kennedy Oral History* (Boston, April 16, 1967), pp. 4–7; Major General Sir Kenneth Strong, *Men of Intelligence* (London, 1970), ch. V; Schlesinger, *A Thousand Days*, p. 248. The misunderstanding and possibly outright deception of Miró Cardona, Chief of the Cuban Revolutionary Council, eventually led to his belief that he had been promised by Adolf Berle and the agency between 15,000 and 30,000 U.S. troops to support the invading Brigade. Taylor, *Taylor Committee Report:* "Memorandum" (May 25, 1961), pp. 3–4.

10. Dulles, *Papers:* "My Answer to the Bay of Pigs," Box 138, pp. 13–37; *Kennedy and the Press:*

The News Conferences, ed. H. Chase and A. Lerman (New York, 1965), January 24, 1963, pp. 368–369; "Robert Kennedy Speaks His Mind," U.S. News & World Report (January 22, 1963), 62; "We Were Promised Planes, Cuban Says," The Miami Herald (January 22, 1963), 1; Hilsman, pp. 33–34; Hugh Thomas, Cuba, or the Pursuit of Freedom (New York, 1971), p. 1210; see Chalmers Roberts, First Rough Draft (New York, 1973), pp. 190–191, for the optimism of General Lemnitzer concerning all Cuban projects, an official optimism evidently engendered by close association with Dulles.

11. Schlesinger, A Thousand Days, p. 251; cf. id., Robert Kennedy, pp. 442–445; Haynes Johnson and others, The Bay of Pigs (New York, 1964), pp. 68–69; H. Johnson and B. Gwertzman, Fulbright: The Dissenter (Garden City, N.Y., 1968), pp. 174–175; Taylor, Taylor Committee Report: "Memorandum No. 1," p. 15; ibid., "Memorandums" (May 1 and 4, 1961), pp. 11–12, (May 3, 1961), pp. 7–9, (May 4, 1961), pp. 7–8; ibid., Pt. 3: "Summary of White House Meetings," p. 2; Theodore Sorensen, Transcript: Kennedy Oral History (Boston, April 6, 1964), pp. 19, 25; Alan Riding, "For Rudderless Costa Rica, a Quixotic Rescue Effort," The New York Times (January 12, 1981), A2.

12. "Fulbright Panel Votes C.I.A. Role," The New York Times (May 18, 1966), 6; cf. David Wise and Thomas Ross, The Espionage Establishment (New York, 1967), p. 171; Victor Marchetti and John Marks, The CIA and the Cult of Intelligence (New York, 1974), p. 342; Foreign and Military Intelligence, Bk. I: Final Report . . .

Select Committee . . . Intelligence Activities (Washington, April 14, 1965), pp. 547–553; and particularly William Colby with Peter Forbath, Honorable Men: My Life in the CIA (New York, 1978), pp. 18–19, 182 ff.

13. Dean Acheson, Transcript: Kennedy Oral History (Boston, April 27, 1967), pp. 6 ff.; cf. Taylor, Taylor Committee Report: "Memorandums" (May 5, 1961), p. 1; ibid., Pt. 3: "Proposed Operation against Cuba," p. 5.

14. Ronald Steel, "Seduction and Betrayal," The New York Review of Books (September 25, 1980), 55; cf. Operation Zapata, p. 267; B. Berle and T. Jacobs, Navigating the Rapids, ed. B. Berle and T. Jacobs (New York, 1973), pp. 729–743; Schlesinger, A Thousand Days, p. 250; Cohen, p. 104.

15. Rusk even claimed that the "modified" plan, when it was finally put into action, would probably not make the first page of The New York Times. Chester Bowles, Promises to Keep: My Years in Public Life 1921–1969 (New York, 1971), pp. 326 ff., 404. Bissell uses the same argument that, at the time, he also believed that the invasion could remain covert and admits to his and Colonel Hawkins's emotional commitment against calling off the operation (as a possible result of their very necessary illusions regarding secrecy). John Ranelagh, The Agency: The Rise and Decline of the CIA (New York, 1986), pp. 371–372.

16. Seymour Hersh, "Hearings Urged on CIA's Role in Chile," The New York Times (September 9, 1974), 3; cf. id., "Firm Rein on Intelligence Units Urged by 2 Ex-CIA Officials," The New York Times (December 11, 1974), 16, for Ray Cline's well-informed testimony;

John Crewdson, "House Committee Finds Intelligence Agencies Generally Go Unchecked," *The New York Times* (January 26, 1976), 1, 14; Ray Cline, *Secrets, Spies and Scholars* (Washington, 1976), pp. 245–254; Colby with Forbath, pp. 13–19, 182 ff.

17. *Cuba: U.S. Department of State Publication #7171* (Washington, April 1961), pp. 1–2; cf. K. S. Karol, *Guerrillas in Power* (New York, 1970), pp. 14–17; Schlesinger, *A Thousand Days*, pp. 245–246; Maurice Halperin, *The Rise and Decline of Fidel Castro* (Berkeley, 1972), p. 95; Smith, pp. 342–343; Richard Welch, Jr., *Response to Revolution* (Chapel Hill, N.C., 1985), pp. 74–76.

18. Taylor, *Taylor Committee Report:* "Memorandums" (May 3, 1961), p. 10; cf. Dulles, *Papers:* "My Answer to the Bay of Pigs," Box 138, p. 37; "Kennedy Tells of Cuban Decision," *The Christian Science Monitor* (December 19, 1962), 146–158; Berle, pp. 738–742; *Alleged Assassination Plots Involving Foreign Leaders: An Interim Report* (Washington, 1975), p. 272; *Executive Sessions of the Senate Foreign Relations Committee, 1961* (Washington,

1984), Vol. XIII, Pt. 2, pp. 63–66; Tristran Coffin, *Senator Fulbright* (New York, 1966), pp. 147–149; author's interview with Allen Dulles (Washington, January 18, 1963); author's interview with Senator William Fulbright (Washington, May 13, 1969); author's interview with General Lyman Lemnitzer (Washington, April 21, 1970); author's interview with Theodore Sorensen (New York, January 23, 1985); Mann, pp. 20–24.

19. Schlesinger, *A Thousand Days*, pp. 251–252.

20. Taylor, *Taylor Committee Report:* "Memorandums" (May 3, 1961), p. 10, (May 4, 1961), pp. 7–12; *Operation Zapata*, pp. 201–203; Dulles, *Papers*, "Disclosures," Box 244; Mann, pp. 20–24; Mann, letters to the author (Austin, Tex., January 19, 1979), p. 1; Berle, pp. 738–743; U. Alexis Johnson, *Transcript: Kennedy Oral History* (Boston, n.d.), p. 1; Vandenbroucke, 482, n. 29; Admiral Arleigh Burke, *Transcript: Eisenhower Oral History* (Abilene, Kans., June 12, 1973), pp. 218–220.

21. Henry A. Kissinger, *The Necessity for Choice* (New York, 1961), pp. 342–343.

VI. *Day of Dupes*

1. William J. Rust and others, *Kennedy in Vietnam* (New York, 1985), p. 125.

2. Stanley Karnow, *Vietnam: A History* (New York, 1984), p. 652.

3. Kenneth Love, *Suez: The Twice Fought War* (New York, 1969), p. 443.

4. Arthur Schlesinger, Jr., *Papers, Memoranda for the President* (New York, April 5, 1961), pp. 1–

15; *id.*, *A Thousand Days* (Boston, 1965), pp. 252–258.

5. General Maxwell Taylor, *Taylor Committee Report and Memorandum for Record of Paramilitary Study Group Meetings*, Pt. 3: "Summary of White House Meeting," declassified April 1985 (Washington), p. 3; cf. Lyman Kirkpatrick, Jr., "Paramilitary Case Study—The Bay of Pigs," *Naval*

War College Review (November–
December 1972): 40–41; *Foreign
Relations of the United States
[FRUS] 1941*, Vol. I: *General: The
Soviet Union*, Department of State
(Washington, 1958), pp. 789–790;
National Security Files (Boston:
Kennedy Library, March 29,
1961), Box 35; Charles Murphy,
"Cuba—The Record Set Straight,"
Fortune (September 1961), 224.
6. Taylor, *Taylor Committee Report:*
"Memorandums" (May 4, 1961),
pp. 10–11; cf. *ibid.*, "Rules of
Engagement of Operation Bumpy
Road," pp. 1 ff.; Admiral R. L.
Dennison, *Transcript: Oral Rem-
iniscences* (Annapolis: U.S. Naval
Academy, August 1975), pp. 348–
349; Taylor, *Taylor Committee
Report*, Pt. 3: "Memorandum for
Mr. Murrow" (April 23, 1961),
pp. 1–3.
7. Bill Moyers, "Open Letter to
Arthur Schlesinger," *The Wall
Street Journal* (New York, July
20, 1977), 10; cf. Schlesinger, *A
Thousand Days*, pp. 254–258;
Chalmers Roberts, *First Rough
Draft* (New York, 1973), p. 188.
Roger Hilsman, Director of Intelligence and Research in the State
Department, was severly rebuffed
by Rusk on his offer of aid at this
time for the customary reason that
security would prevent the consultation of his I-and-R experts
on Cuba. Roger Hilsman, *To Move
a Nation* (Garden City, N.Y.,
1967), p. 31.
8. Pierre Salinger, *With Kennedy*
(Garden City, N.Y., 1966), p. 146;
cf. Louise Fitzsimmons, *The Kennedy Doctrine* (New York, 1972),
pp. 49–51; Tad Szulc, "Anti-Castro Units Trained to Fight at Florida Bases," *The New York Times*
(April 7, 1961), 1–2; Taylor, *Taylor Committee Report:* "Memorandums" (April 24, 1961), pp.
15–16; Roberts, pp. 188–190.

9. Clifton Daniel, "Excerpts from
Speech on Coverage of Bay of
Pigs Buildup," *The New York
Times* (January 2, 1964), 14; cf.
Tad Szulc, articles, *The New York
Times* (April 6–10, 1961); Harri-
son Salisbury, *Without Fear or
Favor* (New York, 1980), pp 151–
163; Turner Catledge, *My Life
and the Times* (New York, 1971),
pp. 260–265; Gilbert Harrison,
*Transcript: Kennedy Oral His-
tory* (Boston: Kennedy Library,
October 6, 1967), pp. 10–11; see
the discussion of this basic issue
for any democracy in Lewis J.
Paper, *The Promise and the
Performance: The Leadership of
John F. Kennedy* (New York,
1975), pp. 251–257.
10. Schlesinger, *A Thousand Days*,
pp. 271–272; cf. David Wise, *The
Politics of Lying* (New York,
1973), pp. 37–38; John Bartlow
Martin, *Adlai Stevenson and the
World* (Garden City, N.Y., 1977),
pp. 624 ff.; David A. Phillips, *The
Night Watch* (New York, 1977),
p. 106.
11. Haynes Johnson and others, *The
Bay of Pigs* (New York, 1964),
pp. 71–77; cf. Hugh Thomas,
Cuba, or the Pursuit of Freedom
(New York, 1971), pp. 994, 1028,
1030, 1213; Harold Macmillan
Pointing the Way 1959–1961
(London, 1972), p. 350; J. Dorschner and R. Fabricio, *The Winds
of December* (New York, 1980),
pp. 166 ff.
12. Schlesinger, *Papers* (April 10,
1961), pp. 2–8, also in Kennedy
Library, Box 65; cf. Schlesinger,
A Thousand Days, p. 254.
13. Arthur Schlesinger, Jr., *Robert
Kennedy and His Times* (Boston,
1978), p. 452; Kirkpatrick, p. 196;
Richard Bissell, Jr., *Transcript:
Kennedy Oral History* (Boston,
April 1967), pp. 33–35; and see
ahead, n. 15; Manuel Peñabaz,

"We Were Destroyed," *U.S. News & World Report* (January 14, 1963), 47; Theodore Sorensen, *Transcript: Kennedy Oral History* (Boston, April 6, 1964), pp. 296–298, 302; John Ranelagh, *The Agency: The Rise and Decline of the CIA* (New York, 1986), pp. 371–372; Richard Bissell, Jr., "Response to Lucien S. Vandenbroucke, the 'Confessions' of Allen Dulles: New Evidence on the Bay of Pigs," *Diplomatic History* (Fall 1984): 380.

14. *Kennedy and the Press: The News Conferences*, ed. H. Chase and A. Lerman (New York, 1965), p. 59; W. W. Rostow, *The Diffusion of Power 1957–1972* (New York, 1972), p. 654.

15. Bissell, "Response to Lucien Vandenbroucke," 380; Taylor, *Taylor Committee Report:* "Memorandums" (April 24, 1961), pp. 5–6, 16, (April 24, 1961, afternoon meeting), pp. 17–20, (May 4, 1961), p. 2; *ibid.*, Pt. 3: "Memorandum for Lt. Colonel B. W. Tarwater" (April 26, 1961), p. 1; *ibid.*, "Memorandum for Admiral R. L. Dennison: Bumpy Road," Enclosure A (April 1, 1961), pp. 186–187; Schlesinger, *Robert Kennedy*, pp. 442, 453; Tom Flaherty, "Anatomy of the Snafu," *Life* (May 10, 1963), 83. Even before this date, some CIA air planners had evidently given up hope of minimal success for whatever marginal air strikes might pass Kennedy's muster, owing to the lack of open U.S. air support. Joseph B. Smith, *Portrait of a Cold Warrior* (New York, 1976), p. 328.

16. Taylor, *Taylor Committee Report:* "Memorandum No. 1," pp. 13–14, 26–27; *ibid.*, "Memorandums" (April 25, 1961), pp. 3–4, (April 28, 1961), pp. 6–8, (May 25, 1961), pp. 1–2; Dennison, pp.

34–367; Schlesinger, *A Thousand Days*, pp. 262, 275; Lucien Vandenbroucke, "The 'Confessions' of Allen Dulles—New Evidence on the Bay of Pigs," *Diplomatic History* (Fall 1984): 370–371.

17. Taylor, *Taylor Committee Report,* Pt. 3: "Memorandum for General Taylor" (April 16, 1961).

18. Schlesinger, *A Thousand Days*, pp. 267–268; Johnson and others, p. 73; Richard M. Nixon. *The Memoirs of Richard M. Nixon*, Vol. I (New York, 1978), p. 288. In justice to the Hawkins report, 20 percent of the Brigade was comprised of former professional Cuban soldiers. Nevertheless, in the Taylor post-mortem, General David Shoup, Commandant of the Marine Corps, considered the invading Brigade to be a bad joke. Taylor, *Taylor Committee Report:* "Memorandums" (May 1, 1961), p. 4, (May 18, 1961), p. 19; *Operation Zapata: The "Ultrasensitive" Report and Testimony of the Board of Inquiry on the Bay of Pigs* (Frederick, Md., 1981), pp. 104–105, 154–155; John Dille, "With a Quiet Curse It All Began," *Life* (May 10, 1963), 34; Robert A. Hurwitch, *Transcript: Kennedy Oral History*, Pt. I (Boston, April–May 1964), pp. 30–53; Peter Wyden, *The Bay of Pigs* (New York, 1979), pp. 125–126, 168–179; Kirkpatrick concluded that the CIA training officers did not mislead the Cuban Brigade on the direct participation of Americans in the invasion. Lyman Kirkpatrick, Jr., *Transcript: Kennedy Oral History* (Boston, April 16, 1967), p. 20, and *id.*, "Paramilitary Case Study," 37.

19. Taylor, *Taylor Committee Report:* "Memorandums" (April 27, 1961, and May 3, 1961); *ibid.*, Pt. 3: "Proposed Operation against

Cuba," p. 2; *ibid.*, "Evaluation of the CIA Cuban Volunteer Task Force," p. 7; *ibid.*, "Sequence of Events" (May 3, 1961), pp. 2–3; *ibid.*, "Memorandum No. 1," pp. 14–15; "America and the 'Common Danger'—Dean Rusk Talks to Michael Charlton," *The Listener* (January 9, 1977), 744; Johnson and others, pp. 88–95; *Executive Sessions of the Senate Foreign Relations Committee, 1961* (Washington, 1984), Vol. XIII, Pt. 2, pp. 26 ff., 42; Wayne Smith, *The Closest of Enemies* (New York, 1987), p. 53.

20. Johnson and others, pp. 86–99; cf. General S. L. A. Marshall's citation of the Somoza letter, Allen Dulles, *Papers, Articles and Briefings* (Princeton: Mudd Library, 1965), Box 138. In 1980, the Sandinistas welcomed Castro in Managua with his beard still intact, as the Cuban leader proudly pointed out. Shirley Christian, *Nicaragua: Revolution in the Family* (New York, 1985), p. 166.

21. Only the original Trinidad plan had considered a junction of the invading force with guerrillas in the Escambray region. Taylor, *Taylor Committee Report*, Pt. 3: "Military Evaluation of the Cuban Plan" (March 11, 1961), pp. 20–33; *ibid.*, "Memorandums" (April 24, 1961), p. 7, (May 1, 1961), p. 7, (May 16, 1961), pp. 4–8, (May 18, 1961), pp. 11–12; *ibid.*, Pt. 3: "Supply Data" (May 23, 1961); *Operation Zapata*, p. 98; *Executive Sessions of the Senate Foreign Relations Committee, 1961*, Vol. XIII, Pt. 1, p. 391.

22. Taylor, *Taylor Committee Report*: "Memorandum No. 1," pp. 12–25; *ibid.*, "Memorandums" (April 24, 1961), p. 103, (afternoon meeting that day), pp. 21–22, (April 25, 1961), pp. 2–3, (May 3, 1961), p. 9, (May 6, 1961), p.

2, (May 8, 1961), pp. 10–31, (May 13, 1961), pp. 9–10; *ibid.*, Pt. 3: "Sequence of Events," pp. 1–2; *Operation Zapata*, pp. 118 ff., 234 ff., 256, 257, 268–279, 322; *Executive Sessions of the Senate Foreign Relations Committee, 1961,* Vol. XIII, Pt. 1, pp. 396–397, 436, 602–611; Bissell, "Response to Lucien Vandenbroucke," 378–379; *American Foreign Policy, Current Documents, 1961,* Department of State Historical Office (Washington, 1965), p. 289. According to a Cuban source, Castro admitted that by the morning of April 17 he had only nine operative planes left and only seven pilots; many of Castro's fighter pilots were still being trained in Eastern Europe for the still-unassembled Soviet MiGs. Maurice Halperin, *The Rise and Decline of Fidel Castro* (Berkeley, 1972), pp. 104–106, esp. p. 106, n. 2.

23. "Roa in U.N. Lays Bombing to U.S.," *The New York Times* (April 16, 1961), 1–3.

24. *United Nations, General Assembly, Official Records, 1961,* Session 15 (New York, April 15–17, 1961); Wyden, pp. 185–188; Schlesinger, *A Thousand Days,* pp. 271–272.

25. Charles Yost, *The Conduct and Misconduct of Foreign Affairs* (New York, 1972), pp. 74–75; author's interview with Charles Yost (New York, December 10, 1973); W. McGaffin and E. Knoll, *Anything but the Truth—The Credibility Gap, How the News Is Managed in Washington* (New York, 1968), p. 22; Richard Walton, *The Remnants of Power: The Tragic Last Years of Adlai Stevenson* (New York, 1968), pp. 32–36; Phillips, pp. 105–106; Martin, pp. 626 ff.; Stewart Alsop, *The Center: People and Power in*

Political Washington (New York, 1968), pp. 195 ff.

26. Karl Meyer and Tad Szulc, *The Cuban Invasion: The Chronicle of a Disaster* (New York, 1962), pp. 123–124; cf. Dulles, *Papers:* "My Answer to the Bay of Pigs," Box 138, pp. 29–31; Taylor: *Taylor Committee Report:* "Memorandums" (April 24, 1961, afternoon meeting), pp. 2–7, (April 26, 1961), p. 4, (May 18, 1961), p. 2; *American Foreign Policy, Current Documents,* 1961, p. 289; *Central Intelligence Agency: Current Intelligence Bulletins,* declassified September 1976 (Washington, April 17, 1961), p. 1.

27. McGeorge Bundy, "Beware of Aiding the 'Contras,' " *The New York Times* (June 12, 1985), A19; cf. Dean Rusk with David Nunnerley, *Transcript: Oral History* (Boston: Kennedy Library, February 9, 1970), pp. 3 ff.

28. Dulles, *Papers:* "My Answer to the Bay of Pigs," Box 138, pp. 2–31; cf. Schlesinger, *Robert Kennedy,* pp. 453–454; and *id., A Thousand Days,* pp. 272–274.

29. Taylor, *Taylor Committee Report,* Pt. 3: "Memorandum for General Taylor," pp. 1–3; *ibid.,* "Military Evaluation of the Cuban Plan," p. 23; *ibid.,* "Sequence of Events," pp. 1–2; *ibid.,* "Memorandum No. 1"; General Maxwell Taylor, *Maxwell Taylor File: Robert F. Kennedy Papers, #1* (Boston: Kennedy Library, October 22, 1969), p. 3; *id., Taylor Committee Report:* "Memorandums" (April 24, 1961), pp. 6, 21, (April 24, 1961, afternoon meeting), pp. 22–23, (April 24, 1961), p. 3, (April 25, 1961), pp. 4–10, (May 1 and 4, 1961), pp. 13–14, (May 6, 1961), pp. 1–3; *Operation Zapata,* pp. 130, 146, 180, 221 ff.; interview with Richard Bissell by David Wise, in "Exiles May Have Hit Central America," *The New York Herald Tribune* (July 21, 1965), 1; Dennison, pp. 49–52, 264 ff.; Kirkpatrick, *Transcript: Kennedy Oral History,* pp. 10–12; *Executive Sessions of the Senate Foreign Relations Committee, 1961,* Vol. XIII, Pt. 1, pp. 504, 516. E. Howard Hunt has written that Cozumel in Yucatán was scratched as a nearby refueling base for the B-26 strikes, both because of the reluctance of the Mexican government and because of the venality of the local officials on the spot. E. Howard Hunt, *Give Us This Day* (New Rochelle, N.Y., 1973), pp. 183–184, 195–200.

30. Tristan Coffin, *Senator Fulbright* (New York, 1966), p. 149.

31. Vandenbroucke, " 'Confessions' of Allen Dulles," 375.

VII. *Bumpy Road*

1. Walter Millis, *The Martial Spirit* (Cambridge, Mass., 1931), p. 12.

2. Martin Blumenson, "General Lucas at Anzio," in *Command Decisions,* Office of the Chief of Military History (New York, 1959), p. 256.

3. "Military Situation in the Far East," in *Hearing before the Joint Senate Committee on Armed Services and Foreign Relations,* 82d Cong., 1st sess., 1951, 1584. For the striking analogies between Bay of Pigs and Dieppe or Suez, see Philip Ziegler, *Mountbattan* (New York, 1985), chs. 14 and 41.

4. *Executive Sessions of the Senate Foreign Relations Committee,*

1961 (Washington, 1984), Vol. XIII, Pt. 1, pp. 405, 416, 446, 598 ff., 614; *Operation Zapata: The "Ultrasensitive" Report and Testimony of the Board of Inquiry on the Bay of Pigs* (Frederick, Md., 1981), pp. 173, 315; General Maxwell Taylor, *Taylor Committee Report and Memorandum for Record of Paramilitary Study Group Meeting:* "Memorandum No. 1," declassified April 1985 (Washington), pp. 18–24; *ibid.,* "Memorandum No. 2" (June 13, 1961), pp. 1–2; *ibid.,* "Memorandums" (April 24, 1961, afternoon meeting), pp. 3–5, 18–19, (April 26, 1961), pp. 6–10, (April 26, 1961), pp. 3–4, (April 27, 1961), pp. 6–7, (April 28, 1961), pp. 2–5, (May 1, 1961), pp. 2–6, (May 2, 1961), pp. 1–6, 9–11, (May 4, 1961), p. 8, (May 8, 1961), pp. 9–10, (May 16, 1961), pp. 2–9, (May 17, 1961), pp. 1–16, (May 18, 1961), pp. 2, 15–16, (May 19, 1961), pp. 9–10; *ibid.,* Pt. 3: "Rules of Engagement," pp. 2–3; *ibid.,* "After Action Report on Operation Pluto" (May 4, 1961), pp. 1–10; Haynes Johnson and others, *The Bay of Pigs* (New York, 1964), pp. 103 ff.; Peter Wyden, *The Bay of Pigs* (New York, 1979), pp. 82–83, 133–138; Admiral R. L. Dennison, *Transcript: Oral Reminiscences* (Annapolis: U.S. Naval Institute, August 1975), pp. 331 ff.; Tad Szulc, *Fidel: A Critical Portrait* (New York, 1986), pp. 544 ff.; Arthur Schlesinger, Jr., *Robert Kennedy and His Times* (Boston, 1978), p. 445; Carlos Franqui, *Diary of the Cuban Revolution* (New York, 1980), pp. 121 ff.; Richard Bissell, Jr., *Transcript: Kennedy Oral History* (Boston, April 1967), p. 9; Lyman Kirkpatrick, Jr., *Transcript: Kennedy Oral History* (Boston, April 16,

1967), pp. 13–15. Another ship, the *Lake Charles,* was not employed at the Bay of Pigs, since it was being saved for another diversion, which was never attempted.

5. Arthur Schlesinger, Jr., *A Thousand Days* (Boston, 1965), pp. 275–276; cf. *id., Robert Kennedy,* pp. 444–448; Johnson and others, pp. 133–152; *Operation Zapata,* pp. 167–169; Taylor, *Taylor Committee Report:* "Memorandum No. 1," pp. 20–31; *ibid.,* "Memorandums" (April 24, 1961, afternoon meeting), pp. 21–26, (April 25, 1961), p. 7, (May 1, 1961), p. 1, (May 4, 1961), pp. 5–10, (May 6, 1961), pp. 1–3; *ibid.,* Pt. 3: "Tarwater Memorandum," p. 2: Kirkpatrick, p. 12; Maurice Halperin, *The Rise and Decline of Fidel Castro* (Berkeley, 1972), pp. 106–107; Jon Nordheimer, "Castro Plays Charming Host on Guided Tour for Yankees," *The New York Times* (August 16, 1979), 2; Wyden, pp. 235 ff.

6. Johnson and others, pp. 151–152; *American Foreign Policy: Current Documents, 1961,* Department of State Historical Office (Washington, June 1965), pp. 295–297; cf. Herbert Dinerstein, *The Making of a Missile Crisis: October 1962* (Baltimore, 1976), pp. 129–134.

7. Kevin O'Donnell and David Powers, *Johnny, We Hardly Knew Ye* (Boston, 1970), p. 274; cf. Wyden, pp. 26 ff.; W. W. Rostow, *The Diffusion of Power 1957–1972* (New York, 1972), pp. 209–210; *Declassified Documents Reference System:* "Memorandum for the President" (Carrollton, Md., April 18, 1961), 556, 1.

8. This communication barrier between the Navy and the CIA still continued under the regime

of Admiral Turner as DCI as late as 1979. Admiral Stansfield Turner, *Secrecy and Democracy: The CIA in Transition* (Boston, 1985), p. 236; Taylor, *Taylor Committee Report:* "Memorandums" (April 24, 1961), pp. 8–9, (afternoon meeting), pp. 23–25, (April 25, 1961), pp. 7–8, (April 28, 1961), p. 5, (May 1, 1961), pp. 1–2, (May 2, 1961), pp. 8–11, (May 3, 1961), pp. 15–18, (May 4, 1961), pp. 2–3, (May 6, 1961), pp. 2–3, (May 17, 1961), pp. 3–8, (May 18, 1961), pp. 4–7, 16–17, (May 19, 1961), p. 5; *ibid.*, Pt. 3: "Rules of Engagement," pp. 3–4 and attached message by General Gray (April 19, 1961); Johnson and others, pp. 60, 153–155; Theodore Sorensen, *Transcript: Kennedy Oral History* (Boston, April 6, 1964), pp. 299–300; Schlesinger, *Robert Kennedy*, pp. 455–458, 471–472; *id.*, *A Thousand Days*, pp. 277–279; author's interview with Richard Bissell (East Hartford, Conn., June 17, 1969); Bissell, p. 40; Kirkpatrick, p. 13; author's interview with Admiral Arleigh Burke (Washington, April 20, 1970); *Operation Zapata*, pp. 92, 146–147, 164–169, 330; Dennison, pp. 352–367; *Executive Sessions of the Senate Foreign Relations Committee, 1961*, Vol. XIII, Pt. 1, pp. 404, 412, 426, 436, 504, 586, 616.

9. *American Foreign Policy, Current Documents*, 1961, p. 299; Johnson and others, p. 147; cf. General Maxwell Taylor, *Swords and Plowshares* (New York, 1972), pp. 183–187; *id.*, *Taylor Committee Report*, Pt. 3: "Briefing on Young Guerrillas" (May 31, 1961), pp. 2–5; *ibid.*, "American Action Report on Operation Pluto," pp. 11–13; *ibid.*, "Memorandums" (May 17, 1961), pp. 1

ff.; *ibid.*, "Memorandum No. 1," pp. 28–29; *Central Intelligence Agency: Current Intelligence Digests and Weekly Summaries* (Washington, April 27, 1961). For Castro's own analysis of the social composition of the Brigade, see Fidel Castro, *Fidel Castro Speaks*, ed. M. Kenner and J. Petras (New York, 1969), p. 75.

10. David Binder, "Castro Said to Foresee a Thaw with U.S.," *The New York Times* (August 3, 1974), 3; cf. José Miró Cardona, "Statement by Dr. Miró Cardona on His Resignation from Cuban Exile Council," *The New York Times* (April 19, 1963), 14; Taylor, *Taylor Committee Report:* "Memorandums" (May 25, 1961), pp. 2–3.

11. *American Foreign Policy, Current Documents, 1961*, pp. 229, 302; cf. Richard Walton, *Cold War and Counter-Revolution* (New York, 1972), pp. 49–54; Arkadi Shevchenko, *Breaking with Moscow* (New York, 1985), pp. 110–117.

12. Richard M. Nixon, "Cuba, Castro and John F. Kennedy," *Reader's Digest* (November 1964), 286–292; cf. *id.*, *The Memoirs of Richard M. Nixon*, Vol. I (New York, 1978), pp. 233–291; "Kennedy Presidential Library Opens Virtually All Its Files," *The New York Times* (August 2, 1971), 6; Schlesinger, *Robert Kennedy*, p. 446; Dwight D. Eisenhower, *Papers:* "Notes by Eisenhower on Luncheon Meeting with President Kennedy at Camp David" (Abilene, Kans., April 22, 1961), Box 8.

13. Nixon, *Memoirs*, Vol. I, pp. 288–290; cf. Arthur Dommen, *Conflict in Laos* (New York, 1967), pp. 196 ff.; Walton, p. 24; Schlesinger, *Robert Kennedy*, pp. 471–472; U. Alexis Johnson, *Tran-*

script: *Kennedy Oral History*
(Boston, n.d.), pp. 5–11.

14. Chester Bowles, *Promises to Keep:
My Years in Public Life 1921–
1969* (New York, 1971), pp. 329–
332; cf. Taylor, *Swords and
Plowshares*, p. 180; Schlesinger,
Robert Kennedy, pp. 446, 471–
472; Harris Wofford, *Of Kennedys and Kings* (New York, 1980),
p. 372.

15. *Alleged Assassination Plots Involving Foreign Leaders: An Interim Report* (Washington, 1975),
pp. 274, 324, 334; cf. *Executive
Sessions of the Senate Foreign*

Relations Committe, 1961, Vol.
XIII, Pt. 1, p. 472; Schlesinger, *A
Thousand Days*, p. 293.

16. *Alleged Assassination Plots*, pp.
205–215, 262–272. This was a
standard cover device of the
agency for attempts at assassination. John Stockwell, *In Search of
Enemies: A C.I.A. Story* (New
York, 1978), pp. 160n., 236–237.

17. *Alleged Assassination Plots*, pp.
212–213, 273; cf. Schlesinger,
Robert Kennedy, pp. 485–492;
Bernard Diederich, *Trujillo: The
Death of the Goat* (Boston, 1978),
ch. X and pp. 180–188.

VIII. *The Perfect Failure*

1. Roger Hilsman, *To Move a Nation*
(Garden City, N.Y., 1967), pp. 61–
63; cf. Victor Marchetti and John
Marks, *The CIA and the Cult of
Intelligence* (New York, 1974), pp.
322 ff.; *The Investigation of the
Assassination of President John
F. Kennedy: Performance of the
Intelligence Agencies*, Bk. V: *Final
Report: Senate Select Committee*
(Washington, April 23, 1976), pp.
6–105. On the other hand, a CIA
analyst put it in 1979 after
resigning, "Policy pretty much
determines reporting rather than
the other way around." Seymour
Hersh, "Ex-Analyst Says C.I.A.
Rejected Warning on Shah," *The
New York Times* (January 7,
1979).

2. Tad Szulc, "Clifford Assays Cambodia Threat," *Life* (May 22,
1970), 34.

3. Martin van Creveld, *Command in
War* (Cambridge, Mass., 1985),
p. 258.

4. Arthur Schlesinger, Jr., *A Thousand Days* (Boston, 1965), p. 289;
cf. Vice-Admiral Lawson Ramage,

Transcript: Oral Reminiscences
(Annapolis: U.S. Naval Institute,
June 1975), p. 405.

5. "CIA Operations: A Plot Scuttled," *The New York Times* (April
28, 1966), 28; cf. Pierre Salinger,
With Kennedy (Garden City, N.Y.,
1966), p. 148; Robert F. Kennedy, *Thirteen Days: A Memoir
of the Cuban Missile Crisis* (New
York, 1969), p. 112; Richard Bissell, Jr., *Transcript: Kennedy Oral
History* (Boston, April 1967), pp.
48–49; Lyman Kirkpatrick, Jr.,
*Transcript: Kennedy Oral His-
tory* (Boston, April 16, 1967), pp.
21–25; Lewis J. Paper, *The
Promise and the Performance: The
Leadership of John F. Kennedy*
(New York, 1975), pp. 156–169;
*Declassified Documents Refer-
ence System:* White House (Carrollton, Md.), 218A, 4.

6. J. K. Galbraith, *Ambassador's
Journal* (Boston, 1969), p. 87; cf.
Thomas Powers, *The Man Who
Kept the Secrets: Richard Helms
and the CIA*, MS (New York,
1977), p. 88.

7. Robert Amory, *Transcript: Kennedy Oral History* (Boston, 1966), pp. 134–135; *The President and the Management of National Security*, ed. K. C. Clark and L. J. Legere (New York, 1969), pp. 176–177; General Maxwell Taylor, *Swords and Plowshares* (New York, 1972), pp. 180–185; *id., Maxwell Taylor File: Robert F. Kennedy Papers, #1* (Boston, 1969), pp. 1–2; Bissell, pp. 46–48; *Central Intelligence Agency: National and Special National Intelligence Estimates (NIE)* (Washington, April 28, 1961), pp. 3–7; David Rosenberg, *Arleigh Albert Burke, Chief of Naval Operations 1955–1961*, MS (Annapolis, 1980), pp. 79–80. Not surprisingly, Richard Bissell has considered Taylor's Cuba study report as a very fair-minded inquiry, unlike what he and Dulles called the hatchet job of the less favorable inquiry on the CIA by Inspector General Lyman Kirkpatrick. On the other hand, Kirkpatrick informed the author that Dulles had deliberately rendered the Cuba study report superficial and ineffective. Telephone conversation with Kirkpatrick (Providence, R.I., December 3, 1973).

8. *Central Intelligence Agency: NIE* (Washington, April 28, 1961), pp. 3–7.

9. Taylor Branch and George Crile III, "The Kennedy Vendetta: How the CIA Waged a Silent War against Cuba," *Harpers* (April 1975), 50–60.

10. Bill Moyers, "Open Letter to Arthur Schlesinger," *The Wall Street Journal* (July 20, 1977), 10; cf. *Alleged Assassination Plots Involving Foreign Leaders: An Interim Report* (Washington, 1975), pp. 104, 214–215; "Warren Was Reportedly Told of CIA Efforts to Kill Castro," *The New York Times* (March 2, 1976), 10; "C.I.A. Memo Says Warren Unit Slighted Leads on Foreign Plot," *The New York Times* (March 21, 1976), 36; Admiral R. L. Dennison, *Transcript: Oral Reminiscences* (Annapolis: U.S. Naval Institute, August 1975), p. 368. Vice-Admiral William Mack denies Robert Kennedy's alleged destruction of records in Mack's own *Transcript: Oral Reminiscences*, Vol. I (Annapolis: U.S. Naval Institute, March 1980); Thomas Powers, letter to the author (South Royalton, Vt., January 23, 1986), 2.

11. Richard Nixon, *The Real War* (New York, 1980), p. 100; Rosenberg, pp. 96–97; William Colby with Peter Forbath, *Honorable Men: My Life in the CIA* (New York, 1978), pp. 200–202.

12. General Maxwel Taylor, *Taylor Committee Report:* "Memorandum No. 1," declassified April 1985 (Washington), p. 11; *ibid.,* "Memorandum No. 3," pp. 1–3; *ibid.,* "Memorandum No. 4," p. 5; *ibid.,* "Memorandums" (April 25, 1961), p. 10, (May 1 and 4, 1961), p. 13, (May 2, 1961), pp. 13–14, (May 3, 1961), pp. 10–12, (May 18, 1961), p. 18, (May 19, 1961), p. 6; Admiral Stansfield Turner, *Secrecy and Democracy: The CIA in Transition* (Boston, 1985), pp. 175, 246–248; *Alleged Assassination Plots*, pp. 121–122; Kirkpatrick, pp. 200–204; *id.,* "Paramilitary Case Study—The Bay of Pigs," *Naval War College Review* (November–December 1972): 40–41; *The President and the Management of National Security*, pp. 76–77, 176–177, 204–205; Rosenberg, p. 81; Hilsman, pp. 78–82; J. F. Campbell, *The Foreign Affairs Fudge Factory* (New York, 1971), pp. 161–165; Senator Henry Jackson, *The*

National Security Council: Jackson Subcommittee Papers on Policy-Making at the Presidential Level (Washington, 1965), pp. 241–242; Robert McNamara, "McNamara Shares Bay of Pigs Blame," The New York Times (February 5, 1968), 9; Colby with Forbath, pp. 73, 200–202; Allen Dulles, The Secret Surrender (New York, 1966), p. 9; "House Select Committee on Intelligence," The Village Voice (February 16, 1976), 83.

13. Taylor, Taylor Committee Report: "Memorandum No. 4," p. 1; Foreign and Military Intelligence, Bk. I: Final Report . . . Select Committee . . . Intelligence Activities (Washington, April 14, 1965), pp. 427, 447, 480; Supplementary Detailed Staff Reports, pp. 51, 70–72, 89; Hanson Baldwin, "The Cuban Invasion II," The New York Times (August 1, 1961), 4; The President and the Management of National Security, chs. IV and V; Theodore Sorensen, Transcript: Kennedy Oral History (Boston, April 6, 1964), pp. 23–24; John Stockwell, In Search of Enemies: A C.I.A. Story (New York, 1978), pp. 159–16on.; Powers, pp. 106, 129; Central Intelligence Agency: NIE, pp. 63 ff., 106.

14. Foreign and Military Intelligence, p. 46; Alleged Assassination Plots, pp. 149–150, 278–295; cf. on how Lyndon Johnson was told by the CIA of the assassination plots against Castro under Kennedy but not of, if any, under himself. John Crewdson, "Nixon Explains His Cryptic Remark about Helms," The New York Times (March 12, 1976), 15; The Investigation of the Assassination of President John F. Kennedy, p. 86; The Intelligence Community, ed. T. Fain and others (New York, 1977), p. 40; Thomas Powers, "The C.I.A. and the President," Commonweal (March 14, 1980), 141.

15. Amory, pp. 24, 121–122, 132–134; Alleged Assassination Plots, pp. 121, 266, 274; cf. E. Howard Hunt, Give Us This Day (New Rochelle, N.Y., 1973), pp. 213–214; Supplementary Detailed Staff Reports, p. 130, n. 38; The Intelligence Community, pp. 44, 694n.

16. Supplementary Detailed Staff Reports, pp. 44–48; cf. The Intelligence Community, pp. 44, 694n., for John Hoizenga's testimony; B. E. Ayers, The War That Never Was (New York, 1976), pp. 21–48; Allen Dulles, The Secret Surrender (New York, 1966), p. 9, for further comments on this perennial intelligence problem. In all fairness, Rusk would admit to the same refusal in the State Department to employ its own intelligence people on the Cuban operation. Taylor, Taylor Committee Report: "Memorandums" (May 4, 1961), p. 12; Hilsman, p. 31.

17. Howard, Regius Professor of Modern History at Oxford, has good cause for these heartfelt remarks. Michael Howard, "Cowboys, Playboys and Other Spies," The New York Times Book Review (February 16, 1986), 6; cf. Christopher Andrew, Her Majesty's Secret Service (New York, 1986), pp. 505–506.

18. Alleged Assassination Plots, pp. 121, 266, 274; Supplementary Detailed Staff Reports, pp. 44–48; cf. Foreign and Military Intelligence, pp. 111–114; Turner, pp. 174 ff., 228, 273; Thomas Halperin, Foreign Policy Crises (Columbus, Ohio, 1971), p. 40, n. 69; Chester Bowles, Promises to Keep: My Years in Public Life 1921–1969 (New York, 1971), pp.

323–324, 333; Major General Sir Kenneth Strong. *Men of Intelligence* (London, 1970), pp. 135–139; David A. Phillips, *The Night Watch* (New York, 1977), pp. 98–112; Ray Cline, *Secrets, Spies and Scholars* (Washington, 1976), pp. 154, 182; Joseph B. Smith, *Portrait of a Cold Warrior* (New York, 1976), pp. 320 ff., 346–355; Ralph Stavins, "The Secret History of Kennedy's Private War," *The New York Times Book Review* (July 22, 1971), 26–32; Kirkpatrick, *Transcript: Kennedy Oral History*, pp. 4–10, 18–19, 23–24, and *id.*, "Paramilitary Case Study," 39–42; *The Central Intelligence Agency: NIE*, pp. 56–72; Bissell, pp. 17–18, 24, 48–49; "Guatemala Ex-Chief Says Kennedy Ordered His Ouster," *The New York Times* (April 17, 1964), 2; Marchetti and Marks, pp. 30–34, 122–123, 326–340, 401; E. Howard Hunt, *Undercover* (New York, 1974), pp. 103, 132; Powers, *The Man Who Kept the Secrets*, pp. 4–5, 92–93, 165; R. H. Smith, *Spymaster's Odyssey: The World of Allen Dulles*, MS (New York, n.d.), ch. 20, pp. 17–18, ch. 23, p. 1, ch. 24, pp. 1 ff., 24, ch. 25, pp. 22 ff., ch. 31, p. 17, ch. 36, p. 2.

19. Lyman Kirkpatrick, Jr., *The Real C.I.A.* (New York, 1968), pp. 195–203; cf. *id.*, *Transcript: Kennedy Oral History*. p. 6; Richard Bissell, Jr., "Response to Lucien S. Vandenbroucke, The 'Confessions' of Allen Dulles: New Evidence on the Bay of Pigs," *Diplomatic History* (Fall 1984): 380; David Martin, *Wilderness of Mirrors* (New York, 1980), pp. 119–120; Sorensen, pp. 301 ff.; Taylor, *Swords and Plowshares*, pp. 190–196; Amory, p. 122. There had been no undue friendship anyway between Kirkpatrick and Allen Dulles, since the former may have been recommended in 1953 by CIA Director Walter Bedell Smith as his successor. Under the influence of John Foster Dulles, in the opinion of one authority, Eisenhower had instead appointed Foster's brother Allen. Townsend Hoopes, *The Devil and John Foster Dulles* (Boston, 1973), pp. 145–146. Indeed, Kirkpatrick's report was simply dismissed by many in the agency as a product of his own disappointed ambitions there. John Ranelagh, *The Agency: The Rise and Decline of the CIA* (New York, 1986), pp. 380–381.

20. Ernest Halperin, *The National Liberation Movement in Latin America*, MS (Cambridge, June 1969), pp. 57–65; Manuel Urrutia Lléo, *Fidel Castro and Castro's Cuba* (Washington, 1962), p. 28; Ernesto Ché Guevara, *Reminiscences of the Cuban Revolutionary War* (New York, 1968), pp. 40 ff.; *Hearings:* "Communist Threat to the United States through the Caribbean," Pt. XIII, *Senate Internal Security Committee* (Washington, 1959–1960), p. 871; Taylor, *Taylor Committee Report:* "Memorandums" (April 24, 1961, afternoon meeting), pp. 13–14.

21. Arthur Schlesinger, Jr., *Robert Kennedy and His Times* (Boston, 1978), p. 524; cf. *ibid.*, pp. 447 ff.; Ranelagh, p. 376.

22. Taylor, *Taylor Committee Report:* "Memorandum No. 1," p. 11; *ibid.*, "Memorandums" (May 1 and 4, 1961), p. 12, (May 3, 1961), p. 13, (May 8, 1961), pp. 12–14, 28–29; *id.*, *Swords and Plowshares*, pp. 190–191; Sorensen, pp. 23–24, 252–253, 305–306; Kirkpatrick, *Transcript: Kennedy Oral History*, pp. 8–10. Disagreeing with most others, CIA iconoclast,

former Director William Colby, cites the agency's secret war in Laos to refute Taylor on the need for military control of large paramilitary operations. Colby with Forbath, pp. 200–201.

23. Dean Acheson, *Transcript: Kennedy Oral History* (Boston, April 27, 1967), pp. 6–7. So good and loyal has Rusk been to Kennedy that he recently said that he would "never build up a record of my own against my own President." "Rusk on the Record," *The Village Voice* (April 16, 1985), 16–17; cf. Bissell, *Transcript: Kennedy Oral History*, p. 44; "Kennedy Presidential Library Opens Virtually All Its Files," *The New York Times* (August 2, 1971), 6; "Rusk a Recluse for about a Year," *The New York Times* (December 30, 1969), 12; "Rusk Assesses Past and Future Soberly," *The New York Times* (March 20, 1969), 5; Taylor, *Swords and Plowshares*, p. 190; Hilsman, pp. 34–60, 314–315; Sorensen, pp. 287 ff.; E. Weintal and C. Bartlett, *Facing the Brink: An Intimate Study of Crisis Diplomacy* (New York, 1967), pp. 148–150; Campbell, pp. 52 ff.; John Henry and William Espinosa, "The Tragedy of Dean Rusk," *Foreign Policy* (Fall 1972): 179; David Halberstam, *The Best and the Brightest* (New York, 1969), pp. 29–37, 67–68; Warren Cohen, *Dean Rusk* (Totowa, N.J., 1980), pp. 92–96, 115; Kevin O'Donnell and David Powers, *Johnny, We Hardly Knew Ye* (Boston, 1970), pp. 281–282; Walter Isaacson and Evan Thomas, *The Wise Men: Six Friends and the World They Made* (New York, 1986), pp. 592–598.

24. Cohen, pp. 101–103; cf. Schlesinger, *Robert Kennedy*, p. 507; William J. Rust and others, *Kennedy in Vietnam* (New York, 1985), pp. 89, 126.

25. In General Maxwell Taylor's phrase. Taylor, *Maxwell Taylor File: Robert F. Kennedy Papers*, #2 (Boston, December 29, 1969), p. 51; cf. George Ball, *The Past Has Another Pattern: Memoirs* (New York, 1982), p. 172.

26. General Maxwell Taylor, *Responsibility and Response* (New York, 1967), pp. 68–69; *id., Taylor Committee Report:* "Memorandums" (May 1 and 4, 1961), pp. 12–14; *ibid.,* "Memorandum No. 2" (June 13, 1961), p. 4; *ibid.,* "Memorandum No. 4," pp. 1 ff.; *id., Swords and Plowshares,* pp. 186–191. Bundy may have failed in his supervisory role at Pigs in part because of refusal to criticize and his personal closeness to both Dulles and Bissell as much as for his sympathies for the Cuban operation per se. Schlesinger, *A Thousand Days,* pp. 296–297, and *id., Robert Kennedy,* pp. 458–459; Henry F. Graff, *The Tuesday Cabinet* (Englewood Cliffs, N.J., 1970), pp. 34, 82, 96; Hilsman, pp. 17–46; I. M. Destler, "The Nixon N.S.C., Can One Man Do?" *Foreign Policy* (Winter 1972): 30; Ball, pp. 172–173; *Foreign and Military Intelligence,* Bk. 1: *Final Report,* pp. 113–114; Gordon Gray, "Memorandum for the President," in Dwight D. Eisenhower, *Papers* (Abilene, Kans., January 11, 1967), p. 11.

27. Taylor, *Swords and Plowshares,* pp. 188–189.

28. *Ibid.,* pp. 188–190; *id., Taylor Committee Report:* "Memorandums" (May 18, 1961), p. 17; author's interview with Taylor (Washington, May 18, 1969) and with Bundy (New York, January 19, 1982); Philip Bonsal, *Cuba, Castro and the United States* (Pittsburgh, 1971), pp. 181 ff.; Ball, pp. 167–168; Sorensen, pp.

304–309; Baldwin, 4; Bowles, pp. 444, 450–451; Dean Acheson, "No Yearning to Be Loved—Dean Acheson Talks to Kenneth Harris," *The Listener* (April 27, 1964), 444.

29. Herbert Matthews, *Fidel Castro* (New York, 1969), p. 219; cf. Sorensen, p. 22.

30. Hilsman, pp. 195–205; Tad Szulc, "Friendship Is Possible, but . . . ," *Parade, Daily News* (April 1, 1984), 6; Charles Yost, *The Conduct and Misconduct of Foreign Affairs* (New York, 1972), pp. 74–77; *The President and the Management of National Security*, pp. 78–81; David Detzer, *The Brink* (New York, 1979), pp. 1–4. For an opposing view, see Dean Acheson, "Dean Acheson's Version of Robert Kennedy's Version of the Cuban Missile Affair," *Esquire* (February 1969), 46.

31. *The Investigation of the Assassination of President John F. Kennedy*, pp. 6, 11–15, 20, 81–84, 100–105. Schlesinger denies this: Schlesinger, *Robert Kennedy*, p. 554n. and ch. XXIII. "White House Tapes and Minutes of the Cuban Missile Crises, . . . ," *International Security* (Summer 1985): 166 ff.; R. Kessler and L. Stern, "Rosselli, Castro and Kennedy," *New York Post* (August 23, 1976), 2; Donald Schultz, "Kennedy and the Cuban Connection," *Foreign Policy* (Spring 1977): 126 ff.; Daniel Schorr, "The Assassins," *The New York Review of Books* (October 13, 1977), 17–22; id., *Clearing the Air* (Boston, 1977), pp. 163 ff.; Edward Jay Epstein, *The Secret World of Lee Harvey Oswald* (New York, 1978), 232–242; Colby with Forbath, pp. 188–190, 213–214, 221; George Lardner, Jr., "Castro Denies Any Plot against Kennedy," *International Herald Tribune* (September 21, 1972), 1–2; Powers, *The Man Who Kept the Secrets*, pp. 180 ff.; Harris Wofford, *Of Kennedys and Kings* (New York, 1980), pp. 414–418, 125; Szulc, "Friendship Is Possible, but . . . ," 6; Lyndon B. Johnson, *The Vantage Point* (New York, 1971), p. 26.

Bibliography

Abel, Elie. *The Missile Crisis* New York: Lippincott, 1966.

Acheson, Dean. "Dean Acheson's Version of Robert Kennedy's Version of the Cuban Missile Affair." New York: *Esquire*, February 1969.

——. "No Yearning to Be Loved—Dean Acheson Talks to Kenneth Harris." London: *The Listener*, April 27, 1964.

——. *Transcript: Kennedy Oral History*. Boston: April 27, 1967.

Agee, Philip. *Inside the Company: CIA Diary*. London: Penguin, 1975.

Alleged Assassination Plots Involving Foreign Leaders: An Interim Report of the Select Committee to Study Governmental Operations with Respect to Intelligence Activities, U.S. Senate. Washington: USGPO, 1975.

Alsop, Stewart. *The Center: People and Power in Political Washington*. New York: Popular Library, 1968.

——. "The Cuban Disaster: How It Happened." Philadelphia: *The Saturday Evening Post*, June 24, 1961.

Ambrose, Stephen. *Eisenhower*, Vol. II: *The President*. New York: Simon & Schuster, 1984.

——. *Ike's Spies: Eisenhower and the Espionage Establishment*. Garden City, N.Y.: Doubleday, 1981.

"America and the 'Common Danger'—Dean Rusk Talks to Michael Charlton." London: *The Listener*, June 9, 1977.

American Foreign Policy: Current Documents, 1961, Department of State Historical Office. Washington: USGPO, June 1965.

Amory, Robert, *Transcript: Kennedy Oral History*, Boston: 1966.

Anderson, Jack. "Six Attempts to Kill Castro Laid to the CIA." Washington: *The Washington Post*, January 18, 1971.

Attwood, William. *The Reds and the Blacks: A Personal Adventure*. New York: Harper & Row, 1967.

Ayers, B. E. *The War That Never Was: An Insider's Account of CIA Covert Operations against Cuba*. New York: Bobbs-Merrill, 1976.

Baldwin, Hanson. "The Cuban Invasion II." New York: *The New York Times*, August 1, 1961.

Ball, George. *The Past Has Another Pattern: Memoirs*. New York: W. W. Norton, 1982.

Batista, Fulgencio. *The Growth and Decline of the Cuban Republic*. New York: Devin-Adair, 1964.

Beck, Kent. "Necessary Lies, Hidden Truths: Cuba in the 1960 Campaign." Washington: *Diplomatic History*, Winter 1984.

Berle, Adolf. MSS: *Papers* and *Diary*. Hyde Park., N.Y., 1953–1954, 1961.

Berle, B., and T. Jacobs. *Navigating the Rapids: From the Papers of Adolf Berle*. Ed. B. Berle and T. Jacobs. New York: Harcourt Brace Jovanovich, 1973.

——. "The Cuban Crisis: Failure of American Foreign Policy." New York: *Foreign Affairs*, October 1960.

Bernays, Edward. *Biography of an Idea: Memoirs.* New York: Simon & Schuster, 1965.
Bernstein, Victor, and Jesse Gordon. "The Press and the Bay of Pigs." New York: *Columbia University Forum,* Fall 1967.
Beschloss, Michael. *Mayday: Eisenhower, Khrushchev and the U-2 Affair.* New York: Harper & Row, 1986.
Bethall, Paul. *The Losers.* New York: Arlington House, 1969.
Binder, David. "Castro Said to Foresee a Thaw with U.S." New York: *The New York Times,* August 3, 1974.
———. " '56 East Europe Plan of CIA Is Described." New York: *The New York Times,* November 30, 1976.
Bissell, Richard, Jr. Interview with Richard Bissell by David Wise, "Exiles May Have Hit Central America." Paris: *The New York Herald-Tribune,* July 21, 1965.
———. "Response to Lucien S. Vandenbroucke, the 'Confessions' of Allen Dulles: New Evidence on the Bay of Pigs." Washington: *Diplomatic History,* Fall 1984.
———. *Transcript: Dulles Oral History,* Mudd Library. Princeton: January 27, 1967.
———. *Transcript: Eisenhower Oral History,* Columbia University Library. New York: 1967.
———. *Transcript: Kennedy Oral History.* Boston: April 1967.
Blasier, Cole. *The Hovering Giant: U.S. Response to Revolutionary Change in Latin America.* Pittsburgh: University of Pittsburgh Press, 1976.
Bloomfield, L. P., and A. C. Leiss. *Controlling Small Wars: A Strategy for the 1970s.* New York: Alfred A. Knopf, 1969.
Bonsal, Philip. *Cuba, Castro and the United States.* Pittsburgh: University of Pittsburgh Press, 1971.
Bowles, Chester. *Promises to Keep: My Years in Public Life 1921–1969.* New York: Harper & Row, 1971.
Braden, Spruille. *Diplomats and Demagogues: Memoirs.* New York: Arlington House, 1971.
Bradlee, Benjamin. *Conversations with Kennedy.* New York: W. W. Norton, 1975.
Branch, Taylor, and George Crile III. "The Kennedy Vendetta: How the CIA Waged a Silent War against Cuba." New York: *Harpers,* April 1975.
Briggs, Ellis. *Anatomy of Diplomacy.* New York: David McKay, 1968.
Bundy, McGeorge. "Beware of Aiding the 'Contras.' " New York: *The New York Times,* June 12, 1985.
———. *National Security Files,* Kennedy Library, Box 35. Boston: February 1961.
———. *President's Office Files,* Kennedy Library, Box 62. Boston: February 1961.
Burke, Admiral Arleigh. *Oral Reminiscences 1955–1961.* Annapolis: U.S. Naval Institute, 1963.
———. *Transcript: Eisenhower Oral History.* Abilene: Eisenhower Library, January 12, 1973.
Campbell, J. F. *The Foreign Affairs Fudge Factory.* New York: Basic Books, 1971.
Castro, Fidel. "Castro Sees Hope for Better U.S. Ties." New York: *The New York Times,* October 27, 1973.
———. "Castro Suggests Amity with U.S." New York: *The New York Times,* January 21, 1961.
———. *Fidel Castro Speaks.* Ed. M. Kenner and J. Petras. New York: Grove Press, 1969.
———. *Transcript: Oral History,* Lee Lockwood. Cuba: Columbia University Library, August 1965.
Catledge, Turner. *My Life and the Times.* New York: Harper & Row, 1971.
Central Intelligence Agency: CIA Information Reports. Declassified 1982. Washington: 1953–1954, 1958–1961.

Central Intelligence Agency: Current Intelligence Bulletins. Declassified September 1976. Washington: 1954–1961.

Central Intelligence Agency: Current Intelligence Digests and Weekly Summaries. Washington: 1953–1961.

Central Intelligence Agency: Memoranda for the Director, 1960–1962. Washington: Office of National Estimates.

Central Intelligence Agency: National and Special National Intelligence Estimates (NIE). Washington: 1949–1961.

The Central Intelligence Agency: History and Documents. Ed. W. M. Leary. University: University of Alabama Press, 1984.

Challener, Richard. *Admirals, Generals and American Foreign Policy, 1898–1914.* Princeton: Princeton University Press, 1973.

Charlton, Michael. "Star Wars." London: *Encounter,* February 1986.

Christian, Shirley. *Nicaragua: Revolution in the Family.* New York: Random House, 1985.

CIA. "How the CIA Built . . . Network for Propaganda." New York: *The New York Times,* December 26, 1977.

"C.I.A. Assassination Unit Described." New York: *The New York Times,* October 4, 1975.

"C.I.A. Memo Says Warren Unit Slighted Leads on Foreign Plot." New York: *The New York Times,* March 21, 1976.

"CIA Operations: A Plot Scuttled." New York: *The New York Times,* April 28, 1966.

The CIA: Past Transgressions and Future Controls. Symposium. Providence: Brown University, October 11, 1975.

"C.I.A. Plot to Kill Castro Described." New York: *The New York Times,* April 30, 1975.

CIA Report on Castro Visit. Washington: April 27, 1959.

Clifford, Clark. "A Vietnam Reappraisal." New York: *Foreign Affairs,* July 1968.

Cline, Ray. *Secrets, Spies and Scholars.* Washington: Acropolis Press, 1976.

Coffin, Tristan. *Senator Fulbright.* New York: Dalton, 1966.

Cohen, Warren. *Dean Rusk.* Totowa, N.J.: Cooper Square Publishers, 1980.

Colby, William, with Peter Forbath. *Honorable Men: My Life in the CIA.* New York: Simon & Schuster, 1978.

Colville, John. *The Fringes of Power: 10 Downing Street, 1939–1955.* New York: W. W. Norton, 1985.

Cook, Blanche. *The Declassified Eisenhower: A Divided Legacy.* Garden City, N.Y.: Doubleday, 1981.

Copeland, Miles. *Without Cloak or Dagger.* New York: Simon & Schuster, 1974.

Corson, William. *The Armies of Ignorance: The Rise of the American Intelligence Empire.* New York: Dial Press, 1977.

Creveld, Martin van. *Command in War.* Cambridge, Mass.: Harvard University Press, 1985.

Crewdson, John. "House Committee Finds Intelligence Agencies Generally Go Unchecked." New York: *The New York Times,* January 26, 1976.

———. "Nixon Explains His Cryptic Remark about Helms." New York: *The New York Times,* March 12, 1976.

———. "White House Not Linked to Plots against Castro." New York: *The New York Times,* November 21, 1975.

Cuba: U.S. Department of State Publication #7171. Washington: USGPO, April 1961.

Cutler, Robert. *No Time for Rest.* Boston: Little, Brown, 1966.

Daniel, Clifton. "Excerpts from Speech on Coverage of Bay of Pigs Buildup." New York: *The New York Times,* June 2, 1964.

Declassified Documents Reference System. Carrollton, Md.: 1976–1979, 1984.

Dennison, Admiral R. L. *Transcript: Oral Reminiscences.* Annapolis: U.S. Naval Institute, August 1975.

Destler, I. M. "The Nixon N.S.C., Can One Man Do?" New York: *Foreign Policy,* Winter 1972.

Detzer, David. *The Brink: Cuban Missile Crisis 1962.* New York: Thomas Y. Crowell, 1979.

Diederich, Bernard. *Trujillo: The Death of the Goat.* Boston: Little, Brown, 1978.

Dille, John. "With a Quiet Curse It All Began." New York: *Life,* May 10, 1963.

Dinerstein, Herbert. *The Making of a Missile Crisis: October, 1962.* Baltimore: Johns Hopkins University Press. 1976.

"Director Colby on the Record." New York: *Time,* September 30, 1974.

Dommen, Arthur. *Conflict in Laos.* New York: Praeger, 1967.

Doolittle Report. MS. Central Intelligence Agency. Declassified April 1, 1976. Washington: The National Archives.

Dorschner, J., and R. Fabricio. *The Winds of December.* New York: Coward, McCann & Geoghegan, 1980.

Draper, Theodore. *Castro's Revolution: Myths and Realities.* New York: Praeger, 1962.

————. "Journalism, History and Journalistic History—An Exchange." New York: *The New York Times Book Review,* December 16, 1984.

————. *Papers on Cuba.* MS. and press clippings. Palo Alto: Hoover War Library, 1958–1961.

Dulles, Allen. *The Craft of Intelligence.* New York: Signet/New American Library, 1965.

————. *Papers, Articles and Briefings,* especially "My Answer to the Bay of Pigs" in several versions. Princeton: Mudd Library, 1965.

————. *The Secret Surrender.* New York: Harper & Row, 1966.

Dulles, John Foster, *Papers.* Princeton: Mudd Library, 1953–1965.

Dunleavy, Steve. "A Cloak or Dagger Duo." New York: *New York Post,* November 1, 1977.

Dunlop, Richard. *Donovan, American Master Spy.* New York: Rand McNally, 1982.

Eden, Sir Anthony. *Memoirs: Full Circle.* Boston: Houghton Mifflin, 1960.

"Editorial." New York: *The Nation,* 1960.

Eisenhower, Dwight D. *Papers* and *Memoranda* from the White House and State Department, including Ann Whitman File. Abilene, Kans.: Eisenhower Library, 1953–1961.

————. *Public Papers of the Presidents: Dwight D. Eisenhower 1960–1961,* Vol. XIII, Pt. 2. Washington: USGPO, 1961.

————. *The White House Years,* Vol. I: *Mandate for Change, 1953–1956.* Garden City, N.Y.: Doubleday, 1963.

————. *The White House Years,* Vol. II: *Waging Peace 1956–1961.* Garden City, N.Y.: Doubleday, 1965.

"Eisenhower-Churchill," *Harkness Memorandum.* In *John Foster Dulles Additional Papers.* Princeton: Mudd Library, July 1, 1954.

Eisenhower: The Diaries. Ed. Robert Ferrell. New York: W. W. Norton, 1981.

"Eisenhower Finds Bay of Pigs Error." New York: *The New York Times,* October 14, 1965.

Epstein, Edward Jay. *The Secret World of Lee Harvey Oswald.* New York: McGraw-Hill, 1978.

Ewald, W. M., Jr. *Eisenhower, the President: Crucial Days, 1951–1960.* Englewood Cliffs, N.J.: Prentice-Hall, 1981.

Executive Sessions of the Senate Foreign Relations Committee, 1959 (Historical Series),

Vol. XI, Eighty-sixth Congress, First Session. Declassified March 1982. Washington: USGPO.

Executive Sessions of the Senate Foreign Relations Committee, 1961 (Historical Series), Vol. XIII, Pts. 1 and 2, Eighty-seventh Congress, First Session. Declassified April and December 1984. Washington: USGPO.

Exner, Judith. *My Story, As told to Ovid Demaris.* New York: Grove Press, 1977.

Fitzsimmons, Louise. *The Kennedy Doctrine.* New York: Random House, 1972.

Flaherty, Tom. "Anatomy of the Snafu." New York: *Life,* May 10, 1963.

Flanagan, Stephen. "Managing the Intelligence Community." Cambridge: *International Security,* Summer 1985.

Foreign and Military Intelligence, Bk. I: *Final Report of the Select Senate Committee to Study Governmental Operations with Respect to Intelligence Activities Together with Additional, Supplemental and Separate Views.* Washington: USGPO, April 14, 1965.

Foreign Relations of the United States (FRUS) *1941,* Vol. I: *General: The Soviet Union,* Department of State. Washington: USGPO, 1958.

Foreign Relations of the United States (FRUS) *1952–1954,* Vol. IV: *The American Republics,* Department of State. Washington: USGPO, 1983.

Foreign Relations of the United States (FRUS) *1952–1954,* Vol. XIII: *Indochina,* Department of State, Pt. 1. Washington: USGPO, 1982.

Franqui, Carlos. *Diary of the Cuban Revolution.* New York: Viking, 1980.

———. *Family Portrait with Fidel: A Memoir.* New York: Random House, 1984.

Freed, Fred. "Cuba, Bay of Pigs." New York: NBC *White Paper,* February 4, 1964.

"Fulbright Panel Votes C.I.A. Role." New York: *The New York Times,* May 18, 1966.

Galbraith, J. K. *Ambassador's Journal.* Boston: Houghton Mifflin, 1969.

Gates, Thomas, Jr. *Transcript: Eisenhower Oral History.* New York: Columbia University Library, August 1967.

Gellman, Irwin. *Roosevelt and Batista: Good Neighbor Diplomacy in Cuba 1933–1945.* Albuquerque: University of New Mexico Press, 1973.

Goldenberg, Boris. "Castroism." Fort Leavenworth, Kans.: *Military Review,* April 1970.

Goldman, Eric. *The Tragedy of Lyndon Johnson.* New York: Alfred A. Knopf, 1969.

Gonzalez, Edward. "The United States and Castro." New York: *Foreign Affairs,* July 1972.

Graff, Henry F. *The Tuesday Cabinet.* Englewood Cliffs, N.J.: Prentice-Hall, 1970.

Gray, Gordon. *Transcript: Eisenhower Oral History.* New York: Columbia University Library, December 7, 1966.

"Guatemala Ex-Chief Says Kennedy Ordered His Ouster." New York: *The New York Times,* April 17, 1964.

"Guerrilla War Is Stressed in Guatemala Troop Training." New York: *The New York Times,* November 20, 1960.

Guevara, Ernesto Ché. *Ché Guevara on Revolution: A Documentary Overview.* Ed. Jay Mallin. Coral Gables: University of Miami Press, 1969.

———. *Reminiscences of the Cuban Revolutionary War.* New York: Grove Press, 1968.

Hagerty, James. *The Diary of James C. Hagerty: Eisenhower in Mid-Crisis 1954–1955.* Ed. Robert Ferrell. Bloomington: Indiana University Press, 1983.

Halberstam, David. *The Best and the Brightest.* New York: Random House, 1969.

Halderman, H. R., with Joseph Di Mina. *The Ends of Power.* New York: New York Times Books, 1978.

Halper, Thomas. *Foreign Policy Crises: Appearance and Reality in Decision Making.* Columbus: Bobbs-Merrill, 1971.

Halperin, Ernst. *The National Liberation Movement in Latin America.* MS. Cambridge: MIT Press, Center for International Studies, June 1969.

Halperin, Maurice. *The Rise and Decline of Fidel Castro.* Berkeley: University of California Press, 1972.

Halperin, Morton. "The President and the Military." New York: *Foreign Affairs,* January 1972.

Harrison, Gilbert. *Transcript: Kennedy Oral History.* Boston: October 6, 1967.

Hearings before the House Subcommittee . . . on Communist Aggression in Latin America. Washington: USGPO, October 8, 1954.

Hearings before the House Subcommittee on Inter-American Affairs, "Communist Threat in Latin America." Washington: USGPO, 1960.

Hearings. "Communist Threat to the United States through the Caribbean," Pts. III, X, and XIII, *Senate Internal Security Committee.* Washington: USGPO, 1959–1960.

Henry, John, and William Espinosa. "The Tragedy of Dean Rusk." New York: *Foreign Policy,* Fall 1972.

Hersh, Seymour. "Ex-Analyst Says C.I.A. Rejected Warning on Shah." New York: *The New York Times,* January 7, 1979.

———. "Firm Rein on Intelligence Units Urged by 2 Ex-CIA Officials." New York: *The New York Times,* December 11, 1974.

———. "Hearings Urged on CIA's Role in Chile." New York: *The New York Times,* September 9, 1974.

Higgins, Trumbull. *Winston Churchill and the Second Front.* New York: Oxford University Press, 1957.

Hilsman, Roger. *To Move a Nation: The Politics of Foreign Policy in the Administration of John F. Kennedy.* Garden City, N.Y.: Doubleday, 1967.

Hilton, Ronald. *Hispanic American Report.* Stamford: November 1960.

Hinckle, Warren, and William Turner. *The Fish Is Red: The Story of the Secret War against Castro.* New York: Harper & Row, 1981.

Hinsley, F. H., and others. *British Intelligence in the Second World War: Its Influence on Strategy and Operations,* Vol. II. New York: Cambridge University Press, 1981.

History of an Aggression: Testimony from the Trial of the Mercenary Brigade. Havana: Editions Vinceremos, 1964.

Hoopes, Townsend. *The Devil and John Foster Dulles.* Boston: Atlantic–Little, Brown, 1973.

Horrock, Nicolas. "Ford Seeks Curb on Data on Plots." New York: *The New York Times,* November 3, 1975.

"House Select Committee on Intelligence." New York: *The Village Voice,* February 16, 1976.

Howard, Michael. "Cowboys, Playboys and Other Spies." New York: *The New York Times Book Review,* February 16, 1986.

Hunt, E. Howard. *Give Us This Day.* New Rochelle: Arlington House, 1973.

———. *Undercover: Memoirs of an American Secret Agent.* New York: G. P. Putnam's Sons, 1974.

Hurwitch, Robert A. *Transcript: Kennedy Oral History,* Pts. I and II. Boston: April–May 1964.

Immerman, Richard. *The CIA in Guatemala: The Foreign Policy of Intervention.* Austin: University of Texas, 1982.

The Intelligence Community: History, Organization and Issues. Public Document Series. Ed. T. Fain and others. New York: R. R. Bowker, 1977.

The Investigation of the Assassination of President John F. Kennedy: Performance of the

Intelligence Agencies, Bk. V: *Final Report: Senate Select Committee . . . with Respect to Intelligence Activities.* Washington: USGPO, April 23, 1976.

Isaacson, Walter, and Evan Thomas. *The Wise Men: Six Friends and the World They Made.* New York: Simon & Schuster, 1986.

Jackson, Senator Henry. See *The National Security Council.*

Janis, Irving. *Victims of Groupthink.* Boston: Houghton Mifflin, 1972.

Jenks, L. H. *Our Cuban Colony: A Study in Sugar.* New York: Arno Press, 1928.

Johnson, H., and B. Gwertzman. *Fulbright: The Dissenter.* Garden City, N.Y.: Doubleday, 1968.

Johnson, Haynes, and others. *The Bay of Pigs: The Leaders Story of Brigade 2506.* New York: W. W. Norton, 1964.

Johnson, Lyndon B. *The Vantage Point: Perspectives of the Presidency 1963–1969.* New York: Holt, Rinehart and Winston, 1971.

Johnson, U. Alexis. *Transcript: Kennedy Oral History.* Boston: n.d.

Kahin, George M. *Intervention: How America Became Involved in Vietnam.* New York: Alfred A. Knopf, 1986.

Kalb, Madelaine. *The Congo Cables: The Cold War in Africa, from Eisenhower to Kennedy.* New York: Macmillan, 1982.

Karnow, Stanley. *Vietnam: A History.* New York: Penguin, 1984.

Karol, K. S. *Guerrillas in Power.* New York: Hill & Wang, 1970.

Kennedy, John F. *Freedom of Communications: Final Report of the Committee on Commerce, U.S. Senate Subcommittee on Communication,* Pt. I: *The Speeches, Remarks, Press Conferences and Statements of Senator John F. Kennedy, August 1– November 7, 1960.* Washington: USGPO, September 13, 1961.

———. *Public Papers of the Presidents: John F. Kennedy, 1961—Concerning the Public Messages, Speeches and Statements of the President.* Washington: USGPO, 1962.

———. *The Strategy of Peace.* Ed. Allan Nevins. New York: Popular Library, 1961.

———. *Why England Slept.* Westport, Conn.: Greenwood Press, 1961.

"Kennedy Cover-Up Denied by Church." New York: *The New York Times,* December 16, 1975.

"Kennedy Presidential Library Opens Virtually All Its Files." New York: *The New York Times,* August 2, 1971.

Kennedy and the Press: The News Conferences. Ed. H. Chase and A. Lerman. New York: Thomas Y. Crowell, 1965.

"Kennedy Tells of Cuban Decision." Boston: *The Christian Science Monitor,* December 19, 1962.

Kennedy, Paul. *The Middle Beat.* New York: Teachers College Press, Columbia University, 1971.

———. "U.S. Helps Train an Anti-Castro Force at Secret Guatemalan Air-Ground Base." New York: *The New York Times,* January 10, 1961.

Kennedy, Robert F. *Attorney General's Papers.* Boston: Kennedy Library, 1961–1964.

———. *Transcript: Oral History.* Boston: Kennedy Library, 1979.

———. *Thirteen Days: A Memoir of the Cuban Missile Crisis.* New York: W. W. Norton, 1969.

"Robert Kennedy Speaks His Mind." Washington: *U.S. News & World Report,* January 22, 1963.

Kessler, R., and L. Stern. "Rosselli, Castro and Kennedy." New York: *New York Post,* August 23, 1976.

Khrushchev Remembers. Ed. E. Crankshaw. Boston: Little, Brown, 1970.

Kirkpatrick, Lyman, Jr. "Paramilitary Case Study—The Bay of Pigs." Newport, R.I.: *Naval War College Review,* November–December 1972.

———. *The Real C.I.A.* New York: Macmillan, 1968.
———. *Transcript: Kennedy Oral History.* Boston: April 16, 1967.
Kissinger, Henry A. *The Necessity for Choice.* New York: Harper & Row, 1961.
Kistiakowsky, George. *A Scientist at the White House.* Cambridge: Harvard University Press, 1976.
Knowing One's Enemies: Intelligence Assessment before the Two World Wars. Ed. E. R. May. Princeton: Princeton University Press, 1984.
LaFeber, Walter. *Inevitable Revolutions: The United States in Central America.* New York: W. W. Norton, 1984.
Laqueur, Walter. *A World of Secrets: The Uses and Limits of Intelligence.* New York: Basic Books, 1985.
Lardner, George, Jr. "Castro Denies Any Plot against Kennedy." Paris: *International Herald Tribune,* September 21, 1972.
Lazo, Mario. *Dagger in the Heart: American Policy Failures in Cuba.* New York: Funk & Wagnalls, 1968.
Leary, William *Perilous Missions: Civil Air Transport and CIA Covert Operations in Asia.* University: University of Alabama Press, 1984.
Leary, William, and W. Stuech. "The Chennault Plan to Save China: U.S. Containment in Asia, Chennault and the Origins of the CIA's Aerial Empire, 1949–1950." Wilmington, Del.: *Diplomatic History,* Fall 1984.
Llerena, Mario. *The Unsuspected Revolution: The Birth and Rise of Castroism.* Ithaca, N.Y.: Cornell University Press, 1978.
Lockwood, Lee. *Castro's Cuba, Cuba's Fidel.* New York: Vintage / Funk & Wagnalls, 1967.
———. *Transcript: Castro Oral History.* New York: Columbia University Library, August 1965.
Lopez-Fresquet, Rufo. *My Fourteen Months with Castro.* Cleveland: World Publishing Co., 1966.
Lyon, Peter. *Eisenhower: Portrait of the Hero.* Boston: Little, Brown, 1974.
McCann, Thomas. *An American Company: The Tragedy of United Fruit.* New York: Crown Publishers, 1976.
McGaffin, W., and E. Knoll. *Anything but the Truth—The Credibility Gap, How the News Is Managed in Washington.* New York: G. P. Putnam's Sons, 1968.
"McGeorge Bundy Is Completing One Job, Preparing for Another." New York: *The New York Times,* May 22, 1979.
Mack, Vice-Admiral William. *Transcript: Oral Reminiscences,* Vol. I. Annapolis: U.S. Naval Institute, 1980.
Macmillan, Harold. *Pointing the Way 1959–1961.* London: Macmillan, 1972.
McMillan, Priscilla. "An Elitist Left Holding the Bag: C.I.A.'s Helms," Pt. III. New York: *New York Post,* October 15, 1978.
McNamara, Robert. "McNamara Shares Bay of Pigs Blame." New York: *The New York Times,* February 5, 1968.
Mallin Jay. "The Call to Arms That Never Came." Miami: *Tropic, The Miami Herald,* March 10, 1974.
Mankiewicz, Frank, and Kirby Jones. *With Fidel: A Portrait of Castro and Cuba.* Chicago: Playboy Press, 1975.
Mann, Thomas. Letters to the author. Austin, Tex.: January 19 and February 5, 1979.
———. *Transcript: Eisenhower Oral History.* New York: Columbia University Library, February 23, 1968.
———. *Transcript: Kennedy Oral History.* Boston: March 13, 1968.
Marchetti, Victor, and John Marks. *The CIA and the Cult of Intelligence.* New York: Alfred A. Knopf, 1974.

Martin, David. *Wilderness of Mirrors*. New York: Harper & Row, 1980.

Martin, John Bartlow. *Adlai Stevenson and the World: The Life of Adlai E. Stevenson.* Garden City, N.Y.: Doubleday, 1977.

Matthews, Herbert. *Fidel Castro.* New York: Simon & Schuster, 1969.

———. *Revolution in Cuba.* New York: Charles Scribner's Sons, 1975.

Mazo, Earl. *Transcript: Eisenhower Oral History.* New York: Columbia University Library, December 7, 1966.

"Memorandum by Thomas Mann for Charles Murphy." MS. Independence, Mo.: Truman Library, December 11, 1952.

Meneses, Enrique. *Fidel Castro.* London: Taplinger Press, 1966.

Meskil, Paul. "C.I.A. Sent Bedmate to Kill Castro in 1960." New York: *Daily News,* June 13, 1976.

———. "Frogman Blew Up a French Ship in Havana." New York. *Daily News,* April 25, 1975.

Meyer, Cord. *Facing Reality.* New York: Harper & Row, 1980.

Meyer, Karl, and Tad Szulc. *The Cuban Invasion: The Chronicle of a Disaster.* New York: Praeger, 1962.

Millet, A. R. *The Politics of Intervention: The Military Occupation of Cuba 1906–1909.* Columbus: Ohio University Press, 1968.

Millis, Walter. *The Martial Spirit.* Cambridge: The Riverside Press, 1931.

Miró Cardona, José. "Statement by Dr. Miró Cardona on His Resignation from Cuban Exile Council." New York: *The New York Times,* April 19, 1963.

Mitgang, Herbert. "Arthur Schlesinger." New York: *The New York Times Book Review,* January 9, 1979.

Moran, Lord. *Taken from the Diaries of Lord Moran: The Struggle for Survival 1940–1965.* Boston: Houghton Mifflin, 1966.

Moyers, Bill. "Open Letter to Arthur Schlesinger." New York: *The Wall Street Journal,* July 20, 1977.

Murphy, Charles. "Cuba—The Record Set Straight." New York: *Fortune,* September 1961.

Murphy, Robert. *Diplomat among Warriors.* New York: Pyramid Books, 1965.

———. *Transcript: Eisenhower Oral History.* New York: Columbia University Library, 1973.

National Intelligence Estimates (NIE). See *Central Intelligence Agency* entries.

The National Security Council: Jackson Subcommittee Papers on Policy-Making at the Presidential Level. Ed. Senator Henry M. Jackson. Washington: 1965.

National Security Files, Box 35. Boston: Kennedy Library, 1961.

Nixon, Richard M. "Cuba, Castro aand John F. Kennedy: Reflections on U.S. Foreign Policy." New York: *Reader's Digest,* November 1964.

———. *Freedom of Communications: Final Report of the U.S. Senate Committee on Commerce, Subcommittee on Communications,* Pt. II: *The Speeches, Remarks, Press Conferences, Study Papers of Vice President Richard M. Nixon, August 1– November 7, 1960.* Washington: USGPO, 1961.

———. *The Memoirs of Richard M. Nixon,* Vol. I. New York: Warner Books, 1978.

———. *The Real War.* New York: Warner Books, 1980.

———. *Six Crises.* Garden City, N.Y.: Doubleday, 1967.

"Nixon Rebutted by White House." New York: *The New York Times,* March 21, 1962.

"Nixon Watergate Tapes." New York: *Time,* August 19, 1974.

Nordheimer, Jon. "Castro Plays Charming Host on Guided Tour for Yankees." New York: *The New York Times,* August 16, 1979.

O'Donnell, Kevin, and David Powers. *Johnny, We Hardly Knew Ye: Memories of John*

Fitzgerald Kennedy. Boston: Little, Brown, 1970.

Operation Zapata: The "Ultrasensitive" Report and Testimony of the Board of Inquiry on the Bay of Pigs. Frederick, Md.: University of Publications of America, 1981.

Paper, Lewis J. *The Promise and the Performance: The Leadership of John F. Kennedy.* New York: Crown Publishers, 1975.

Parkinson, F. *Latin America, the Cold War and the World Powers: A Study in Diplomatic History 1945–1973.* Beverly Hills, Calif.: Sage Publications, 1974.

Parmet, Herbert. *J.F.K.: The Presidency of John F. Kennedy.* New York: The Dial Press, 1983.

Peñabaz, Manuel. "We Were Destroyed." Washington: *U.S. News & World Report,* January 14, 1963.

Pentagon Papers, The, Senator Gravel ed., Vol. II. Boston: Beacon Press, 1971.

Philby, Kim. *My Silent War.* New York: Grove Press, 1968.

Phillips, David A. *The Night Watch: Twenty-five Years of Peculiar Service.* New York: Atheneum, 1977.

Powers, Thomas. "The C.I.A. and the President." New York: *Commonweal,* March 14, 1980.

———. *The Man Who Kept the Secrets: Richard Helms and the CIA.* New York: MS, 1979.

Prados, John. *Presidents' Secret Wars: CIA and Pentagon Covert Operations since World War II.* New York: William Morrow, 1986.

The President and the Management of National Security: A Report by the Institute for Defense Analyses. Ed. K. C. Clark and L. J. Legere. New York: Praeger, 1969.

The President's Foreign Intelligence Advisory Board (PFIAB). Washington: The Hal Foundation, 1981.

President's Office File, 1961 / McGeorge Bundy Papers. Boston: Kennedy Library.

Rabe, Stephen. "The Johnson (Eisenhower) Doctrine for Latin America." Washington: *Diplomatic History,* Winter 1985.

Ramage, Vice-Admiral Lawson. *Transcript: Oral Reminiscences.* Annapolis: U.S. Naval Institute, June 1975.

Ranelagh, John. *The Agency: The Rise and Decline of the CIA.* New York: Simon & Schuster, 1986.

Ransom, H. H. *Central Intelligence and National Security.* Cambridge: Harvard University Press, 1958.

———. *Report to the President by the Commission on CIA Activities within the United States.* Washington: USGPO, June 1975.

Riding, Alan. "For Rudderless Costa Rica, a Quixotic Rescue Effort." New York: *The New York Times,* January 12, 1981.

Rivero, Nicolas. *Castro's Cuba: An American Dilemma.* Washington: Luce Press, 1962.

"Roa in U.N. Lays Bombing to U.S." New York: *The New York Times,* April 16, 1961.

Roberts, Chalmers. *First Rough Draft.* New York: Praeger, 1973.

Rosenberg, David. *Arleigh Albert Burke, Chief of Naval Operations 1955–1961.* MS. Annapolis: U.S. Naval Institute Press, 1980.

Rositzke, Harry. *The C.I.A.: Past Transgressors and Future Controls.* Providence, R.I.: Monograph on National Security Affairs, Brown University Symposium, October 11, 1975.

———. *The CIA's Secret Operations.* New York: Readers's Digest Press, 1977.

Rostow, W. W. *The Diffusion of Power 1957–1972: An Essay in Recent History.* New York: Macmillan, 1972.

Rubottom, Roy R., Jr. *Transcript: Dulles Oral History.* Princeton: Mudd Library, 1967.

Ruiz, Ramón Eduardo. *Cuba: The Making of a Revolution.* New York: W. W. Norton, 1968.

Rusk, Dean, with David Nunnerley. *Transcript: Oral History*. Boston: Kennedy Library, February 9, 1970.

"Rusk a Recluse for about a Year." New York: *The New York Times*, December 30, 1969.

"Rusk Assesses Past and Future Soberly." New York: *The New York Times*, March 20, 1969.

"Rusk on the Record." New York: *The Village Voice*, April 16, 1985.

"Russia Defies Monroe Doctrine." New York: *The New York Times*, July 13, 1960.

Rust, William J., and others. *Kennedy in Vietnam*. New York: Charles Scribner's Sons, 1985.

Salinger, Pierre. *With Kennedy*. Garden City, N.Y.: Doubleday, 1966.

Salisbury, Harrison. *Without Fear or Favor*. New York: New York Times Books, 1980.

Schlesinger, Arthur, Jr. *A Thousand Days: John F. Kennedy in the White House*. Boston: Houghton Mifflin, 1965.

————. *Papers, Memoranda for the President*. New York: March 15, 1961, and April 5 and 10, 1961.

————. *Robert Kennedy and His Times*. Boston: Houghton Mifflin, 1978.

Schlesinger, Stephen, and Stephen Kinzer. *Bitter Fruit: The Untold Story of the American Coup in Guatemala*. Garden City, N.Y.: Doubleday, 1982.

Schorr, Daniel. "The Assassins." New York: *The New York Review of Books*, October 13, 1977.

————. *Clearing the Air*. Boston: Houghton Mifflin, 1977.

Schultz, Donald. "Kennedy and the Cuban Connection." New York: *Foreign Policy*, Spring 1977.

Senate Internal Security Subcommittee Hearings, Pt. III. Washington: USGPO, November 5, 1959.

Shawcross, William. *Sideshow: Kissinger, Nixon and the Destruction of Cambodia*. New York: Simon & Schuster, 1979.

Shevchenko, Arkadi. *Breaking with Moscow*. New York: Alfred A. Knopf, 1985.

Smathers, Senator George. *Transcript: Oral History*. Boston: Kennedy Library, March 31, 1964.

Smith, Earl T. *The Fourth Floor: An Account of the Castro Communist Revolution*. New York: Random House, 1962.

Smith, Joseph B. *Portrait of a Cold Warrior*. New York: G. P. Putnam's Sons, 1976.

Smith, R. H. *OSS: The Secret History of America's First Central Intelligence Agency*. Berkeley: University of California Press, 1972.

————. *Spymaster's Odyssey: The World of Allen Dulles*, MS. New York: n.d.

Smith, Robert F. *The United States and Cuba: Business and Diplomacy, 1917–1960*. New Haven: Yale University Press, 1960.

Smith, Wayne S. *The Closest of Enemies: A Personal and Diplomatic Account of U.S.-Cuban Relations since 1957*. New York: W. W. Norton, 1987.

Sorensen, Theodore. *Transcript: Kennedy Oral History*. Boston: Harper & Row, April 6, 1964.

Soviet Relations with Latin America 1918–1968: A Documentary Survey. Ed. Stephen Clissold. London: Oxford University Press, 1970.

State Department Memoranda. Abilene, Kans.: Eisenhower Library, 1954–1961.

Stavins, Ralph. "The Secret History of Kennedy's Private War." New York: *The New York Times Book Review*, July 22, 1971.

Stebbens, Richard. *The United States in World Affairs 1961*. New York: Harper & Row, 1961.

Steel, Ronald. "Seduction and Betrayal." New York: *The New York Review of Books*, September 25, 1980.

Stein, Jean. *American Journey: The Times of Robert Kennedy*. New York: Harcourt Brace Jovanovich, 1970.

Stevenson, Adlai. *Papers.* Princeton: Mudd Library, December 6 1960.

Stockwell, John. *In Search of Enemies: A C.I.A. Story.* New York: W. W. Norton, 1978.

Strategy for Conquest: Communist Documents on Guerrilla Warfare. Ed. Jay Mallin. Coral Gables: University of Miami Press, 1970.

Strong, Major General Sir Kenneth. *Men of Intelligence.* London: Ginger-Cassell, 1970.

Supplementary Detailed Staff Reports on Foreign and Military Intelligence, Bk. IV: *Final Report of the Select Senate Committee to Study Governmental Operations with Respect to Intelligence Activities.* Washington: USGPO, April 14, 1976.

Szulc, Tad. "Anti-Castro Units Trained to Fight at Florida Bases." New York: *The New York Times,* April 7, 1961.

―――. Articles. New York: *The New York Times,* April 6–10, 1961.

―――. "Clifford Assays Cambodia Threat." New York: *Life,* May 22, 1970.

―――. *Compulsive Spy: The Strange Career of E. Howard Hunt.* New York: Viking, 1974.

―――. "Cuba on Our Mind." New York: *Esquire,* February 1974.

―――. *Fidel: A Critical Portrait.* New York: William Morrow, 1986.

―――. "Friendship Is Possible, but . . ." New York: *Parade, Daily News,* April 1, 1984.

―――. "The Politics of Assassination." New York: *New York Magazine,* June 23, 1975.

―――. "U.S. Sees Invasion Fears." New York: *The New York Times,* May 6, 1964.

Taylor, General Maxwell. *Maxwell Taylor File: Robert F. Kennedy Papers, #2.* Boston: December 29, 1969.

―――. *National Security File,* Box 61, Country Series. Declassified October 18, 1976. Boston: Kennedy Library.

―――. *Responsibility and Response.* New York: Harper & Row, 1967.

―――. *Swords and Plowshares.* New York: W. W. Norton, 1972.

―――. *Taylor Committee Report and Memorandum for Record of Paramilitary Study Group Meetings.* Pts. 1 and 2 declassified June 21, 1978; Pt. 3 declassified April 1985. Washington: May 17, 1961–June 18, 1961.

Thomas, Hugh. *Cuba, or the Pursuit of Freedom.* New York: Harper & Row, 1971.

―――. "The U.S. and Castro, 1959–1962." New York: *American Heritage,* October–November 1978.

Tuchman, Barbara W. *The March of Folly.* New York: Alfred A. Knopf, 1984.

Turner, Admiral Stansfield. *Secrecy and Democracy: The CIA in Transition.* Boston: Houghton Mifflin, 1985.

Twining, General Nathan. *Transcript: J. F. Dulles Oral History.* Princeton: Mudd Library, March 16–19, 1965.

United Nations, General Assembly, Official Records 1961. New York: April 1961.

United Nations, Security Council, Official Records. New York: 1954 and 1961.

United States–Vietnam Relations 1945–1967. Department of Defense Study. Washington: USGPO, 1971.

"U.N. Sets Hearings on Cuba's Charge of U.S. Aggression." New York: *The New York Times,* January 2, 1961.

Urrutia Lléo, Manuel. *Fidel Castro and Castro's Cuba: An American Dilemma.* Washington: Praeger, 1962.

Vandenbroucke, Lucien. "The 'Confessions' of Allen Dulles—New Evidence on the Bay of Pigs." Washington: *Diplomatic History,* Fall 1984.

―――. "The Decision to Land at the Bay of Pigs." New York: *Political Science Quarterly,* Fall 1984.

Volsky, George. "Cuba Exiles Recall Domestic Spying and Picketing for C.I.A." New York: *The New York Times,* January 4, 1975.

Walton, Richard. *Cold War and Counter-Revolution: The Foreign Policy of John F. Kennedy.* New York: Viking, 1972.

———. *The Remnants of Power: The Tragic Last Years of Adlai Stevenson.* New York: Coward, McCann, 1968.
"Warren Was Reportedly Told of CIA Efforts to Kill Castro." New York: *The New York Times,* March 2, 1976.
Weintal, E., and C. Bartlett. *Facing the Brink: An Intimate Study of Crisis Diplomacy.* New York: Charles Scribner's Sons, 1967.
Welch, Richard, Jr. *Response to Revolution: The United States and the Cuban Revolution 1959–1961.* Chapel Hill: University of North Carolina Press, 1985.
"We Were Promised Planes, Cuban Says." Miami: *The Miami Herald,* January 22, 1963.
Weyl, Nathaniel. *Red Star over Cuba.* New York: Devin-Adair, 1960.
White House Memoranda: Meetings with the President. Abilene, Kans.: Eisenhower Library, 1958–1961.
"White House Tapes and Minutes of the Cuban Missile Crises, Executive Meetings, October 1962." Cambridge: *International Security,* Summer 1985.
Wise, David. "Exiles May Have Hit Central America." Paris: *The International Herald Tribune,* July 21, 1965.
———. *The Politics of Lying.* New York: Random House, 1973.
Wise, David, and Thomas Ross. *The Espionage Establishment.* New York: Random House, 1967.
Wofford, Harris. *Of Kennedys and Kings: Making Sense of the Sixties.* New York: Farrar, Straus & Giroux, 1980.
Wohlstetter, Roberta. "Kidnapping to Win Friends and Influence People." London: *Survey,* Autumn 1974.
Wyden, Peter. *The Bay of Pigs.* New York: Simon & Schuster, 1979.
Yost, Charles. *The Conduct and Misconduct of Foreign Affairs.* New York: Random House, 1972.
Zapata, see *Operation Zapata.*
Ziegler, Philip. *Mountbatten.* New York: Alfred A. Knopf, 1985.

Interviews

AMORY, ROBERT, Washington, 1977.
BISSELL, RICHARD, East Hartford, Conn., June 17, 1969.
BONSAL, PHILIP, Washington, November 3, 1971.
BUNDY, MCGEORGE, New York, January 19, 1982.
BURKE, ADMIRAL ARLEIGH, Washington, April 20, 1970.
DULLES, ALLEN, Washington, January 18, 1963.
FULBRIGHT, SENATOR WILLIAM, Washington, May 13, 1969.
GOODPASTER, GENERAL ANDREW, Alexandria, Va., March 26, 1985.
HILTON, RONALD, Stamford, Calif., May 3, 1984.
JEBSEN, JENS, New York, October 17, 1975.
KIRKPATRICK, LYMAN, Providence, R.I., December 3, 1973.
LEMNITZER, GENERAL LYMAN, Washington, April 21, 1970.
MURPHY, ROBERT, New York, 1977.
SORENSEN, THEODORE, New York, January 23, 1985.
TAYLOR, GENERAL MAXWELL, Washington, May 18, 1969.
YOST, CHARLES, New York, December 10, 1973.

Index